Relativism and the
Foundations of Liberalism

ST ANDREWS STUDIES IN PHILOSOPHY AND PUBLIC AFFAIRS

Founding and General Editor:
John Haldane
University of St Andrews

Volume 1:
Values, Education and the Human World
edited by John Haldane

Volume 2:
Philosophy and its Public Role
edited by William Aiken and John Haldane

Volume 3:
Relativism and the Foundations of Liberalism
by Graham Long

Volume 4:
Human Life, Action and Ethics:
Essays by G.E.M. Anscombe
edited by Mary Geach and Luke Gormally

Volume 5:
The Institution of Intellectual Values:
Realism and Idealism in Higher Education
by Gordon Graham

Relativism and the Foundations of Liberalism

Graham Long

St Andrews
Studies in
Philosophy and
Public Affairs

ia

IMPRINT ACADEMIC

Published in the UK by Imprint Academic
PO Box 200, Exeter EX5 5YX, UK

Published in the USA by Imprint Academic
Philosophy Documentation Center
PO Box 7147, Charlottesville, VA 22906-7147, USA

ISBN 1-84540-004-6

A CIP catalogue record for this book is available from the
British Library and US Library of Congress

Cover Photograph:
St Salvator's Quadrangle, St Andrews by Peter Adamson
from the University of St Andrews collection

Contents

Acknowledgements

I would like to thank John Horton and Tim Gray for their helpful comments on the doctoral thesis that forms the backbone of this book. I owe a particular debt of thanks to Simon Caney, my doctoral supervisor. Without his support, and his detailed and helpful criticisms, my original thesis would never have come about. I would also like to thank Keith Sutherland at Imprint Academic and Noel O'Sullivan for their help in bringing this work to print. My thesis was written whilst holding an AHRB doctoral studentship; the work of preparing this book for publication was done during my British Academy Postdoctoral Fellowship. I would like to thank both bodies for their support. Lastly, I owe a special debt to Emma for all her help and love.

For Mum and Dad

Preface

'For too many philosophers', Graham Long writes, 'relativism has taken the form of a spectre that must be laid to rest'. Contemporary liberal thinkers in particular, he observes, are especially troubled by the fear that the universal values on which they often rely appear to be threatened by relativism.

Prompted by the prevalence of relativist attitudes, Long offers a new analysis of the debate between relativists and universalists. This includes a searching discussion of 'reasonable disagreement', a central concept in contemporary liberal debate. In addition, Long contends that relativism is perfectly compatible with a 'contingent' defence of universal values, as well as with a 'political' defence of liberal ones.

But how, more precisely, can relativism account for moral justification in a way which allays the fear it frequently inspires? In an extended analysis of this fundamental question, Long offers a reworked relativism that focuses on the crucial role of a moral agent's own perspective in the exercise of justification. This element means, it is true, that no moral or political judgment can be credited with the completely unassailable character for which leading critics of relativism often yearn. And it means, more generally, that we must accept that there will always be 'situations where compelling reasons for me fail to be compelling reasons for others'. What it does not mean, however, is moral subjectivism. That would only follow if relativism were necessarily reductionist (reducing values to arbitrary subjective feelings, intuitions or personal preferences) or nihilistic (claiming that all values are worthless). Although some relativists have made such claims, the relativism Long defends completely rejects them. In his formulation, relativism is nothing more than the acknowledgement of a truth which only a dogmatist denies: that different people may hold different moral positions which are equally justifiable. This truth, Long argues, lies unacknowledged in contemporary liberal thought. Arguments for liberal toleration and neutrality can, and should, be founded on relativism.

Finally, Long makes clear that just as his rehabilitated relativism does not entail subjectivism, neither does it undermine the integrity of moral practice. Quite the reverse, a fear of relativism may actually do moral harm by encouraging a wild goose chase, in the form of a 'search for unassailable, immutable, eternal values' that turn out not to exist.

Here, then, is far more than a conceptual disquisition. Long's book is in fact an eloquent and closely reasoned call for a reinterpretation of relativism which presents it in a positive light. Seen in this light, it provides a means of which we can make our own values more, not less secure, whilst simultaneously providing the foundation for an ideal of political toleration which permits others to do the same with theirs.

Noël O'Sullivan
University of Hull

Chapter 1

Introduction

Obi-Wan: What I told you was true, from a certain point of view.

Luke: A certain point of view?

Obi-Wan: Luke, you will find that many of the truths we cling to depend greatly on our point of view.[1]

This kind of casual relativism about morality — the idea that things 'depend greatly on our point of view' — is deeply embedded in our culture. When we turn to survey the wide array of life practices adopted by people in our society and across the globe, 'it's all relative' is a cry not restricted just to issues of taste or preference but also applied to questions of culture or morality. Just as the early anthropologists were staggered by the degree of diversity present in humanity, the culturally diverse state we are in encourages an attitude of relativism, at least on the part of some. This relativism with respect to moral diversity finds various expressions — things are 'true for them', we 'shouldn't judge others', 'no view's better than any other'. Moral relativism holds to the possibility that people can have different but equally good moral lives. But there is a countervailing view of other cultures or moralities also present in society. Some phenomena in history and in today's world produce a different reaction. 'What they did was wrong, pure and simple' 'pure evil' 'beyond the pale' — labels often applied to genocide, for example. These two attitudes, one of a relativist suspension of judgement, and another demanding the imposition of judgement, are in conflict both within and between individuals and societies. How can these two attitudes be combined (if indeed they can), and where does the line lie between acceptance and criticism?

Approaching this question from a concern with relativism, as I will, raises several issues straightaway. For relativism has often

[1]   George Lucas, *Return of the Jedi*.

been thought obviously false, or pernicious, or both. Controversy continues between those who see relativism as straightforwardly true, and those who see it as patently false, and has done since the debate between Socrates and Protagoras described in the *Theaetetus*. This debate seems to have become more entrenched of late, as resistance to postmodernism has prompted strident criticism of any kind of 'subjectivism'. Whilst we might meet relativism in our everyday life, and whilst it does not lack for theoretical defenders, it remains nevertheless a dirty word to many contemporary analytical philosophers.[2] To get anywhere near the bottom of this debate requires first a distinguishing of types of relativism and an explanation of the ways we might come to see things as 'relative'. Second, and relatedly, there needs to be an examination of what is at issue between the relativist and his/her opponent. Lastly, there remains a question as to whether a successful defence of some variety of relativism can be mounted.

I aim to provide a fresh contribution to this debate. My aim is to examine some of the conceptual issues and present relativism, or at least one variety of relativism, in a new way. In so doing I clarify the relations between relativity and those elements which are often taken to be its opposites — universality and objectivity. The discussion probes some of the complexities involved, and aims to suggest and justify a distinctive and overlooked relativist position. I then go on to examine some of the implications of such a proposal for political philosophy, and in particular liberalism.

Thus, in addition to the controversy over the feasibility of relativism, my work enters another controversy about the nature and desirability of what has been termed 'political liberalism'. The character and justification of the liberal response to diversity has been the centrepiece of another debate in recent years. Can liberalism provide an account of how to deal with diversity and, equally important, can it provide a justification for that account? I aim to clarify the relationship between relativism and these two questions, concluding that relativism is important to both and can make an especially significant contribution to the latter.

Relativism and the political liberal response to diversity are related in a number of ways. As I have already mentioned briefly, a link is often posited between relativism and cultural diversity. Is diversity an argument for relativism — either direct proof, or a phenomenon that is best explained by relativism? Relativists have advanced both of these theses over the years, and in this

---

[2]   The philosophers on both sides that I am thinking of here are quoted and discussed at length at the beginning of chapter two, where I discuss conceptions of relativism in much more detail.

book I will say something about such positions. Furthermore, relativism has been used to justify an attitude of tolerance to diverse moralities — an attitude that has been turned against relativism by its critics as sanctioning an 'anything goes' approach to morality. Thus, I need to address the question of whether relativism results in liberal tolerance and neutrality, nihilism, or neither. Another link between political and moral theory here is the involvement of a metaethical theory often associated with liberalism — reflective equilibrium. Initially introduced by John Rawls in *A Theory of Justice*, the method of reflective equilibrium constitutes an attempt to get our moral views in order, so that our judgements are supported by theories, and these theories are in turn supported by our judgements. This emphasis on coherence, I suggest, is helpful in a defence of relativism.

The political component of the book also arises from my conviction that relativism is supportive of contemporary liberal claims concerning the nature of moral justification. Relativism is not opposed to liberal commitments, nor need it undermine them; instead it can, and does, serve to underwrite contemporary arguments for liberal principles. Thus, the concern with political philosophy is motivated by the need to clarify what follows from relativism, and to discuss the relationship between relativism and cultural diversity. I examine this relationship through the lens of contemporary liberalism, because contemporary 'political' liberalism is focused on the need to respond to this diversity. Introducing questions of political theory in the second part of the book also allows me to respond to the fear of relativism expressed by many thinkers.

From the discussion of these issues arise my two key claims. First, *metaethical relativism provides a plausible account of moral justification*. Second, *metaethical relativism is not only consistent with the claims of contemporary liberalism, but underpins those claims*. To explain and offer support for these two claims, the book is split into two parts. The first of these concerns the defence of relativism and the nature of the debate between relativism and universalism. The second concerns contemporary liberalism and its relationship with relativism. The two parts are interdependent. If I cannot show in the first part that relativism is a plausible account of moral justification then the question of its implications for liberalism is, in a sense, void. Part of the plausibility of relativism, I suggest, lies in its ability to support and cohere with plausible moral and political principles. If relativism stands in opposition to liberalism then this opposition may provide a good reason to reject it, so that the project of the first half may still fail.[3] The question of the plausibility of relativism cannot be separated from its implications for our moral life, and political principles (including liberal ones) are important features of people's moral lives. Before moving into an outline of the structure of my argument, I want to set its key issues in context by giving initial characterisations of the touchstones of the book: relativism and political liberalism.

Relativism

Before outlining the structure of my argument for relativism, an attempt must be made here to clarify what relativism is, in particular the kind of relativism I am primarily concerned with. The classic definition of relativism takes it as denying that in any particular sphere of inquiry there are truths that hold regardless of circumstances or viewpoint. This might sound a purely negative definition, but relativism posits the alternative that truths[4] are 'relative' in some sense. I do not intend to offer any precise taxonomy of relativism here. There are already many catalogues of the way in which relativism has been applied to a number of different areas of thought. For example Harré and Krausz (1996), distinguish between four senses. 'Semantic relativism' makes the claim that meaning is language-relative. 'Ontological relativism' is the view that existence is relative to conceptual systems. 'Aesthetic relativism' holds that judgements are relative to culture or epoch. 'Moral relativism' claims that morality is relative to framework or culture. An attempt to discuss all the typologies of relativism, and to determine where certain thinkers sit within them, would be a lengthy and problematic exercise. The common core of these catalogues of relativism lies in the view that truth is 'relative-to' certain features of the terrain in each of these dimensions of thought. Thus, Kuhn and Feyerabend would maintain that there are many different and incommensurable scientific paradigms (Kuhn, 1970, Feyerabend, 1975). Anthropologists such as Winch have maintained that even logic is 'only intelligible in the context of ways of living and modes of social life' (Winch, 1958, 100). I am not concerned here to advance either of these positions. Instead, my analysis centres on the claim that *morality* is relative.

---

[3]   I say 'may' because it isn't obvious that we should reject a plausible account of morality because it has unpalatable consequences. Nevertheless, the charge that relativism undermines strong commitments to liberal ideas such as human rights has been used as a reason to reject it, as I shall discuss later.

[4]   Or justifications, as I go on to note in chapter two.

The relativism I will discuss concerns morality or ethics, but even here I will draw a distinction between ethical and metaethical relativism. Ethical relativism is a normative project, an attitude or principle intended to guide our actions in dealing with diversity. Metaethical relativism is instead a position about the nature of morality. Metaethical relativists have variously taken truth or justification in morality to be relative to cultures, moral frameworks, or systems of moral rules, and I discuss these variants in chapter two. In particular, metaethical relativism specifies what we understand as moral justification, how it proceeds and what we can expect of it. As I will go on to show, the kind of relativism I advocate has links with conceptual relativism, which makes judgements relative to conceptual schemes or frameworks. However, I do not examine the question of whether relativism is appropriate only for ethics, or should instead be adopted as a general theory covering all areas of thought. Any in-depth discussion of all these different relativisms lies outside the scope of this work, and I want to suggest that relativism about morality can be conceived of independently of any grand relativist plan.

Political Liberalism

Recent years have seen a turn in liberalism towards questions of how to respond to diversity within society. It ought to be made clear that I examine liberalism in this book not as an economic regime, or an analysis of real-world states, but instead as a distinctive political philosophy. Within this political philosophy, a concern for the priority of justice has been augmented by a recognition of diversity in ways of life or 'conceptions of the good' within a single society. In this book, I pick out and examine a particular strand of liberal thought that has been termed 'political liberalism'. This kind of liberalism has been set out by, amongst others, Brian Barry, Charles Larmore and John Rawls. The approach aims not just to reach a stable liberal consensus amongst diverse groups in society, but also makes this diversity central to the argument. In so doing, liberalism needs to characterise or explicate diversity in 'conceptions of the good', just as relativism does. Once I have attempted a defence of relativism as a plausible metaethical theory, I apply relativism in an examination of political liberalism. I think relativism holds special relevance for the claims political liberals make about the nature of reasonable diversity. A similar claim has been made before, by some of liberalism's most vehement opponents — for example Unger's claim that liberalism rests on the 'subjectivity of values' (Unger, 1976).[5] As I have noted, many liberals will resist any association of relativism with liberalism, for they believe that relativism undermines the primacy of our moral commitments (Dworkin 1996, Nagel 1997). However, my analysis suggests that a more open commitment to a theory of moral justification would help counter criticisms of political liberalism.

Outline of the Argument

Having indicated my main goals, I now want to set out an overview of my argument.

In chapter two I focus on contemporary defences of relativism. I begin by expanding the distinction between moral and metaethical relativism. Whilst the first aims to be action-guiding, the second constitutes a theory about the nature of morality and especially moral justification. I concentrate on this type of relativism, identifying it with the key claim that 'there is no single justified morality'. I examine the defences of this claim offered by David Wong and Gilbert Harman, before briefly discussing the views of Richard Rorty. Rorty, whilst continually disavowing the epithet 'relativist', nevertheless makes key relativist claims. I evaluate the ability of these views to explain aspects of our moral experience — our reaction to moral horror, moral disagreement, and demands for moral truth. I argue that whilst all of these thinkers can provide answers to these questions, they do so at too great a cost. In particular, neither Wong nor Harman's approach allows us to criticise horrific moralities without importing too great a degree of universalism into their theory. In the course of my analysis, I identify two further problems for a relativist account. The first is the problem of theory choice indeterminacy — summed up in Harrison's charge that if relativism is correct, we are left in a position where 'heads I'll be a Kantian, tails I'll be a utilitarian' (Harrison, 1979, 135). The second problem concerns moral criticism. Relativism must explain what our attitude should be towards equally justified but incompatible moralities, allowing

---

[5]   The similarity between Unger's 'subjectivity of values' and relativism lies in the way that both are thought to undermine strongly universalist or objectivist accounts of values. Strauss makes a similar claim about liberalism being in crisis because it has abandoned its absolutism (Strauss, 1961, 140 quoted in Fishkin 1984, 156). Fishkin argues that the only way to avoid the conclusion that 'liberalism self-destructs as a coherent moral ideology' is to achieve a change 'in our common expectations about the character of an objective morality' (Fishkin, 1984, 157). In some ways, I conceive of this book as engaged in an activity of this kind, an examination of both moral experience and liberalism.

us to not only criticise moralities which are 'beyond the pale' but also those that are equally justified.

Chapter three introduces and analyses the opponents of relativism; those theorists who advocate what I term universalist accounts of morality. Thus, they affirm that in some sense there *is* a single justified morality. Thomas Nagel explicates this as some moral reasons having universal force. Jürgen Habermas holds that discourse about justice presupposes some 'inescapable' commitments to a moral core. Stuart Hampshire makes the moral universals more contingent, and grounds them in human nature or human rationality. I move on to identify a new approach which I term 'contingent universalism' that relies on the ability of humanity to converge around common and hence universal norms. All of these approaches are problematic to varying extents, often because of their uneasy relationship with moral diversity. An examination of contingent universalism also shows how close some universalist approaches are to relativist ones. Contingent universalism can vary in the link it posits between claim (1) that people's morals converge on a moral core and claim (2) that the moral core is universal in status.

Having criticised universalism, and existing contemporary defences of relativism, chapter four turns to the method of reflective equilibrium to try to solve some of the problems identified with relativist approaches. I take the method, as sketched by John Rawls and expanded by Norman Daniels, as an example of a coherentist approach to moral justification. After analysing the nature of the reflective equilibrium methodology, I argue that one interpretation of the coherence methodology supports a kind of relativism which I term 'coherence relativism', and begin the task of discussing how such an approach can cope with the features of our moral life that I identified in chapter two. I indicate how coherence relativism can obtain objectivity and how, drawing on a variety of sources such as Bernard Williams and Samuel Scheffler, coherence relativism suggests an answer to questions of theory choice indeterminacy.

Chapter five extends the work of the previous chapter by looking at how coherence relativism can deal with further elements of our moral life against which I tested contemporary relativist approaches. I begin by looking at the kind of criticism a relativist could offer of other moralities. I draw a distinction between the justification of a morality and the application of it. My argument is that the relativist, much like the universalist, can apply her morality even where it cannot be justified, though ideally we should aim for justification to underpin the application of our morality. However, whilst relativism allows people to criticise, compelling justification for that criticism will not always be available. I then discuss in detail how the relativist might be able to respond to horrific moralities. As part of this discussion, I examine implications for the idea of tolerance. Whilst some people take it as axiomatic that we can identify relativism with tolerance — indeed, that relativism requires us to tolerate too much — others have dismissed the view that relativism can have any implications for toleration as 'absurd' (notably Bernard Williams). I argue that relativism can support an argument for toleration when conjoined with the view that moral justification is relevant to judging whether or not to tolerate.

Chapter six begins the second part of the book by turning from questions of tolerance to questions of state neutrality. This chapter does the groundwork for my argument in chapter seven that political liberalism rests on a relativist foundation, by examining the concept of neutrality and the justifications offered for it in liberal theory. I distinguish, as suggested by Colin Bird and Charles Larmore, between neutral and non-neutral justifications of state neutrality. Non-neutral justifications are those such as Mill's, that base a commitment to neutrality on a controversial value such as individuality or autonomy. I suggest that existing 'neutral' liberal defences of neutrality based on ideas of reasonableness and equal respect — such as those mounted by Rawls and Larmore — are problematic.

Chapter seven focuses on the character of the justification for neutrality offered by political liberals. I identify the core claims of the argument, and argue that these must rest on a foundation which — contra the claims of political liberals — is controversial and involves metaethical questions. I undermine the claims of political liberals that the argument is uncontroversial by indicating how a kind of confused proto-relativism already features in political liberal arguments. I suggest that relativism provides a natural foundation to this kind of liberalism, answering liberal worries about scepticism and helping to specify the key liberal idea of reasonableness. The chapter concludes by speculating on some of the possibilities for such an explicitly relativist liberalism.

Method

In this introduction, I have set out the key concerns of the book and its structure. My methodology has so far been implicit in the discussion: here I want to highlight three key aspects of my particular methodological approach.

First, I have already indicated that the book is concerned with theoretical analysis and argument across the fields of metaethics, ethics, and political philosophy. While it is commonly thought that moral philosophy in some sense 'sets the boundaries' for political philosophy, there has been an increased tendency to get on with the examination and application of moral principles, thinking that this can be separated from asking questions of the nature of morality, of moral truth and justification (Rawls, 1999a). However, the book operates on the basis of several links between these areas. In chapters five, six and seven, I will examine the implications of theories of moral justification for moral and political arguments. I argue there that we cannot exclude metaethical questions from a thorough assessment of political philosophies.

Second, my analysis makes use of reflections on our common moral experience. For many thinkers I examine, these constitute the raw material for moral, political and even metaethical philosophy. Amongst those thinkers are, for example, John Rawls, Thomas Nagel and David Wong. This, however, is not to disguise the disagreements about what should constitute the data and what the role of such data is in the argument. The points of agreement and disagreement will become clear in the analysis of particular theories. What must be said at this stage is that my own analysis also makes widespread use of the convictions, judgements and the experiences that help constitute our moral life. I assume that they form, in the absence of a good reason to reject them, a basic test or data set on which to work. Behind my arguments lie a set of common assumptions about such moral experiences; they can be more or less important or prevalent, more or less correct, and the justifications offered for them, or which they constitute in turn, can be good or bad, strong or weak. These are the kinds of terms in which I evaluate competing theories of moral justification and competing analyses of moral and political arguments.

Third, it follows that if I make my arguments in these terms, many of my arguments will appear irrelevant to those who reject the content or the very idea of common moral experience. Some might do this, for example, because they deny that our moral judgements ever come with or demand justification, or they deny that anything can be said about the moral lives of persons other than ourselves. For these people, imposing these kinds of formulas or relations on moral relations necessarily simplifies and distorts. Others will argue that moral beliefs can be reduced to psychology, the analysis of power-relations, or class interest. Whilst I think there is something to be said for explanation and analysis of morality that takes these forms, I believe there remains a sense in which we can study morality *qua* morality, though not in ignorance of the way that these factors may feature in our moral views. As a tradition, relativism has often itself been accused of reducing morality to something else. I will deny that relativism, or our study of morality in general, ought to be reductionist in character. In response to these critics, I am relatively unconcerned that some of my arguments will possess force only for those who endorse some common features of moral life. My argument, after all, is premised on the idea that these features will be common to a wide constituency of people. Whether they are, or not, is for the reader to decide.

Part 1

Chapter 2

Relativism

Introduction

In this chapter, I intend to examine metaethical relativism as an analysis of our moral experience in general, and of our experience of moral disagreement and diversity in particular. This will form the first part of my argument, developed through part one, that relativism is the best analysis of our moral experience. The work of this chapter is divided into sections, each dealing with a specific component of my argument. The first deals with the definition of relativism. To illustrate my analysis here, I look at the views of Richard Rorty. Rorty argues strongly against relativism, yet I want to claim that he proposes a version of relativism himself. The second addresses the kind of strategies that have been used to justify relativism, and the strategy that I will employ in my examination of contemporary relativist views here. The third applies this strategy by examining two advanced expositions of relativism, by David Wong and Gilbert Harman. This process includes considering various common, and not so common, challenges to relativism, the most important of which arise out of its need to cope with the intuitive demands of the way we live our moral lives, and use moral language.

Relativism and Its Enemies

The label 'relativism', as I noted in the introductory chapter, is attached to many packages of beliefs and ideas, some more consistent than others. People in many different areas of philosophy and the social sciences have termed themselves and others relativists. I am specifically concerned in this chapter with relativism in the moral sphere. I have suggested the common thread to relativism is the presentation of a positive view denying certain understandings of universal truth or justification (and certain understandings of objectivity) and substituting considerations of relativity instead. Thus, the relativism which I wish to examine is roughly the idea that — with regard to morality — truth, validity and justification are relative to people's moral beliefs and values.[1] Different relativists will provide different interpretations of this claim, offer different arguments for it, and draw different implications from it. I will defend the claim in this work that *there is no single uniquely justified morality*. So how does my definition fit amongst other interpretations of relativism?

Moral relativism has had a rocky road as an idea. Bernard Williams dismissed a version of it, for example, as 'the anthropologist's heresy, the most absurd view ever to be held in moral philosophy' (Williams 1973, 34). Figures in contemporary political philosophy have lined up to proclaim that they have avoided the 'trap of relativism', for example Brian Barry and Alasdair MacIntyre.[2] I believe this fear and loathing to be a result of a failure on the part of critics to appreciate the diversity of relativist approaches. This can partly be explained by the time-honoured philosophical practice of criticising the most easily criticised version of an argument. Tilley, for example, claims to refute in one short article twenty-seven varieties of relativism but fails to consider *at all* the metaethical relativism that is my concern here (Tilley, 1998). As I will briefly discuss in chapter four, the most incautious defenders of relativism are open to an easy refutation on grounds of inconsistency. Indicative of scepticism and relativism's apparent popularity in modern culture, defenders of relativism are often not professional philosophers. I think this has two consequences. First, relativism is sometimes presented in a way, or in spheres, not conducive to philosophical analysis and second, relativism is often dismissed as a simplistic or unenlightened view. It seems notable in this regard that the main encounter of many professional philosophers with relativism comes through their students. Blackburn, for example, talks of a poor, simplistic 'freshman relativism' as something to be 'pitied' (Blackburn,

---

[1]   I do not wish to assert that terms such as these can be used interchangeably. Rather, I list three terms here to be inclusive in the light of the fact that different moral relativists have different understandings of the relationship of their ideas to these terms, and different understandings of the terms themselves.

[2]   Barry is especially, and characteristically, scathing about relativism (Barry, 2000, 132–3); MacIntyre, 1988, 352–3. Relativism in general has a long history of being dismissed as absurd or incoherent. See Plato's discussion of Protagoras in the *Theaetetus* (Plato, 1990). More recent critics of relativism as being inconsistent or self-refuting include Putnam (1981) and Margolis (1991). Geertz cites a long list of the excesses of anti-relativists in Geertz,1989, 15–25.

1999, 217). Joseph Raz mentions the related phenomenon of the 'deep roots of value scepticism' among students (Raz, 1994, 98). As was briefly indicated earlier, Williams associates it with anthropologists as a false inference drawn from apparent difficulties in cross-cultural interpretation — and indeed, there continues a lively and scholarly debate in anthropology about relative and universal values.

Increasingly, some critics see relativism as part of the 'assault' by postmodernism on ideas of truth or logic and linked ideas in ethics. For example, Norris talks of an 'ultra-relativist orthodoxy' in postmodernism (Norris, 1996, xvi). Ronald Dworkin similarly cites the idea that 'our most confident convictions . . . are just our convictions' as part of a view that 'wearing names like 'post-modernism' and 'anti-foundationalism' and 'neo-pragmatism' now dominates fashionable intellectual style' (Dworkin, 1996, 87). Macklin concludes that 'extreme ethical relativism is the prevailing postmodern view' (Macklin, 1999, 45). Whether taken as part of a general attempt to relativise standards of justification, or advanced purely in the moral realm, relativism of roughly the type that I want to examine is often positioned in opposition to 'professional' analytical philosophy. This characterisation of simplistic incoherence on one side and quick dismissal on the other, of an opposition between analytical philosophy and the subjectivism 'epidemic in the weaker regions of our culture' (Nagel, 1997, 4) is, however, misleading. My aim here is to examine and critique contemporary systematic and thoughtful approaches to relativism.

The first task of this chapter is to differentiate between different kinds of relativism concerning morality. I will propose that 'relativism', as commonly understood by its critics, is not the type of relativism that I will defend. This raises the question of whether the relativism I am defending is properly called relativism at all. I start by explaining in more detail the split between normative and metaethical relativism. This allows me to draw an initial distinction between the kind of relativism I am defending and a different kind entirely.

Normative Relativism

Normative relativism holds that 'it is wrong to pass judgement on those who have substantially different values, or to try to make them conform to one's values, for the reason that their values are as valid as one's own' (Wong, 1991, 442). This view has occasionally been termed 'cultural relativism', as it was associated especially with twentieth century anthropologists such as Herskovits;

however, I believe we can draw a distinction between two aspects of cultural relativism. In this section I will discuss only the first. These anthropologists drew a *normative* conclusion of non-interference from the evidence of massive moral diversity they encountered.[3] In my experience, however, this kind of idea — about moral relativism justifying toleration — is a fairly common view. It is a view that, as I will argue later, can be explained and rendered coherent. Normative relativism is a view about what kind of attitude, or action, is justified towards others with very different moral views; it aims to guide our moral action. However, it is not in itself a view on how we justify this particular moral belief. In other words, normative relativism is a 'first order' claim about the *content* of morality. The second aspect of the cultural relativists' position is a view about the nature of morality that served to underpin their conclusion of non-interference. This more interesting aspect of moral relativism, that I will term *metaethical relativism*, is a view about how we justify our moral beliefs in the first place, i.e. a 'second order' view.[4]

Metaethical Relativism

My central concern is with metaethical rather than normative relativism. Metaethical relativism claims centrally that concepts such as truth or justification are relative to standards, cultures or frameworks that legitimately differ. Harman identifies the key claim as being that 'conflicting judgements can be equally correct or equally justified' (Harman, 1982, 308).[5]

One way of interpreting this claim is that culture determines what is good or bad, that moral goodness and badness are reducible to cultural norms. Here, then, is the second component of cultural relativism, an account of metaethical relativism holding that "'right' means (can only be coherently understood as meaning) 'right for a given society'" (Williams, 1973, 34). This kind of rela-

---

[3] Herskovits, in *Cultural Relativism: Perspectives in Cultural Pluralism*, cites Kroeber: "This anthropological principle [that each society should be evaluated on its own terms] leads, it is true, to a relativistic or pluralistic philosophy — a belief in many values rather than a single values system." (Kroeber, 1950, in Herskovits 1972). For an excellent discussion of Herskovits' relativism, see Fernandez in *Ethos* 1990.

[4] For the commonly used distinction between first and second order questions, see Mackie, 1977, 16–9.

[5]   Flew offers a similar definition of relativism; ' to be a relativist about value is to maintain that there are no universal standards of good and bad, right and wrong' (Flew, 1984, 303). Note that this claim, like the one I will examine, does not straightforwardly entail that all moralities are equally good, or that 'good' must be given a functional definition.

tivism, on Foot's account, 'identifies a moral utterance with an assertion of psychological or sociological fact' (Foot, 1979, 4). A cultural account of this kind identifies what is morally right with what is deemed good by that society. In recent years, Michael Walzer has been interpreted as making this kind of claim, for example when he writes 'a given society is just if its substantive life is lived in a certain way — that is, in a way faithful to the shared understandings of its members' (Walzer, 1983, 313). However, I will suggest later that his view also has a 'contingent universalist' component.[6] This use of 'right' is not an account of metaethical relativism that can be defended, and is quite distinct from the type of relativism I seek to defend.

Another relativist thesis which has been advanced by some, but has also been the subject of disproportionate attention, is the claim that *all moralities are equally true or justified*.[7] If this is what must be meant by 'relativism' then, as will become clear below, I am not defending relativism at all. At this point, having given an account of all the varieties of relativism I will *not* be defending, many critics will simply pack up and go home disappointed. However, I want to argue here that I am not performing some kind of semantic trick. Critics who believe that these are the *only possible* interpretations of relativity, which is after all what I take relativism to be about, are taking a conception of relativism which is too narrow and impoverished. Too many reject the concept of relativism because they identify it *only* with one of the theories above.

The kind of relativism about morality that I will defend can be summed up in Wong's phrase 'there is no single, true morality' (Wong, 1986, 1). Instead, there are a number of moralities, at least some of which cannot be found objectively superior or inferior, either because there *is* no objective standpoint or because, from an objective standpoint, these competing moral systems share the same form and amount of justification. One elaboration of this is the view that whilst moral rules or standards are relative, in the end either some moral standards will be shared (though not enough to yield a single true morality), or that some shared non-moral standards will be important. This chapter is centrally concerned with what kind of reasons can be offered for thinking

---

[6] Another, perhaps more popular view of Walzer, is that he is plainly self-contradictory on this claim. I will argue in chapter three that relativism and contingent universalism can be compatible: Walzer can be a relativist but believe that there is, in some sense, a common moral core.

[7] We shall see in this chapter and chapter five that Gilbert Harman has been understood as holding a version of this claim.

this is the correct view of morality; i.e., how this theory of justification can in turn be justified. Amongst metaethical relativists, I count such thinkers as David Wong, Gilbert Harman, Clifford Geertz, and perhaps Richard Rorty and Bernard Williams.[8] This account still aims to make truth or justification relative to rules, frameworks or standards, but crucially it does *not* claim that *all* moralities are equally good. Instead, some rules or frameworks will be more justified than others.

Before I go any further, I should make it clear that I do not straightforwardly identify this kind of relativism with the 'pluralism' advocated by thinkers such as Isaiah Berlin. I take pluralism as the view that values are incommensurable: there is a plurality of values amongst which no single order of merit can be constructed (Berlin, 1991, 79). Pluralism, however, says nothing about the way we go about identifying and justifying these incommensurable values. For the pluralist there may be a single universal morality, but one that is composed of incommensurable values. Whilst relativists will hold that some opposing values can be equally justified, the focus of relativism is the account of justification on which this is possible. Some variety of pluralism may be an outcome of some kind of relativism, and vice-versa, but there is no necessary link between the two.[9] As Berlin notes:

> The fact that the values of one culture may be incompatible with those of another, or that they are in conflict within one culture or group or in a single human being at different times . . . does not entail relativism of values, only the notion of a plurality of values not structured hierarchically (Berlin, 1991, 80).[10]

One important further difference with the prevalent image of relativism amongst its critics is that when I come to offer my argument for relativism, I will claim that this is an argument about *justification* rather than *truth*. Whilst arguments about whether beliefs are '*true*-for' dominate classical discourse, some thinkers cast relativism as a justificatory position. For example, MacIntyre characterises relativism as a view about 'rational justification'

---

[8]   Richard Rorty does not want to call himself a relativist — since relativists believe that 'every coherent view is as good as every other' (Rorty, 1991, 42). His protestations not withstanding, however, it seems to me that Rorty does subscribe to the idea that there is no single true morality. I discuss this idea shortly. Williams affirms a limited 'relativism of distance', holding that a kind of suspension of judgement from our society does hold where the morality we are considering is one which does not present a possible alternative to our own. (Williams 1985, 157–73)

[9]   See, for example, Galston, 1999, e.g. 770.

[10]   However, I wouldn't want to claim that Berlin means exactly the same as I do by 'relativism'.

(MacIntyre, 1988, 364), and Harman has also defended relativism as a view on justification (Harman, 1979). I want to claim that metaethical relativism can be isolated from debates over the nature of truth. The relativism I will advocate operates in the realm of the justification of truth-claims to other people and ourselves. It is centrally concerned with beliefs and reasons rather than how we establish the relationship between justified belief and truth.[11] We can say something about the nature of justified belief without establishing whether there are moral facts or truths, and what these truths look like.

In the language I will introduce later, this does not make my position entirely 'neutral' between different conceptions of morality. The analysis I propose at least assumes some weak foundation, that is, I will be making judgements on whether views are justified, mistaken, relevant, appropriate, and even correct, where correctness refers to strong interpersonal justification, or objectivity.[12] But I believe we can say all these things without getting involved with what it means for something to be true — whether truth is redundant in ethics, merely to be given an affirmative use, or whether we should adopt a correspondence or coherence theory of truth. Many relativists do supply analyses of truth in these kinds of terms, and I set these out briefly when I discuss their arguments. However, I believe the relativist position can be stated without recourse to this terminology. Thus, the core relativist claim that I defend later is that *there is no single justified morality*. The main advantage of this emphasis on justification is that it helps to concentrate the argument on debates which are already controversial enough without engaging with another equally controversial question. The rest of my arguments stand or fall independent of the existence and character of moral truth.

In these ways, the relativism I will examine and defend here may well be different from the image of relativism held by many of its opponents and some of its defenders. Not all relativism's defenders will conceive of relativism in the terms I have outlined, but it is my contention that the most prominent contemporary

[11] This is not a novel position. Gerald Gaus makes an identical claim in the introduction to *Justificatory Liberalism*, and my position here follows his analysis (Gaus, 1996, 5-10).

[12] I have sympathy with the description Gaus offers of this view as 'weak cognitivism' (Gaus, 1996, 8), where I take strong cognitivism to make the additional claim that moral views are 'either true or false' (Flew, 1984, 65) in their relation to some kind of moral reality. Strong cognitivism thus clearly rules out emotivist or affirmatory accounts of morality. However, I eschew this terminology here — setting out the territory I will be defending already seems a contentious enough exercise.

defenders of relativism do. It may well be the case that I am defending a less outlandish version of relativism, but it still claims a strong element of relativity for our moral beliefs. Critics of relativism will be comforted to see that I still affirm some of the 'freshman' premises that appear so incredible. For Rorty, my analysis *will* allow a sense in which two coherent views can both be equally good. Indeed, I will argue shortly that Rorty is also committed to a version of this claim. For Dworkin, I will maintain that our most confident convictions are *just* convictions.

To see the way in which different conceptions of relativism have caused confusion, I want to propose that despite Richard Rorty's opposition to the term 'relativism', he is nevertheless committed to the kind of metaethical relativism I am talking about. This will come as no surprise to thinkers who have long consigned Rorty to the ranks of 'subjectivists'.[13] The argument I make here serves two purposes. First, it serves as an example of the kind of distinctions drawn between relativist and non-relativist accounts. Second, Rorty gives us a preliminary idea of what a metaethical relativism of the kind I have described here might look like.

Rorty Against Relativism

Rorty provides an analysis of three relativist theses. He claims that those terming themselves relativists hold one of these three views.

(1) 'Every belief is as good as every other'

(2) 'True' is an equivocal term, having as many meanings as there are procedures of justification.

(3) 'There is nothing to be said about either truth or rationality apart from descriptions of the familiar procedures of justification which a given society — ours — uses in one or another area of enquiry.'[14]

Of these, the first view is 'self-refuting', and the second 'eccentric'. The third has no reason to be termed relativist at all, according to Rorty. From the relativist side, very few relativists believe unqualifiedly (1) that every belief is as good as every other. I have suggested above that only some relativists advance this claim, and certainly very few contemporary ones do — precisely

---

[13] For thinkers such as Nagel, subjectivism has a broad usage that includes relativists and indeed any sceptics about moral universality (Nagel, 1997, 4).

[14] I take these three statements from Rorty, 1991, 23.

because, without careful qualification, the view represented by (1) is indeed self-refuting, not to mention morally bankrupt. On (2), Rorty comments that the 'term 'true' . . . means the same in all cultures' (Rorty, 1991, 23), but different objects are taken as fulfilling the different criteria established for it. Elsewhere, he writes 'there are some terms, — for example, 'the true theory', 'the right thing to do' — which are intuitively and grammatically singular, but for which no set of necessary or sufficient conditions can be given which will pick out an unique referent' (Rorty, 1979, 373). The relativist who adopts talk of 'truth' can mean exactly this when she says that 'X is true for you but not for me'. Her claim is that X and not-X are both true, relative to what Rorty calls different 'procedures for assigning the terms' (Rorty, 1991, 23). She need not go 'eccentrically' any further than this. The relativist response I outline here is very similar in content to Wong's claim, outlined shortly, that there are various descriptions of adequate moral frameworks, and that moral truth consists in correspondence with these frameworks. A relativist could think, on (3), that one of the things that can be entailed within a society's procedures of justification is the view that other people's norms were also justified. Beliefs about the kinds of factors that render a judgement justified can form part of the make-up of a culture. Indeed, I would argue that this is one under-recognised consequence of Rorty's approach which he ignores in his haste to be 'ethnocentric'. Allowing that 'ethnocentrism' justifies allows that other people's ethnocentrism will also justify.

Rorty the Relativist

I want to maintain that Rorty is committed to versions of claims (1), (2), and of course ethnocentric claim (3); indeed, I believe that (3) requires Rorty to accept a version of claims (1) and (2). Before analysing Rorty's ethnocentric proposal, and showing in detail how his view is relativistic, I want to offer an initial consideration for thinking of Rorty as a relativist. On (2), that truth is an equivocal term, we should note that Rorty is committed to what Gaus calls a 'relativism of reasons' (Gaus, 1996, 39), similar to Harman's view that our moral claims do not necessarily provide other people with compelling justifications. That is, he allows that 'we cannot justify our beliefs to everybody, but only to those whose beliefs overlap ours to some appropriate extent' (Rorty, 1991, 31, footnote 13). A good justification for us need not be a compelling justification for anyone else. There is no 'God's eye view' from which one position is objectively justified and another is not. Instead, 'objectivity should be seen as conformity to the norms of justification we find about us' (Rorty, 1979, 361). Given Rorty's link between justification and 'commendatory' truth — which I will discuss later in this chapter — we can further say that what we justifiably commend as true need not be justifiably commended as true by others (or, in shorthand, the things true for me need not be true for you). Thus, in one sense, truth does have as many uses as there are different procedures of justification, and Rorty is committed to the claim that there is no single uniquely justified (or true) morality — the claim that I have offered as fundamental to one kind of metaethical relativism.

What allows Rorty to deny his account constitutes a variety of relativism is his claim that it instead constitutes ethnocentrism. Rorty could claim, in response to my description of him as relativist, that (3) we cannot say anything about procedures of justification or truth apart from the ones held by our society. This ethnocentrism is problematic as a response to accusations of relativism, as I will now demonstrate.

Rorty rejects the idea that 'we must believe that every coherent view is as good as every other, since we have no outside touchstone for choice amongst such views' (Rorty, 1991, 42). He holds that 'we do not infer from 'there is no way to step outside communities to a neutral standpoint' that 'there is no rational way to justify liberal communities over totalitarian communities'' (Rorty, 1991, 42). Instead, our 'necessarily ethnocentric answer simply says that we must work by our own lights' (Rorty, 1991, 42). But I think this response implies that 'own lights' are capable of justifying — and one of the perceptions of other cultures is precisely that they have their 'own lights'. In this sense, I believe that Rorty is committed to a modified version of (1); that in a sense, 'every ethnocentrised ('justified-by-own-lights') belief is as good as every other'. This is not to say that we can attain a neutral standpoint from which other cultures share the same kind of justification. From within our culture, we recognize that 'own lights' justify (our own lights would justify, whatever they were), and that other cultures have 'own lights' (this, presumably is what makes them 'other'; they would not be if they had 'our lights'). We can infer, without stepping outside our culture, that other cultures are justified by our standards of justification. Cultures may be thought of as equipping their members with both some sort of internal perspective and an external one on the culture as one amongst many. How we react to this is a different matter. I think that some ethnocentric affirmation — the idea that our culture values certain fundamental values not preferred by others — can provide a reason to affirm one culture as better than another. But

Rorty ignores the way that the standard of justification he advocates is precisely one which, in his terminology, has a univocal meaning but a diversity of reference (Rorty, 1991, 23) — a version of claim (2). Therefore, ethnocentrism is problematic because it does not escape categorisation within the kind of relativism I am trying to defend, and Rorty does advance what I want to class as a relativist thesis.

Agent and Appraiser Relativism

Before I go on to discuss possible justificatory strategies and common problems found with relativist analyses, I want to discuss one commonly drawn distinction within moral relativism, which I mentioned briefly during my discussion of normative relativism. It has often been thought that relativism comes in *agent* and *appraiser* types. I want to discuss this distinction briefly here, and suggest that this distinction is not sufficient as a taxonomy of relativism. The distinction was introduced by David Lyons (1976). For Lyons, *agent*-group relativism 'may be understood as the notion that an act is right if, and only if, it accords with the norms of the agent's group' (Lyons, 1976, 109). Conversely, *Appraiser*-group relativism holds that 'a moral judgement is valid if, and only if, it accords with the norms of the appraisers social group' (Lyons, 1976, 109).

As Lyons notes, this gives us two different sets of standards that morality can be relative *to*. The second will allow us to assess the actions of members of other moralities as wrong, despite the fact that a given action might be right-for-them. The first, in contrast, does not allow us to make this judgement. If it is right-for-them, it is right, and we cannot gainsay it. Agent group relativism is analogous to the position often expressed on matters of etiquette, 'when in Rome, do as the Romans do'.

Exactly what is at issue in this popular distinction within relativism is unclear. Both appraiser- and agent-group relativism are based within metaethical relativism, resting as they both do on the idea that there is no single true morality (Sturgeon, 1994, 84). Each can be viewed as a particular specification of this claim, as each establishes a criterion for moral justification which specifies which moralities are to be treated as equally valid. However, in addition to being a claim about the nature of moral justification, both agent- and appraiser-group relativism are action-guiding, in the sense that they tell us as least partly what is right and what is wrong. As they straddle this line between status and content claims, their nature and relationship with the metaethical/normative distinction resists easy analysis.

Agent-group relativism can be conceived of as related to normative cultural relativism, since both stem from the idea that 'good in' equates to 'good for' a particular society. However, on closer analysis, we can see that the norms of the group in question will have a crucial impact on the consequences that either approach has for moral action. The norms of an agent's group may require criticism of and intervention in other moralities. In this case, agent-group relativism does not support an attitude of normative relativism. To see this, imagine that we are trying to make an agent-relative judgement about another society's morality. If one of their norms is that 'people should not hesitate in making judgements on the morality of other societies, based upon their own' then this gives us the opportunity to do more than live and let live. Conversely, the norms of *appraisers* might be that agents'-groups should decide their own moralities and should not be criticised — in other words, an appraiser-group relativist could be a normative relativist. In this case, we could look at another society as appraisers, and being guided by *our* norm that we should not criticise other moralities, conclude that their practices were 'good for them'.

The idea that these two conceptions are mutually exclusive, a way to divide the territory of relativism, is misleading. Appraising is a moral act, which requires moral agency. Because of this, all appraisers are thus agents and vice-versa. The agent-appraiser distinction is thus puzzling and its relationship to the meta-ethical/normative distinction less than straightforward. Some metaethical relativists will endorse either an agent- or an appraiser- approach. For example, cultural metaethical relativism fits the criteria of agent-relativism, since it holds that for an action to be good is for an action to reflect the cultural norms of an agent's society. However, not all relativist views can be classified so neatly. This is partly because the distinction between agent and appraiser relativisms covers an element of metaethical relativism (a view about moral justification) and normative relativism (the attitude we should take towards others). Whilst having action-guiding implications, neither agent nor appraiser relativism is a complete template for a morality without a further specification of the norms involved. I will go on to argue in chapter five that by closely examining the notions of justification and criticism, we can make sense of a metaethical relativism which advocates *both* agent- and appraiser- relativisms in various circumstances. Thus, the choice between the two is not an either/or one, and the distinction does not suffice as a classificatory device.

This brief discussion of agent and appraiser relativism raises an important question concerning the possibility of social criticism. Relativism holds that moral judgements are relative to frameworks, but it has often been asked *whose framework* these moral judgements are relative to. For Lyons, it is a group of people, of which the agent or appraiser is a member. A common objection to relativism, as I mention below, is that because it says what is right relative to group X is right *period*, it takes no account of social criticism — of individuals having different moralities from the group. If no morality can be correct apart from the norms of the society of which I am a member, then there seems no ground upon which I can criticise those norms without necessarily being wrong. Before I embark on my analyses of Harman and Wong's arguments below, it should be stated that neither take this step and that both accounts are largely immune to this objection. However, Richard Rorty's approach does possess this problem. It can be found in his idea that (to use his terminology) if only one person S asserts p in a society where everybody else affirms the opposite of p, he or she is *unwarranted* in holding p. He writes, 'of course, p might be true. S may be the unhonoured prophet of some social movement or intellectual revolution whose time has not yet come' (Rorty, 1998, 50). Rorty not only appears to have relativist beliefs, here he also encounters a problem which afflicts some variants of relativism: the impossibility of social criticism. Both Harman and Wong avoid this criticism by referring to moral beliefs and frameworks that can be understood as being held by individuals or communities. On their accounts, we can consistently describe someone who disagrees with the prevailing view as justified. By contrast, Rorty seems to be saying that the individual is unwarranted, or unjustified, in holding a view opposite to that which prevails in their society. This answer is considered (rightly) counter-intuitive by opponents of relativism. Surely, if as Rorty admits, p might be true, then S could be justified in holding it even if everyone else did not?

So, in this chapter and in general, I will take the approach that moral judgements are relative to a set of rules or a framework which may be held by one person alone or more than one. Whilst such framework-relativity might map largely onto distinctions between 'cultures', conceived on a group rather than individual level, the analysis can be individuated to deal with particular people's moral frameworks. It makes the framework rather than the 'shared-ness' of the framework the focus of analysis.

In the preceding sections, I have argued that there are different accounts of the central motivating insight of 'relativity'. I have distinguished the variant that I wish to defend, the claim that there is no single justified morality, from other accounts. In particular, I have suggested that relativism is intelligible as a thesis about justification as well as truth, and that relativism need not claim that all views are equally good. I have distinguished it both from normative relativism and pluralism. Furthermore, I suggested that the agent-appraiser distinction, which is often imposed on relativism, is insufficient as a classificatory device.

Moral Relativism, Absolutism, Universalism, Objectivism, Realism

Though I have made some general remarks in the introduction as to where relativism is situated vis-à-vis the alternatives, a complete analysis requires that we explore its relation to other concepts which occupy similar territory. In metaethics, there are a number of theories that contend with relativism as the correct view of moral justification, and these invoke ideas of moral absolutes and universals, objectivity and realism. However, the terms which denote these analyses are used by different thinkers in different ways. Whilst the relations between these terms will be discussed at various points — for example, universalism in chapter three, objectivity in chapter four — there is at least the need for some basic definitions. Thus, I want to introduce here the ideas of universalism or absolutism, objectivism and realism. I will use the term '*universalism*' to denote the position sometimes called absolutism — that there are universally valid moral values, and hence that in direct opposition to relativism, there is a single true or justified morality. For my purposes, Universalism also captures better the appeal to the 'view from everywhere' which is at the heart of contemporary defences of a single true morality, such as those by Hampshire, Nagel and Caney discussed in chapter three. Absolutism, to my mind, already has one usage with regard to morality, in the sense of absolute values which are incapable of being overridden in moral decision-making.[15] *Objectivism* consists of the claims that (1) 'true moral judgements describe a subject matter that is independent of the thoughts and feelings of finite, sentient beings' and (2) 'that at least some moral judgements can be supported by evidence that any knowledgeable and rational individual would have to accept' (Arrington, 1989, 193). *Realism*, I take to be the view that moral claims can be true or false. This differs from objectivism, which has a distinct view about what it is for a moral belief to be true.

---

[15]   As opposed to consequentialism or theories of a moral calculus.

These distinctions are highly contestable, and any of the more complex positions I will examine here are hybrids. For example, Wong holds that there is such a concept as moral truth, and his theory has — I hope to show — objectivist and universalist leanings. I will myself argue later that relativism can be compatible with some conceptions of objectivity. Likewise, universalists need not affirm realism and objectivity by virtue of being universalists. There is no easy overlap between these terms in the debate — indeed, part of my purpose here is to offer some clarification of the relationship between relativism and these other ideas.

How to Justify Relativism

Having briefly highlighted other sophisticated views of morality, we are in a better position to assess the relativist case. Relativism, as the idea that there is no single uniquely justified morality, is far from self-evident. Before examining the justifications for relativism provided by Wong and Harman, I offer in this section an overview of the possible justifications. I examine two primary strategies for the justification of metaethical relativism, each of which is exemplified by one of these two contemporary relativists. The two strategies are linked in various ways, yet I think there is sufficient distance between the two that they can be examined as distinct. I shall term one of them 'relativism as best explanation' and the other 'relativism as reasonably required'. These two terms denote different relationships to our everyday moral experience — the first embracing it, the second standing at a distance from it. The two can support each other, as I shall show with regard to Harman's work. I should also make clear that because the focus in my analysis of contemporary relativism is our moral experience, I will not examine in any depth various other aspects of these relativist strategies. Both Harman and Wong make many interesting and controversial claims — notably comparative ones about the relative failure of universalist analyses — in the course of their defences of relativism, and I cannot hope to do them all justice in the space afforded by this chapter. I take up some of the comparative points in chapters three and four.

Relativism as Best Explanation

One strategy in defence of relativism is to argue that relativism is the best explanation of our moral experience in general or of moral disagreement in particular. For relativists, who often stress the immense diversity of moral systems, moral disagreement is characteristic of that experience. I take accounting satisfactorily for common features of our moral lives to be a central task for any relativist theory. As this chapter and the next will show, this is the crucial battleground between relativists and universalists. Universalists will claim, as we shall see, that our experience of morality has a universal appearance which relativists cannot account for. Relativists (in addition to the common claim that relativism provides a better explanation of moral disagreement) must show that relativism can account for this appearance, or else take the radical step of denying the relevance of this appearance. Because relativism is often taken as an unlikely or counter-intuitive theory, the relativist's strategy here is to take our moral phenomenology head on. The justification of relativism is, on this account, inseparable from the reply to some of the most common objections.

Wong makes some useful comments on the strategy of best explanation. He takes the strategy of best explanation to demand a solution to the problem of 'the main difficulty in explaining moral experience: reconciling the features of experience suggesting that morality is objective with other features suggesting that it is subjective' (Wong, 1986, 1). Amongst examples of what he terms moral objectivity, Wong says 'note that we commonly call moral beliefs true or false, we give arguments for or against these beliefs, and that we judge these arguments to be good or bad' (Wong, 1986, 2). He writes,

> The principle of best explanation requires us to translate moral language in such a way that the resulting explanation of behavior connected with the use of this language be coherent with our total explanation of what human beings are like and the way they deal with the world (Wong, 1986, 116).[16]

The sense in which I want to use the idea of best explanation is related to Wong's by the stress it places on being the best total explanation of human moral *experience* — 'what humans beings are like and how they deal with the world' (Wong, 1986, 116). Roughly outlined, for my purposes in this chapter it means explaining our intuitions about the way we moralise satisfactorily, and indeed better than competing theories (though this comparative element must be the work of later chapters). It accepts our moral experience and asks how we can paint a coherent and attractive relativist picture of it, an explanation of our moral life that is consonant with and supports metaethical relativism. This

---

[16] It should be noted that whilst Wong makes general reference to an idea of best explanation, he also means by it something quite specific. It is a reference to his principle of translation, which he raises with regard to how we can understand the moral language of others.

does not mean, however, that all of our intuitions with regard to the making of moral judgements have to be validated. A relativist explanation could, as Wong notes, instead plausibly reconcile features of our intuitions with a relativistic outlook by explaining how we can hold incorrect, incomplete, or inadequate views as part of our moral experience. What this engagement with our moral experience requires is something I will examine in more detail shortly.

Relativism As Reasonably Required

Gilbert Harman, by contrast, exemplifies a different strategy. It is linked to the first by the desire to explain, but in this case it explains by largely *disregarding* our moral experience, and instead explains what actually *is*. As we shall see, Harman draws an analogy from relativity in physics to show that moral language as we usually use it is incomplete. Harman is emphatic that his argument is not about what moral agents *mean*. He writes, 'recall that moral relativism is not by itself a claim about meaning. It does not say that speakers always intend their moral judgements to be relational in this respect . . . moral relativism is a thesis about how things are and how things aren't!' (Harman, 1996, 17). Relativism, for Harman, is validated in a way that does not refer to the content of our moral intuitions. Instead, it is justified by reference to the world-as-it-is, which may be very different to what we think, intend, or mean. It may require large-scale revision of the way we understand our moral thinking.

Thus, whilst both approaches attempt to explain, their points of reference are very different. One proposes relativism as the best explanation of our experience, and the other proposes it as the best explanation of how things really are, independent of our perceptions. For Harman's analysis to be persuasive, it will have to explain in what way our moral experience is irrelevant or incomplete and why we came to think it so. Nevertheless, the main thrust of the argument is an appeal to 'how things are' (Harman 1998a, 161).[17]

My strategy for this chapter is to consider both approaches from a methodology of my own, which could be seen as a variant of the best explanation approach. The only way to justify relativism, I would suggest, is (1) to prove its internal consistency, (2) to show how it explains satisfactorily (in a broad sense) our moral

---

[17] I argue in my analysis of Harman that he backs down slightly from a strongly counter-intuitive position by introducing a quasi-absolutist analysis of moral language, which nevertheless fails ultimately to provide a plausible account of a relativist's moral life.

experience, and (3) to show how it is superior in these respects to other conflicting metaethical theories. Objectives (1) and (2) can be met through an exposition of relativism, the intuitions it must satisfactorily explain, the criticism it faces, and how these can be answered. The third can be met by a critical examination of opposing views, and for my purposes here these are varieties of universalism. In this chapter I find both Wong and Harman's views wanting in the light of these first two objectives. In the next, I argue that universalist analyses also fail to compel assent. I then move on to elaborate in chapters four and five a distinct relativist approach which answers the problems I find with contemporary defences of relativism here. My approach will proceed first by outlining three common features of our moral experience which any theory of moral justification must deal with, and which have proved sources of important challenges to relativism. I then examine Wong and Harman's theories and interrogate their responses to these three challenges, in order to arrive at a fuller account of them and see more clearly where problems may lie. In the process of this examination, I draw out two additional features of our moral experience, and discuss these as further problems for the two theories. I then leave the troubles of relativism to discuss in chapter three the universalist alternatives to a relativistic view of morality. The work of setting out a relativist position which accounts for our moral experience satisfactorily will be carried out in chapters four and five.

Common Features of Our Moral Experience

I will begin this analysis by outlining three common features of our moral experience which have been thought to pose a problem for relativism. I shall refer to these as our expectations regarding *moral disagreement, moral truth,* and *moral horror.* These are interlinked, as my analysis will show. On the first two, relativism stands accused of both incoherence and violence to our considered moral experience. On the third, it stands accused merely of the latter charge, although perhaps in a way that is more graphic.

Moral Disagreement

Any relativistic view has to deal with the idea of moral disagreement. The presence of apparently irresolvable disagreements has been taken as evidence of relativism, but relativism also has to explain what is going on when two (or more) people disagree. In a genuine moral disagreement, each of the parties is convinced that the other is wrong. If relativism says there is no single true or justified morality, it is quite possible for both of the people to be right, and there to be no 'fact of the matter'. But as far as both parties are concerned there certainly is a fact of the matter, otherwise there would not be a disagreement. Relativism, it is charged, vitiates disagreement by making the confrontation between different moral judgements illusory. 'It is as if I had said 'This is brown' and you had replied 'It is not!' but each of us was referring to a different object; making our subsequent remonstrations and arguments over the matter pointless' (Stout, 1990, 92). Thus, the first challenge for relativism is: does it satisfactorily explain our intuition that disagreements, in order to be *disagreements* in a real sense, must involve two contradictory points of view?

Moral Truth

Linked to this, a second apparent problem for relativism is our deeply held belief that our views on many issues are correct or true, and true in a sense which entails that the opposite view is false. On a standard conception of truth, it is not possible both for 'p' and 'not-p' to be true simultaneously. However, for relativists, what truth consists in, and whether moral beliefs really are 'true' in the above sense, are very much open to question. Relativists tend to analyse 'morally true' as 'true relative to A' and 'true relative to B'. We must ask whether this is a sufficient or satisfactory meaning of true for the purposes of moral discussion. Another response, as I suggested in the introduction to this chapter, is to propose a relativist thesis concerning moral justification which remains broadly neutral with regard to theories of truth. Nevertheless, the relativist thinkers I examine here do provide distinctive theories of truth, and to cast their theories instead as being entirely about moral justification runs the risk of seriously mischaracterising their positions. Thus, there are three strong reasons why an examination of relativist theories of truth serves an important purpose here. First, the need to get a full and accurate picture of their theories; second, to see what potential relativist analyses of truth could look like; and third, to illustrate the advantage to relativists of being able to avoid such a contentious subject that divides philosophers along an axis quite distinct from questions of relativity and universality. In summary, whilst it would be disingenuous of me to render Wong and Harman's theories here as being about moral justification rather than truth, the main thrust of my work will speak only on justification.

This does not mean that I can entirely avoid the concern that, to my mind, underpins the issue of moral truth. There seems to be a real question over whether relativism renders morality somehow arbitrary or whimsical, a statement of personal preference alone. If something and its opposite can both be successfully justified then morality surely loses its force or authority. This more basic charge of arbitrariness cannot be ducked by any plausible relativist approach. When I come to set out my particular relativist proposal, I will discuss this issue in chapter four as a question about whether a relativist view can be thought *objective*.

Moral Horror

The third 'moral horror' objection concerns the implications of relativism for moral criticism. The objection here is that relativism erodes our sense of moral outrage or horror and our ability to criticise those moralities that horrify us. Scanlon, for example, notes the objection that relativism undermines 'the confidence we have or would like to have in our condemnation of wrongful conduct and of those who engage in it' (Scanlon, 1995, 228). It is commonly held that we have deep-seated moral beliefs that some actions undertaken by members of other societies with different moralities are very wrong. However, it would seem that the worst a consistent relativist can say of someone else's evil is 'I disapprove most strongly of their actions and it goes against the morality which is true-for-us, though it may be justified by the morality which is true-for-them'. This, many universalists contend, is not enough. For relativism to satisfy our intuitions, it has to allow us to criticise (and justify action) in certain circumstances. Relativism must allow us to think some moralities 'beyond the pale'. Indeed, there is a wider issue for the relativist here concerning moral criticism in general. I will develop in this chapter a concern about criticism not only in cases of moral horror, but also cases where moralities are equally justified. If relativism renders at least some moralities equally good, then this raises the question of what kind of criticism we can offer of *any* other morality, let alone extreme cases.

Thus, to sum up these three issues as initial criteria for a successful relativist approach;

(1) Relativism must explain what happens when two people have a deep moral disagreement, and in what sense it is a disagreement.

(2) Relativism must allow our moral positions to be true (or at least non-arbitrary).

(3) Relativism must allow us to criticise adequately those moralities that we find abhorrent.

David Wong's Conception of Moral Relativity

Wong's justification is based on (1) a discussion of moral language, (2) a functional argument from what morality — any morality — is supposed to do, and (3) a discussion of differences between moralities that shows how relativism can account in a superior way for deep differences in moral beliefs within and between moral systems. I will briefly set out each of these components in turn.

(1) Wong feels it is incumbent on relativism to explain how it can be accommodated into moral language.[18] This I take to be addressing something like the second challenge to relativism that I outlined above. Drawing on the work of Tarski and Davidson, his analysis of moral language aims to show how different moralities can have different truth conditions because there are many possible extensions to the concept of an adequate moral system. Wong takes as the backdrop for his work the correspondence theory of truth, and reconciles this with relativity by allowing moral truth to vary according to the individual or society's interpretation of an 'adequate moral system'. He analyses statements of the form 'A ought to do X' and 'X is a good Y' in terms of 'rules and standards of moral systems that people have developed to resolve internal and interpersonal conflicts . . . in the end, the true nature of the rules and standards depends on the criteria for adequacy of moral systems that people lay down in fixing the reference of "adequate moral system"' (Wong, 1986, 71–2). Wong's theory makes the truth of moral statements correspond to, and thus relative to, rules that are not independent of 'human will and invention' (Wong, 1986, 72).

(2) Turning now to Wong's functional argument, this begins with an account of how he perceives the role and nature of morality. Wong sees a morality, or adequate moral system, as a system of rules for regulating interpersonal conflict in a satisfactory way. He argues firstly that a number of different moralities can fulfil this function satisfactorily, so there may be more that one morality which fulfils the functional requirements of being an adequate moral system. For example, he says,

> Human beings have needs to resolve internal conflicts between requirements and to resolve interpersonal conflicts of interest. There are constraints on what a morality could be like and still serve these needs. These constraints are derived from the physical environment, from human nature, and from standards of rationality, but they are

---

[18]   I am not particularly concerned here with this part of Wong's analysis. The real thrust of my analysis here, and I think the real power of Wong's argument, lies elsewhere.

not enough to eliminate all but one morality as meeting those needs (Wong, 1986, 175).

I think this claim about the function of an adequate moral system is crucial in allowing Wong to explain those features of moral life which are 'objectivity-suggesting'. However, I want to suggest below that the reason for its success in this respect is also the source of a problem for Wong. He allows for the 'objectivity-suggesting' features of our moral life by building a degree of universalism into his theory.

If we now consider (3), Wong's third central claim is that relativism offers the best account of moral disagreement. Wong takes the disagreement between and within virtue-based theories (such as Confucian and Aristotelian moral systems) and rights-based theories (egalitarian liberalism), as examples of deep moral disagreement. It is worth noting here that a large part of Wong's argument on this point is negative. He systematically delineates, and then eliminates, common absolutist or universalist analyses of moral disagreement and moral diversity. For example, Wong contends that the difference in the interpretation of, and the value placed on, the ideal of freedom in various virtue-based and rights-based moralities cannot be explained by holding one side to be in error, or by the difference being due to ignorance of the true nature of freedom. Wong suggests that 'relativists could argue by elimination' to justify relativism, taking the systematic failure of universalists to explain away disagreement to indicate that 'the failure is likely to be incurable' (Wong, 1986, 175). Thus, he is drawn to the conclusion that the relativist analysis, proved reasonable by his work on moral language and supported by the argument from function, is the best explanation of our moral experience of diversity.

Before I move on to examine how Wong deals with the challenges to relativism posed by the features of our moral life that I identified earlier, certain limitations of Wong's approach ought to be recognised. By taking particular disagreements and showing the failure of universalists to explain them, Wong leaves open the possibility that other disagreements can be solved. Thus, the universalist can claim that on *some* moral issues there is a single objectively true moral answer, but that a universalist morality, like any theory, has grey areas. Indeed, as I will note in the next chapter, universalists such as Nagel and Hampshire do not think that our moral lives are exclusively governed by moral universals. Second, Wong only identifies three strategies on the part of universalists. The first of these is a claim of environmental relativity, i.e. that the same morality is interpreted differently or adapted to particular circumstances. The second response argues that disagreement is due to error or ignorance on one or more sides, and is therefore in principle amenable to resolution. Third, that disagreement is 'beyond human powers to settle at this time' (Wong, 1986, 171). There may be other strategies available to the universalist which escape Wong's refutation. In a similar vein, Stout contends that Wong has underestimated the potential of these three universalist responses (Stout, 1990, 92-97). I discuss these strategies, and the possibility of the universalist invoking other explanations, in chapter three.

Wong is also concerned to show how his relativist analysis fits with the commonly accepted features of our moral life. Examining how he deals with these elements illuminates elements of his strategy, and gives some idea as to how relativists might answer universalist claims about the three key features of our moral life outlined above — moral disagreement, moral truth and moral horror.

The first of these issues is moral disagreement. Wong certainly wants to deny a key claim of moral objectivism, that 'when two moral statements conflict as recommendations to action, only one statement can be true' (Wong, 1986, 1). Instead, he is committed to providing an account upon which two conflicting beliefs can *both* be true. However, here Wong runs into a version of the problem I indicated earlier. Sturgeon, for example, has argued that on a relativist interpretation of disagreement both sides are right in what they say, but wrong in thinking that their disagreement was a 'real' one. Relativism, says Sturgeon, 'reconstrues the beliefs so that the inconsistency disappears' (Sturgeon, 1994, 81).

A relativist interpretation of a disagreement between X and Y might look something like this:

X 'relative to my moral system, agent O should have the abortion in situation p'

Y 'relative to my moral system, agent O should not have the abortion in situation p'.

Sturgeon is right in the sense that there is no logical conflict between these two alternatives. A relativist will hold it is possible for both X *and* Y to be correct here. Once the inconsistency disappears, however, it appears the two parties X and Y must be mistaken in thinking there was a real disagreement between them. Therefore — Sturgeon contends — relativism explains a disagreement by saying it did not really exist to begin with, something which would seem odd to both the parties (Sturgeon, 1994, 81).

Wong's response is to point out that there is, in a different sense, a very real and important conflict between X and Y's alternatives. He argues that both views 'may have the illocutionary force of prescription and they would be *conflicting* prescriptions' (Wong, 1986, 45). It is *impossible* for an agent O to do what is recommended to him by both X and Y. Thus, the two do conflict as recommendations to action. Wong terms this situation one of 'pragmatic' disagreement (Wong, 1986, 45). As Arrington writes in his analysis of Wong's position, 'although there is no logical disagreement here, the two speakers are not just talking past one another ... such conflict is genuine, but it is pragmatic rather than logical' (Arrington, 1989, 228).[19] Wong can simply give a 'particular interpretation' of moral disagreement, rather than denying it really exists. To my mind, this interpretation is close to what we *do* actually say on these difficult questions. People might accept there is widespread disagreement about whether abortion is right or not, and hence feel the need to qualify their statement with something like 'I believe ...' or 'according to my moral beliefs ...'. Whilst there need be no logical conflict, there is a disagreement at quite a deep level about which of these two sets of values, pro- or anti-abortion, should be held by all and form the basis for public policy; this is enough for the disagreement to be meaningful.

I now want to consider Wong's response to the second of the three charges. We have already seen that Wong allows two people with mutually inconsistent views both to have 'true' views. Wong's view has been described as the position that '"X is a good Y" has one set of truth conditions for one of the speakers and another set for the other' (Arrington 1989, 229). However, he is not committed to the view that *all* moralities will equally contain the moral truth. There are, says Wong, good and bad arguments for moral positions (this is one of the features of moral objectivity which Wong believes his theory incorporates). Some of these criteria for a good argument are things such as consistency and coherence, but more interesting is his idea that some moralities can be excluded because they fail to regulate internal and interpersonal conflict satisfactorily. For example, 'one of the primary functions of a morality is the resolution of interpersonal conflict. A system of rules that allowed torture for amusement could not possibly achieve this function' (Wong, 1986, 60).

---

[19] Scanlon, whilst noting this alternative, also gives the possibility of viewing disagreement *as if* it were between universalist positions (Scanlon, 1995). For my criticisms of this position, see Harman's introduction of quasi-absolutism below.

This last argument gives Wong a response to the third of our problems — whether his relativism allows us to criticise morally horrific practices. He can hold that since such moralities fail his criterion of regulating interpersonal conflict, they can be criticised because they are less justified than our own. However, I believe that this resolution comes at a high cost to the relativity of Wong's argument. Historically, it has been very easy to regulate interpersonal conflict in a variety of abhorrent (to us) yet effective ways. Examples of this include the burning of heretics or witches, or caste-based societies such as feudal Japan, where in a practice known as *Kirisutegomen* a samurai could kill commoners at will without threat of punishment. I would argue that unless we value-load the concept of 'regulating interpersonal conflict' to a significant extent, Wong's prohibition on torture appears arbitrary. As Devine has pointed out,

> If one group of persons enjoys what is sometimes called strategic superiority over another — in other words, if it enjoys the ability to impose whatever terms is pleases upon the other group — a system of rules that permitted members of the superior group to do whatever they pleased with members of the inferior group might well settle conflicts both within each of the two groups and between the two groups as a whole (Devine, 1987, 136).

More importantly however, it points to a large universalist element in Wong's theory. The successful resolution of internal and interpersonal conflict becomes a criterion for acceptability which applies to everyone, and this criterion is not purely procedural — since Wong notes that certain types of resolution will be unacceptable. Thus, Wong's theory can be seen to incorporate a substantive moral judgement about the validity of moral systems. This kind of outer limit on what counts as an adequate moral system leaves him open to objections that he is in fact specifying some sort of uniquely true or justified moral system — that an adequate moral system must be a *fair* moral system. There is, strictly, still room here for Wong's claim that it does not determine a *uniquely fair* moral system. Nevertheless, Wong is using a moral claim to determine which moral frameworks are justified. He is applying universal moral norms as an important element in his relativist account of moral justification, and this is incompatible with his relativist framework.

Moral Choice and Criticism

As well as this important problem concerning Wong's response to moral horror, two further problems are generated by the multiplicity of justified moral systems that Wong's system yields. In addition to the challenges posed by moral disagreement, truth and horror, I believe that a response to these two questions is crucial for any relativist approach. First, we are left with a question concerning the limits of justified moral criticism. This asks how, if at all, we can be justified in criticising other adequate moral systems that possess the same amount of the same kind of justification. We have seen that Wong allows for strong criticism of *abhorrent* moralities, but Wong is silent on this particular question. He indicates that hopefully we will be

> exhilarated by the wide range of human possibility to live in different ways and to become different people . . . it is not obvious that we cannot learn to accept that what is morally true for us is in part determined by our specific historical and cultural environment (Wong, 1986, 175).

But this gives us little guidance about the scope of justified criticism available to us, and about the question of whether our moral judgements are altered in form, content or scope. Two important questions need to be answered here. First, if we know there is a competing equally valid moral system, will not our criticisms of it — the judgements we pass — be undermined? Second, shouldn't we acknowledge this when we judge others?[20] Wong can offer one of two possible approaches to these problems. The first response is simply to say that metaethical relativism *should* make our moral beliefs less certain, and to that extent, us holding our moral beliefs with a great deal of certainty is a bad thing. Relativism could require a kind of modesty about our moral beliefs. The second alternative is to say that we can be relativists but insist that we can still criticise strongly *enough*. On the relativist account, it seems that all we can ever say is 'your actions are wrong according to my set of moral rules; I have examined your set of moral rules and find them wanting', and Wong's proposal allows us to say exactly that. He could contend that this was strong enough to fulfil the requirements of our moral experience. However, it is not clear from his work what our justification could be for rejecting another morality which is as 'true' or justified as our own. What could prompt criticism if we accept that the morality we are criticising is equally valid? Any moral assessment of another's position is undercut by the knowledge that there is no real problem with their moral system. This important concern about moral criticism is left unanswered by Wong.

---

[20]   Arrington makes a similar point when he asks 'should we not be brought up short by the fact that moral systems are social creations rather than competing descriptions of some independent moral reality?' (Arrington, 1989, 238).

A second related problem, also left unsolved by Wong, concerns exactly how we *decide* between these equally true moralities. This I will term the problem of indeterminacy in moral theory choice. Universalists have argued that if we are left with a number of equally justified moralities, we have no basis on which to decide between them. Wong's criteria of being consistent, coherent, and fulfilling the functions of an 'adequate moral system', will only limit our choice, not remove the need for any choice at all. If we have any rational choice between competing moral theories, for example if we can choose to reject a rights-based morality in favour of a virtue-based one, then Wong does not tell us how our choice should be guided. Theory choice between those moralities that 'make the grade' is to be left underdetermined. We are given no guidance as to which we should hold, nor (if they are equally justified) could any such guidance be given. We are left in a situation that mimics the parody of relativism 'heads I'll be a utilitarian, tails I'll be an egoist, and if it stands on its edge I'll be a Kantian' (Harrison, 1979, 135). In my view this is a crucial criticism of relativism, and one that I believe Harman (who I will examine next) is also vulnerable to.[21]

Summary

Wong offers a strong account of one kind of metaethical relativism. He suggests that relativism can cope with various features of our moral life which indicate objectivity, and that relativism can explain those features which indicate relativity much more easily than can universalism. Wong's account advances the relativist's case, providing a coherent characterisation of moral disagreement and recognising the need for relativism to cope with criticism of moralities 'beyond the pale'. However, I believe that Wong incorporates a degree of universality that may make his claim about the absence of a single true morality problematic. He does this by specifying a substantive moral baseline for what is to count as an adequate moral system. Only certain ways of regulating interpersonal conflict are truly moral. I have also argued that he fails to provide explanations of two other crucial issues. First, he lacks a thoroughgoing account of the possibility and extent of moral criticism. Second, he lacks an explanation of theory choice in a situation characterised by this kind of relativism.

---

[21] I want to return to this issue in the conclusion of this chapter in order to discuss possible solutions — in particular the one that I will put forward in chapter four, which will arise from an examination of Rawls' idea of reflective equilibrium.

Harman and Relativism —
Relativity as Reasonably Required

Having evaluated Wong's attempted vindication of relativism, I turn now to a second. I have suggested that Wong's argument exemplifies one strategy in justifying relativism. Gilbert Harman, by contrast, suggests another approach. Harman has in the past advanced a limited relativist thesis concerning the evaluation of others' actions, which held that certain moral judgements about rightness and wrongness made sense only in relation to an agreement about rules of conduct. According to Harman, 'an action may be wrong in relation to one agreement but not in relation to another' (Harman, 1975, 3). For Harman this limits the kinds of criticisms we can make of evil men such as Hitler, since we might characterise Hitler as not having any reason which could motivate him to refrain from his evil acts (Harman, 1975, 7). Harman argues that it is a problematic move to assign compelling reasons to people who have different moral understandings or agreements. The analysis of reasons is an important component of relativism. Indeed, because the relativist position I will advance in chapters four and five operates purely as an account of justification, reasons are central to my analysis there. However, here I want to discuss his most recent contribution to the debate on relativism, which is stronger in its premises and conclusions whilst still having this element concerned with reasoning. It is also more complex, introducing a number of different ideas and arguments. Harman makes two linked claims about moral relativity.

(1)   'Moral right and wrong (good and bad, justice and injustice, virtue and vice, etc.) are always relative to a choice of moral framework. What is morally right in relation to one moral framework can be morally wrong in relation to a different moral framework.'

(2)   'And no moral framework is objectively privileged as the one true morality' (Harman, 1996,1).

I want to argue here that whilst we have good reason to accept the first claim — framework-relativity — he does not establish the second claim.

Harman's strategy is twofold. Firstly, he argues that relativity, while not conclusively proved, is made more probable because of widespread moral diversity. Relativism arises out of the most plausible explanation of the diversity. Thus he is committed to the claim, denied by universalists (as my discussion of Caney's argument in chapter three will illustrate) that 'it is unlikely that any nontrivial moral principles are universally accepted in all societies' (Harman, 1996, 8). The presence or absence of moral diversity, and what exactly this presence or absence signifies is a matter of some debate between universalists and relativists.[22] This issue surfaces again in the next chapter and I attempt a resolution, drawing on Daniels' analysis, in chapter four. Harman says that some disagreement and diversity rests on basic differences which universalism cannot satisfactorily explain. Interestingly, he does not then follow this up with a detailed analysis, like Wong's, of the inadequacies of universalist analyses of moral diversity.

Instead, he then turns to argue by analogy from general relativity that scientific judgements and moral judgements alike are both relative to frameworks. Harman holds that 'there is no such thing as absolute motion, apart from one or another system of coordinates' (Harman, 1996, 13). Similarly, 'a given act can be right with respect to one system of moral coordinates and wrong with respect to another system of moral coordinates. And nothing is absolutely right or wrong, apart from any system of moral coordinates' (Harman, 1996, 13).

Of course, one particular set of moral coordinates is going to be 'especially salient' to any particular person — their own. What people tend to take to be absolute rightness or wrongness is really relative to their moral schema. This, it should be noted, is 'not by itself a claim about meaning. It does not say that speakers always intend their moral judgements to be relational in this respect' (Harman, 1996, 17). As I noted above, Harman takes relativism to be a position about how things really are, a position that seems to disregard the way we use moral language. He clearly draws his thoughts on this from the idea that 'Einstein's theory does not make a claim about speakers' intentions. It does not claim that speakers intend to be making relational judgements when they speak about mass or simultaneity. The claim is, rather, that there is no such thing as absolute simultaneity or absolute mass' (Harman, 1996, 18). However, Harman provides very little evidence as to *why* we should suppose that morality is like science with regard to relativity. Depending on our interpretation of the nature of science and of morality, the disanalogies between the two could be many and various; it is not immediately clear that what is true of relativity in science need be true with regard to morality. What is needed is *evidence* for the claim that moral judgements are necessarily relativistic.

---

[22] As I note in chapter three, some universalists point to the extent of *agreement* as a basis for a common morality.

A start on providing such evidence could lie in pointing to the widespread scientific work on the impact on perception of the perceiver's mental state and beliefs.[23] If the framework of the perceiver necessarily influences what is perceived, and our perception of a situation influences our moral judgement in a situation, then it might be thought our moral judgements necessarily have a subjective or relativist element. In addition, every example of a sphere in which relativistic considerations impinge strengthens that argument from analogy.

Despite the need for evidence that moral judgements are relativistic in the same way as judgements of speed, Harman's point that moral judgements typically form parts of frameworks may be undeniable. Moral judgements, as I will discuss in chapter three, ideally fit into a coherent whole. Our judgements require reasons to back them up, and the absence of any justification provided by other judgements, facts and theories, would seem to rob them of this element. My contention is that this element is one we recognise from our moral life. We have to know at the time that we say something to be the case, *why* we say that something is the case, in order for us to think our belief justified. Indeed, being able to supply reasons in support of our view is surely key to any idea of justification at all. Thus, it is a bold move to deny Harman's observation that all judgements ought to be relative to frameworks, i.e. be part of systems of supporting reasons, if they are to claim justification.

We can accept Harman's first claim, that all moral judgements ought to be understood as relative to a moral framework. However, this, by itself, does not serve to justify Harman's second claim. We cannot jump from (1) all moral judgements are relative to a moral framework to (2) there is no objectively privileged moral framework. Absolutists and universalists could admit (1) but say that nevertheless, all moral judgements ought to be made and justified relative to the single *correct* moral framework. For example, a religious person might say 'of course my judgement is relative to a framework in which the Bible is the word of God and should be followed, but I believe this precisely because it is the *only correct* moral framework.' Thus, Harman has to argue, partly by analysing moral disagreement in a similar way to Wong, that all moral judgements should not be seen as relative to *one* universally correct moral framework. Not only, says Harman, is relativism of this kind a better explanation of moral disagreement, but

---

he also denies the claim of universalists that 'when a moral requirement applies to someone, that person has compelling reasons to do what he or she is required to do' (Harman, 1996, 45).

By shifting his approach to the realm of reasons, Harman makes a claim about the nature of moral justification which mirrors his use of moral truth, and returns to the territory of his original relativism. Harman replies to the universalist that for a morality to be universal, there have to be compelling reasons for people to believe and follow it. Through an analysis of attempts to provide compelling reasons, such as those of Gewirth and Nagel, he finds the project unsatisfactory. In doing so, he is suggesting that reasons and justifications are relative to frameworks, just as judgements about mass are. Like Wong, his argument depends on criticism of opposing positions about moral reasoning to establish relative plausibility, and I examine the thinkers he criticises in chapter three. Whilst merely noting this reasons-based aspect of his approach here, I take the relativity of reasons up in more detail in chapter five. There I expand and defend it as part of my defence of a distinct form of relativism.

I now want to show more clearly some of the implications of Harman's view by examining how he copes with the three problems that I initially posed for relativist analyses, and the two further issues I raised in my discussion of Wong. The first of these is moral disagreement. In his discussion of moral disagreement, Harman takes the example of disagreement between two relativists over the morality of raising animals for food. He writes:

> In some sense, they disagree with each other, but moral relativism does not appear to provide them with an easy way in which to express their disagreement. Each agrees that raising animals for food is wrong relative to the first moral framework and that raising animals for food is not wrong relative to the second (Harman, 1996, 32).

Harman's initial response to this disagreement is that the two people are bargaining about what rule *is* to apply in this circumstance. They are not bargaining 'over what the rules morally ought to be in some non-relativistic sense of 'morally ought'' (Harman, 1996, 33). However, Harman acknowledges that pure relativism does not allow the expression of moral disagreement. Thus, initially Harman seems to fall foul of Sturgeon's criticism that relativists start from the fact of pervasive moral disagreement, and end up explaining why there is no disagreement at all (Sturgeon, 1994). His relativism does produce a counter-intuitive response to moral disagreement.

However, Harman toys with a possible alternative approach which would allow relativists to express disagreement. Drawing on the work of Hare (1972) and Blackburn (1993), he terms this approach quasi-absolutism, and takes it to involve appealing 'only to ingredients that are acceptable to a moral relativist in order to construct a way of using moral terminology that mimics the absolutist usage' (Harman, 1996, 34).[24] Harman explains this process as one in which 'the relativist projects his or her moral framework onto the world and then uses moral terminology as if the projected morality were the single true morality, while at the same time admitting that this way of talking is 'only if'' (Harman, 1996, 34). On this account, the relativist rejects universalist backing for our use of moral language and instead substitutes a background acceptable to relativism, but keeps the use and meaning of moral language constant. Similarly, Blackburn explains in his defence of quasi-realism that quasi-realists can employ notions of moral facts, truth and objectivity largely without alteration. 'Can the quasi-realist say such things? I have just said them' (Blackburn, 1999, 217).

Whilst this might silence many universalist criticisms of relativism that centre on the inability of relativism to speak of moral facts, truth and objectivity, it also appears puzzling and problematic.[25] On the one hand, the adoption of quasi-absolutist language to express views may have the advantages of solving Sturgeon's problem and providing a sense in which relativists disagree. Thus, utilising quasi-absolutism, Harman's approach does less violence to our intuitions about moral disagreement. It says that by using language just as if we were universalists, we could give a universalist, and thus satisfactory, account of moral disagreement.[26] The mimicking of universalism, as we shall see, provides Harman with simple responses to other criticisms arising from elements of our moral experience. However, the seemingly ad-hoc adoption of quasi-absolutism also has costs. To adopt an approach which simulates universalism purely so that we can allow for our everyday moral experience is an admission of desperation or defeat. Harman admits that he is unsure whether the central assertion of quasi-absolutism, that 'words can be given meaning by being given a use' (Harman, 1996, 34) is correct. Even

---

[24] Blackburn details the thesis he terms 'quasi-realism' in Blackburn (1993).

[25] In fact, because of these problems, I am doubtful about the ability of this response to satisfy universalist critics.

[26] Although it is by no means obviously the case that this would completely satisfy universalist critics either. Blackburn makes an example of a case where, with regard to particularly powerful moral imperatives, quasi-realism is still thought to 'smell of sulphur' (Blackburn, 1999, 225). For such a universalist view, see Dworkin (1996).

if it is, it is disingenuous of the relativist to use language as if universalism were correct whilst simultaneously asserting that it is not. Quasi-absolutism admits that we use moral language in a universalist way, and advocates the best course to be to mimic this usage. This is perhaps conceding too much to the universalist. As we shall see in chapter three, universalist positions such as Nagel's, and perhaps Habermas', start from this supposition, that our moral experience is ineluctably universalist or objective in character. I will argue in chapters four and five that there is an alternative to quasi-absolutism that, drawing on an examination of the way in which we employ reasons in moral argument and our expectations of the power of such reasons, does not involve such concessions.

Having introduced quasi-absolutism as part of Harman's account of moral disagreement, I want to return to the schema of this section by looking at Harman's response to the other questions raised by our moral experience. Harman's initial response to questions concerning the nature of moral truth does not invoke quasi-absolutism, and appears counter-intuitive,. On his account, moral statements such as 'X is wrong' are incomplete, though not necessarily untrue. Like in the case of pre-Einsteinian physics, says Harman, 'it would be mean-spirited to invoke an error theory' (Harman, 1996, 4) and thus conclude that all such moral statements are false. Instead, they are incomplete because they do not include a relation to a system of reference, and 'the only truth there is in this area is relative truth' (Harman, 1996, 4).

Thompson takes Harman to be denying that moral sentences have truth-conditions, i.e. that moral sentences cannot be true or false (Thompson, 1996). However, I do not think we need take this view, for two reasons. The first is that in saying that moral claims are 'merely incomplete', Harman is ambiguous as to whether moral sentences can be true or false. A second reason is that Harman could respond by saying that they are 'relatively true'. Harman goes on to develop a quasi-absolutist response of this kind, denying that the truth in question is absolute or objective. This position is analogous to Wong's view that different adequate moral systems have different truth conditions. The difference is that on an ordinary level of discourse, the employment of quasi-absolutism allows us to use 'truth' exactly as if it were absolute.

A third issue to which I have suggested that the relativist must respond is our reaction to moral horror. Here again, the introduction of quasi-absolutism complicates Harman's views. Harman says, 'there is no single true morality. There are many different moral frameworks, none of which is more correct than the others' (Harman, 1996, 5). On a natural interpretation of Harman's statement, he is arguing that (1) instead of one true morality, there are many and (2) no morality is more correct than any other. On another understanding, the 'equal correctness' clause is meant only to apply to those many true moralities. There remains on this account a further set of moralities that are *not* equally correct.[27] Harman has subsequently qualified his account in favour of the latter interpretation. Whilst all moral frameworks are equally correct, nevertheless some apparent instances of moral frameworks are not actually successful moral frameworks at all. Within the realm of the many correct frameworks, however, there appears little hope of forceful moral criticism. Again, Harman flies in the face of our intuitions here, and is left with two possible responses. The first is simply to say that our intuitions are wrong; after all, Harman is attempting to describe reality rather than our perception of it. The second is a quasi-absolutist solution, which allows a kind of *appraiser* relativism[28] on which we can judge others by our own relative moral standards (Harman, 1996, 62-3). We can attempt to do more than appraise, however. We can also try to change the view of the person we are criticising. If we are attempting to convince, to provide compelling reasons, then these must come from within the morality of the agent whom we are criticising (*agent* relativism). Here, Harman reintroduces his earlier characterisation of relativism:

> The critic can express certain evaluations of the agent in relation to the critic's moral framework, like 'Hitler was a great evil.' And the critic can make reason-implying judgements in relation to the critic's moral framework, like 'Hitler was doing the morally right thing for a nazi to do.' But the critic cannot make objective reason-implying judgements in relation to his (the critic's) morality. The critic will not be able to say, for example, 'it was morally wrong of Hitler to have acted in that way' (Harman, 1996, 62).

The difficulty comes in moving from appraisal — 'Hitler was a great evil' to making 'reason-implying judgements' that would provide Hitler with a reason to change his view. For Harman, the latter kind can only come relative to the framework of the agent.

In chapter five, I will look more closely at the possibility of giving reasons that can force a change in someone's view. For now, I want to emphasise that quasi-absolutist terminology allows Harman's approach a response to the fourth issue concerning criti-

---

[27] Harman does not provide a clear conception in *Moral Relativism and Moral Objectivity* of what will separate correct from incorrect moralities.

[28] or in Harman's terminology a *critic*-relativism (Harman, 1996, 62).

cism of other justified moralities. It provides an account of the kind of criticism we can make of other equally justified cultures, an account which I suggested Wong lacks. This is nothing more that we should expect, given that quasi-absolutism amounts to the adoption of all the appearances of universalism. However, despite providing a response on this issue, the adoption of quasi-absolutism comes with significant costs and problems for the relativist.

Furthermore, quasi-absolutism is vulnerable to the fifth problem of theory choice indeterminacy, just like Wong's account. If all, or a selection of moralities are equally justified, why should we want to, or be justified in wanting to, pretend that our morality has any superiority? Faced with a selection of competing moralities, how can we decide between them? Whilst quasi-absolutism offers the possibility of moral criticism, it nevertheless leaves undetermined which of the moral theories on offer we should choose as the basis from which to offer such criticism. As with Wong, the question of indeterminacy in theory choice remains unresolved.

I want to contend that the main problem with Harman's theory is his readiness to do some real violence to our intuitions on certain key points (unless we accept quasi-absolutism). Our moral statements are incomplete; disagreement does not exist once you recognise the incompleteness of our moral statements, and judgement of outsiders is impossible, *unless* we accept quasi-absolutism — a move that constitutes a kind of suspension of disbelief. The cost of being a relativist is very high on Harman's account, unless we all pretend to be universalists. For the relativist, this is surely not the most desirable outcome.

Rorty's Relativism

This chapter has so far concentrated on the work of Wong and Harman, and has illustrated the kinds of issues and problems that a relativist approach must face. In the final part of this chapter, I want to return to Rorty's view. When outlining his view in the introduction, I claimed that Rorty is a relativist of the kind I am examining here, despite his protestations to the contrary. It is only appropriate that before concluding the chapter I examine what Rorty's responses might be to the same kinds of issues about our moral experience. His approach shares interesting similarities and differences with those I have examined so far, illustrating their comparative strengths. I want to examine how Rorty deals with our intuitive demands for (a) an explanation of the way in which moral statements can be true, and (b) a response to moral horror. A response to this latter concern also indicates how he might cope with the issues surrounding equally justified moralities that I identified in my discussion of Wong. Missing here is an account of how Rorty would deal with moral disagreement. This is because Rorty does not address this as a key concern. Nevertheless, because of his views on social criticism that I discussed earlier in the chapter, it may be that this is not a major independent issue. If his account allows one party to be wrong or unwarranted in holding a view, and if we can characterise moral disagreement in this way then there is no problem here for Rorty. As I have also suggested, however, this view is problematic in the extent to which it (dis)allows social criticism. Here I will discuss only (a) and (b).

(a) Whilst Harman and Wong have given an account of how things can be 'true-for', on first glance Rorty appears to deny the need for any determinate theory of truth — for this is part of Rorty's anti-representationalist project. He agrees with Davidson that 'we should not say that truth is correspondence, coherence, warranted assertibility, ideally justified assertibility, what is accepted in the conversation of the right people, what explains the convergence on single theories in science, or the success of our ordinary beliefs' (Davidson, quoted in Rorty, 1998, 11). In particular, he wants to argue that there is no independent test of the correspondence of something with reality (Rorty, 1998, 6). Rorty thinks that his pragmatism, at heart, can consist simply in the dissolution of the traditional problematic about truth (Rorty, 1991, 127). We should take these remarks, I would contend, to apply to truth in all fields, and perhaps in morality more than anywhere else.

Despite this position, Rorty is certainly offering an account of the recommended usage of 'true' and 'truth', including the truth of moral judgements and statements. This is an account which denies truth an explanatory value but gives it an 'endorsing' use (Rorty, 1991, 128), in particular as a term designating well-justified belief, since 'the pattern that truth makes is the pattern that *justification to us* makes' (Rorty, 1998, 25). For Rorty, knowledge or truth is 'simply a compliment paid to the beliefs we think so well justified that for the moment further justification is not needed' (Rorty, 1991, 24). He is not offering any of the alternatives listed by Davidson above, but he is nevertheless recommending a different and better meaning to the word 'truth', as when he says that '[James] could have gone on to say that we have no criterion of truth other than justification' (Rorty, 1998, 2). Thus, Rorty's claim to have no theory of truth should not be taken to mean that Rorty does not want to advocate a particular account of truth as being the best.[29]

(b) Rorty's response to moral horror is facilitated by his ethnocentrism. Because Rorty straightforwardly believes that our own lights justify, we are placed in a strong position from which to criticise other moralities. 'Postmodernist bourgeois liberalism' (Rorty, 1991, 197), Rorty contends, is the best belief system. It is justified by our lights, and we should not hesitate in judging others by it. We operate 'from the networks we are, from the community with which we presently identify' (Rorty, 1991, 202). However, his comments about the difficulty of justification — that something can be justified for us but not by another set of lights — leaves matters unclear. Exactly how much force will our criticisms have if other societies need not feel any compunction to heed them? Because Rorty's account places so much emphasis on ethnocentrism, it seems little meaning can be given within his theory to the idea of equally justified moralities, and thus the problem of limits to moral criticism. Nonetheless, I argued earlier in this chapter that Rorty does share with his fellow relativists a commitment to justification being network- or community-relative. Because of this, I am unsure that Rorty can successfully escape this problem.

Likewise, the problem of indeterminacy in theory choice apparently does not even arise within Rorty's theory; we have the lights of our own society, and going against them to choose a different theory is 'unwarranted'. Because we choose from the position of the society of which we are a part, with which we 'presently identify', there appears to be no room for theory choice at all in Rorty's view, and hence no room for criticism that theory choice is underdetermined to find a foothold.[30] Instead, this lack of any external perspective on our own society — Rorty says that 'a child found wandering in the woods, the remnant of a slaughtered nation . . . has no share in human dignity' (Rorty, 1991, 201) — means theory choice is *over*-determined, and Rorty is left with

[29] On this issue, I have some sympathy with Putnam's comment that 'most of the time anyway, Rorty really thinks that metaphysical realism is wrong. We will be better off if we listen to him in the sense of having fewer false beliefs; but this, of course, is something he cannot admit that he really thinks' Putnam, 1990, 25).

[30] We might have to choose between competing interpretations of our own lights, but this is a much smaller question than that of choosing between different sets of lights.

the classic relativist problem concerning the possibility of societal criticism.[31]

To summarise this section, I have argued Rorty can be characterised as a relativist. He affirms as part of his ethnocentrism, like other metaethical relativists, that there is no single justified (or true) morality. His relativism is backed up by a notion of truth that lends itself to recommendatory use, identifying it with justification (which he variously talks of as being constituted by 'coherence' or 'convenience', as I will discuss in chapter five). Rorty's ethnocentrism does not provide clear guidelines as to the description of moral disagreement, or our response to moral horror. On the latter, he leans towards Harman's position that we can criticise freely, though this criticism need not be compelling to others.

Conclusion

This chapter has set out to examine contemporary defences of metaethical relativism, as constituted by various relativistic accounts of moral truth, reasoning and assessment, and 'ethnocentrism'. I have suggested that these defences are united by the claim that there is no single true or justified morality and I have offered summaries of the way two strategies for justifying this claim might run. This chapter demonstrates that relativists can provide ways to deflect many common versions of the charge that relativism fails to do justice to the reality of our moral experience. Wong offers us an account of how people can pragmatically disagree, and how by building in a minimal standard, the relativist need not say that all moralities are as good as each other, even the ones we find appalling.[32] Harman provides an innovative argument by analogy to relativity in physics which might, fully developed, prove difficult to refute. He also indicates a way to think of relativism in terms of the denial of universal reasons which, I will suggest in chapter five, is a powerful way to characterise the central relativist claim.

However, the approaches of both thinkers also share problems. I have suggested that both make too great a concession to their universalist critics: Wong, by giving considerations of universal basic requirements for adequate moralities too thick a content, Harman by adopting quasi-absolutism as the 'way out' of incom-

---

[31]   To say that there is no problem within Rorty's theory here is not to say that there is no problem *with* Rorty's theory. The issue raised by social criticism is that societies are *not* univocal.

[32]   Nevertheless, I have been critical of the particular minimal standard Wong offers. I will go on to suggest in chapters four and five that we can indeed find a minimal standard, but one that differs from Wong's.

patibility with our intuitions. In chapters four and five I sketch my alternatives to these choices and provide reasons why I believe the alternatives to be superior. I have also suggested that both Wong and Harman's theories share a problem about criticism and theory choice within the circle of moralities that are justified on a relativist account. We are left with a worry about the way relativism threatens people's sense 'that they have adequate grounds for believing their way of life is justified, and for preferring it to others' (Scanlon, 1995, 230). There are two aspects to moral criticism. Moral criticism is not just important with regard to fundamentally objectionable moralities. We must also explain the kind of criticism, if any, we can pass on those moralities which are as justified as our own, but that we nevertheless do not agree with. In conjunction with this, we have to provide some reasons why we ought to hold on to our own morality rather than switch to another which is equally justified. This chapter has also briefly discussed Rorty's theory. Rorty's bullish assertion of ethnocentrism, that we should just 'get on with it' because we are committed to our standards being the correct ones, perhaps points the way towards a resolution of these issues, a resolution I attempt in chapters four and five. Thus, in addition to the issues that I identified at the start of the chapter — of (a) moral disagreement, (b) moral truth, and (c) horror — I have highlighted two further concerns, (d) criticism of other justified moralities and (e) theory choice indeterminacy.

The fact that all three thinkers are committed to a particular view of truth underlines another of my contentions; that given the sophisticated ongoing debate about what constitutes truth, provided the relativist can give some account of what is happening when someone *claims* that something is true, there is no reason why relativism cannot remain detached from this debate. Nevertheless, even a relativism which avoids questions of truth must allow relativised moral views to have force beyond being mere statements of personal preference. The way in which relativism can attain some kind of objective force is discussed in chapter four.

Missing from my analysis in this chapter was any examination of 'the competition', and the analysis of the many varieties of universalism is where I must turn next. This chapter aimed to dispel ideas that relativism was patently inadequate in dealing with our moral experience, but also to illustrate the tensions and problems for contemporary relativist approaches that arise from trying to deal with it. The next chapter attempts little in the way of a similar structure, aiming instead to show and examine a range of alternatives to relativism grouped under the heading of 'universalism'. The purpose tying together these analyses of universalism is the task of illustrating possible relationships between universalism and relativism.

Chapter 3

Universalism

Introduction

Having examined some of the core features of relativism, this chapter turns to an examination of competing views of our moral experience. These can be characterised, according to the schema that I laid out in the introduction, as universalist views. I take the core of the universalist position to be the belief that there is a single true morality. Alternatively, if we eschew reference to a complete moral system, then there are at least uniquely valid moral principles that apply to everyone. Thus, truth and justification in the moral sphere is not relativistic. This need not equate, as many universalists have noted, to the view that *all* moral principles must be universal.[1] Furthermore, the grounds on which universalists assert this can vary greatly between positions. In this chapter, I will begin by examining four distinct kinds of universalism, indicating different ways in which values can be thought of as universal. (1)Nagel's argument claims that we must recognise the force of universally binding reasons in assessing moral actions. (2)Habermas' claims that we cannot escape the claim of objectivity made in moral language. (3)Hampshire's position that makes certain moral principles universal 'merely' because they are common to human beings, or rational for them to hold. I then move on to examine further (4) the idea of a contingent basis in a common moral experience as a justification of universal moral norms, a move that I term 'contingent universalism'.

---

[1] Of the positions I examine in this chapter, none of the theorists advance this maximally strong claim. Hampshire, for example, speaks of granting 'universal necessity' only to 'basic procedural justice' (Hampshire, 1989, 77). The argument of Habermas will grant universality only to some basic rules, and Nagel argues, as I will go on to show, only that there is an ineluctable core of universality in morality; relativism '*usually* fails to convince' (Nagel, 1997, 103, my italics).

All of these theories account for our moral experience in ways different to the relativist. I examined in the last chapter how relativists must account for our use of moral language to express disagreement and abhorrence. The universalist tends to begin with this phenomenon, perceiving our moral life as containing claims or intuitions that present themselves with the status of universal commandments. Our moral experience consists partly in criticising others on grounds of universal values. Thus Caney concludes 'in affirming some moral judgements we are affirming judgements that we believe hold universally' (Caney, 1999, 23). But what is it for a judgement to be universally correct? And why should we think, though we might *intend* our moral judgements to bind others, that they in fact *ought* to? The approaches I discuss below propose distinctive answers to these questions. I conclude the chapter by surveying the relationship between universalism and relativism; starting with positions that almost *define* themselves by opposition to relativism, part of the purpose of this chapter is to examine whether universalist and relativist positions can ever converge.

Of course, the selection of four universalist proposals in this chapter is not meant to be exclusive as an examination of such a popular and sophisticated philosophical position as universalism. There are many defences of universally binding moral rules that I will not discuss here. Notable absentees include Alan Gewirth's argument from rational agency, and some variety of Platonism. Other thinkers hold positions along the lines of the ones I set out here, though with some distinctive features. For example, Ronald Dworkin (1996), as he notes himself, takes a very similar approach to Nagel. Likewise, there are strong links between the universalisms of Martha Nussbaum and Stuart Hampshire. My choice of thinkers to focus on here is influenced by a desire to provide a representative overview of contemporary approaches, and also by the prominence (or perhaps notoriety) of some of these thinkers.

Thomas Nagel's Universalism

Thomas Nagel offers a distinctive variety of universalism with reasons rather than values at its centre. Nagel has been interpreted as initially advancing a fairly modest position. This claims that 'objective' (or, as he later called them 'agent-neutral') considerations such as 'that acting would relieve someone's pain' can be 'genuine reasons to act' (Darwall et al, 1992, 135).[2] He expands this claim into one about the power of agent-neutral reasons in the phenomenology of our moral experience. Nagel's insistence on the presence and power of agent-neutral reasons is, as I will show, where his opposition to relativism lies. He aims to provide an account of the existence of universally valid moral reasons. Just as part of Harman's account of moral relativity centred on the lack of compelling cross-cultural reasons, so Nagel's approach conversely affirms the presence of reasons which are universal — compelling to everyone — and objective (though the sense in which they are objective is something I will discuss shortly). Whilst there is not necessarily a conflict between accounts of relativity and objectivity (as I will go on to examine in chapter four), there is nevertheless a conflict between relativity and Nagel's conception of objectivity. Rather than offer us an account of the content and justification of a single true morality, Nagel is concerned to affirm a single true model of morality and body of moral reasons that leaves no room for relativism. Nagel's account, we might say, is an account of universalist moral *justification*, just as Harman's discussion of reasons aims to be an account of relativist justification.

Whilst the content of Nagel's precise position has changed over time,[3] the common core of it is that reason possesses universal authority (Nagel, 1997, 3). Reasons are necessarily an attempt to say objectively what anyone in a certain situation ought to do. Such reasoning is a product of our faculty of practical reason. For Nagel, reason is thus authoritative and normative (it ought to, and can, motivate our action). Our moral life demands explanation not merely in a causal sense — such as a psychological explanation of why we do things — but also in a normative or justificatory sense, which must provide the reasons for our action.

---

[2]   In this section I will often use the terms 'objective' and 'agent-neutral' as interchangeable. A full analysis of the ambiguities present in the content of 'objectivity' is undertaken in chapter four, though I point to ambiguities in Nagel's conception in the final part of my analysis. For now, I take Nagelian objectivity to involve standing back from the particular. Whilst I do not think Nagel would be happy to say that objectivity means 'mind-independence', it is perhaps independent of any *particular* mind.

[3]   For example, *The Possibility of Altruism* (Nagel, 1978) argued that agent-relative reasons must be agent-neutral reasons as well; Nagel retracts this as a general argument in *The View From Nowhere* (Nagel, 1986). Whilst *The View From Nowhere* makes references to objective moral reasons as the best explanation of our moral life, the emphasis in *The Last Word* is much more on first-order moral argument (e.g. Nagel, 1997, preface).

Nagel uses pain as evidence for, and an example of, the way our life contains reasons of universal authority. For Nagel, there is a difference between 'pain is unwelcome' as a merely personal motivation, and 'pain is bad' as an objective reason for action for any agent even when it is not their own pain at issue. Nagel's argument concludes that (1) there are universal moral reasons, and (2) at least some of these reasons are agent-neutral — ought to be compelling to any person simply as a member of humanity regardless of particular circumstances. Agent-neutral reasons, therefore, provide reasons for moral action that we cannot deny without denying our agenthood.[4] They 'depend on what everyone ought to value, independently of its relation to himself' (Nagel, 1991, 40). This reference to what everyone *ought* to value illustrates Nagel's opposition to relativism, since relativism would say that there need be no content to the set of reasons that ought to be valued by everyone. The relevant contrast here for Nagel is with *agent-relative* reasons. Nagel also allows for reasons of this kind, 'specified by universal principles which nevertheless refer ineliminably to features or circumstances of the agent for whom they are reasons' (Nagel, 1991, 40).

We can note three strongly related central features of Nagel's argument for these propositions. (1) It rests largely on the undermining of opposing theories that doubt this conclusion — thus, much of Nagel's argument is involved in rejecting scepticism or subjectivism. (2) Part of the argument is that objective, universally valid moral reasons are the best explanation of our experience of morality. (3) It takes the best argument for objective moral truths to 'come from within morality' rather than 'the metaethical level' (Nagel, 1997, preface). The idea is that any non-objective perspective 'will eventually collapse before the independent force of the first order judgements themselves' (Nagel, 1997, 103).[5] Nagel's view is sophisticated and cannot be dismissed lightly, partly because of some points that Nagel himself raises about what it would take to dismiss it. In later chapters, I discuss in detail some of the charges Nagel lays against subjectivist accounts of objectivity as interpersonal agreement. I argue there that Nagel fails to

---

[4]   His argument here appears to share some features with that of Alan Gewirth in *Reason and Morality* (1978).

[5]   I take Dworkin to be making a similar point when he argues that 'The thesis that there is no right answer to the question whether abortion is wicked is itself a substantive moral claim, which must be judged and evaluated in the same way as any other substantive moral claim.' (Dworkin, 1996, 89). The sceptic cannot but operate inside objective morality, and his protestations to the contrary are 'pointless, unprofitable, wearying interruptions' (Dworkin, 1996, 139).

undermine the subjectivist position, and that there is an account of objectivity and objective reasons which can make sense of our moral life without taking a Nagelian transcendence approach. Here I want briefly to outline some of the areas requiring clarification in Nagel's positive argument for the existence of objective moral reasons. The presence of these universal reasons constitutes Nagel's central challenge to the relativist.

The difficulty of refuting Nagel's position can, I think, be underlined by examining exactly what Nagel claims for his theory, and what — he claims — would be required to undermine it. There are several elements here. First, Nagel argues that the burden of proof in debates over objectivity lies with those who deny the appearance of objectivity. Thus, he writes that 'a defeasible presumption that values need not be illusory is entirely reasonable until it is shown not to be' (Nagel, 1986, 143). The burden is on the anti-objectivist to provide a conclusive argument against the idea of objective value. This stance ties in with Nagel's position that universality is the best explanation of moral appearances. Second, Nagel's position is not that all values need be objective, but that all values cannot be subjective (Nagel, 1997, 80-81). Thus, all that Nagel must maintain for his argument to be successful is that *at least some* values are objective. This position is one that will be hard to refute, partly because of the difficulty in examining exactly what objectivity requires. To refute Nagel, it must be conclusively proved that there are no objective values. Third, it will not do as an argument against Nagel to point out that the drive for objectivity is itself a 'subjective', finite, human-held faculty because Nagel affirms this himself. He writes 'The ambition to get outside ourselves has obvious limits . . . whatever we do we remain subparts of the world with limited access to the real nature of the rest of it and ourselves' (Nagel, 1986, 6). Sometimes we will meet the limit of our objective faculty, other times Nagel allows that we can be mistaken, and think things objective which in fact are not. Fourth, it will not do to argue against Nagel by saying that he has failed to impugn the position of sceptics and subjectivists, for Nagel does not claim that he has conclusively justified the existence of objective truths. For example, he notes in *The View From Nowhere* that 'nothing said here will force a reductionist to give up his denial of normative realism' (Nagel, 1986 148). In addition, after Nagel's vigorous arguments to dismiss subjectivist positions in *The Last Word*, Nagel ends on a curiously ambivalent tone with the 'unfortunate note' that 'unless something positive can be put in that space [of relativising qualifications], we will be left with subjectivism after all' (Nagel, 1997, 35).

Nevertheless, I believe there are limitations in Nagel's approach that weaken its relative plausibility compared to the alternatives. To this end, I want to consider three aspects of what I take to be his positive argument for the objectivity of value. The *first* is the strategy of best explanation that Nagel sometimes uses, which I will consider especially with regard to the idea of moral disagreement. The *second* is Nagel's contention that in creating an objective standpoint we leave the subjective behind. The *third* is Nagel's use of pleasure and pain as a paradigmatic clear-cut case of objective and agent-neutral reasoning. To some extent, all of these areas are intertwined. Furthermore, I do not think that any of the problems I will raise necessarily defy resolution, or will force Nagel to give up his position. Nevertheless, I think they point out complexities, assumptions and limitations of his method that make his account less straightforwardly reasonable.

(1) Best Explanation and Moral Disagreement

For Nagel, objective moral reasons are the best explanation of our moral life. The explanation Nagel thinks we must provide is normative or justificatory rather than psychological or causal: psychological accounts of why we act morally cannot tell the whole story. Nagel maintains that

> Any defender of realism about values must claim that the purely psychological account is incomplete, either because normative explanations are an additional element or because the are somehow present in certain types of psychological explanation — perhaps in a way like that in which explanations of belief by logical reasoning can be simultaneously causal and justificatory (Nagel, 1986, 145).

Normative explanation is required, because to dispense with explaining normative judgements in terms of objective normative truths is 'too radical a denial of the appearances' (Nagel, 1986, 146). Nagel will argue that the best explanation of the fact that our moral judgements lay claim to universal validity is that some in fact *do possess* universal validity.

In the previous chapter, I examined the way in which relativists have characterised moral disagreement. Here I want to ask the same question of Nagel. Nagel holds that moral disagreement, like other disagreements over questions of objective value, is a consequence of various factors, including (1) social pressure, (2) lack of rational grounding for beliefs and (3) strong interests affecting opinions on the disputed question, which I take to be some kind of considerations of 'bias'.[6] In particular, says Nagel, (3) is present 'throughout ethics to a uniquely high degree' (Nagel, 1986, 148). Nagel sees agreement on ethical questions, especially in the face of such interests, as suggesting 'that something real is being investigated' (Nagel, 1986, 148). He writes 'the fact that people can to some extent reach agreement on answers which they regard as objective suggests that when they step outside of their particular individual perspectives, they call into operation a common evaluative faculty' (Nagel, 1986, 148). This common evaluative faculty, when operating correctly, 'provides the answers' (Nagel, 1986, 148).

One might ask why we should share Nagel's presumption that *disagreement* can be explained away as a result of pressure whilst *agreement* is interpreted as the result of the correct operation of this evaluative capacity. That people reach agreement on something might just indicate the operating of the same social pressures. Furthermore, the same result could be achieved by evaluative faculties operating in many different ways rather than the use of one common method — these faculties need not evaluate in the same way according to the same criteria, but could still agree on the result.[7] Likewise, disagreement could just as easily be taken as evidence that the common evaluative faculty could issue in multiple equally justified conclusions. Why has disagreement been ruled inadmissible as evidence of a plurality of faculties or answers whilst agreement has been readily acknowledged as evidence for a single faculty and unique objective reasons? The only answer I can provide is that not only is our moral life evidence for objective value, but that the presence of objective value underpins the way we draw evidence from our moral life. In its harshest form, this argument charges that whilst Nagel felt it an argument against subjectivism that it constituted a radical denial

---

[6] Nagel runs together 'the fact that morality is socially inculcated and that there is radical disagreement about it' (Nagel, 1986, 147). I take the considerations I list to be relevant to both these linked phenomena.

[7] Of course, the more often and systematically consensus occurs (without the consensus being due to strong mutual interests), the more we might think it was due to the presence of a single evaluative faculty. But we are still left with the alternatives (a) that prudence would dictate the same consensus, given considerations of the iterative nature of social relationships (b) that it is not a single faculty of 'practical reasoning' but instead the interaction of multiple ones and (c) that this consensus was entirely determined by our human nature. Whilst I am not saying that any of these would necessarily be advocated by a relativist, they still remain possibilities which some critics might believe, and which Nagel does not consider.

of appearances, clearly some appearances are to be welcomed whilst others are to be denied, depending on their consistency with Nagel's conclusion. Nagel's argument, on this account, is circular — though this is not necessarily a bad thing. We should expect any theory to admit some conflicting evidence and reject other examples, but this is a problem if Nagel's selection and interpretation of the evidence is heavily influenced by the assumption that his conclusion is correct.[8] I think this is one way in which Nagel's proclamation of objective value is a self-fulfilling prophecy, proving the existence of objective value in morality from an assumption that moral reasons are objective.[9]

A Nagelian reply could take the form that we should only count agreement or disagreement if it would persist in an ideal situation where various pressures were ruled out. *Undistorted* agreement or disagreement would be the proof of moral universals. However, such an account might be unattractive to Nagel because it gives too much justificatory weight to considerations of interpersonal agreement and disagreement. It also seems at odds with other elements of his best explanation approach, in that it constitutes a greater denial of the appearances of moral experience.[10] The onus here would also be on the Nagelian to provide an explanation of the criteria that would be used to determine when agreement or disagreement violates the standards of such ideal conditions. This might move the approach further in the direction of what I term contingent universalism, an idea that I discuss later in this chapter.

So far, I have been arguing that Nagel's selective approach to the initial data of moral views which agree and disagree is suspect, questioning his claim that an evaluative faculty is the best explanation of all the evidence. Perhaps the notion of distortion by strong interests can come to Nagel's aid on this question. If we can indeed rule out much disagreement because of the interests it

---

[8] This criticism says in effect that because Nagel rules inadmissible any evidence of disagreement which might invalidate his argument, his theory is 'too true to be good' (Sparkes, 1991, 116).

[9] I discuss this claim more fully later in this section, in order to distinguish it from unobjectionable coherentism.

[10] My claim here is that it would partly undermine Nagel's reliance on appearances. Weeding out which factors would or would not be admissible in an ideal moral debate situation adds another complex layer into the argument. This is a question I discuss in detail in the section on 'contingent universalism' later in this chapter, and in chapter four. My point here is that getting at an undistorted moral experience involves going much further than, say , ruling out judgments made when we are frightened or drunk.

enshrines, and judge some exercises of our moral evaluative capacity flawed whilst others correct, then we have a means to determine whether moral disagreement should be admitted as evidence of the correct functioning of such a faculty or not. However, I think invoking the idea of distortion by interests has problems attached. The examples Nagel uses of these distorting strong interests are instructive — debates over the theory of evolution, the Dreyfus case, genetics and IQ (Nagel, 1986, 148). Though Nagel's cases are unclear in this regard, we may want to distinguish between beliefs, such as anti-Semitism, and the interests which might function improperly as reasons for such beliefs. Strong material interests should not, we generally contend, form the basis of moral judgements. Thus, they constitute an explanation or reason that can actually undermine a belief. Self-interest or the interests of one's group, Nagel appears to feel, underlies much disagreement and invalidates it as evidence.[11] However, on this account we could take the evolution case to indicate that, for Nagel, sincere belief in God as literal creator of the world has underlying costs or interests rendering the view (and thus any resulting disagreement) irrational. My point here is that regarding the continuing adherence of creationists to a certain creed as motivated by interests — for example the psychological costs of sacrificing a belief or group pressure against letting the belief go — is uncharitable to say the least. It might even be 'uncharitable' towards the anti-Semite to impute that her argument is purely based on material interests rather than a sincere belief that Jews are inferior.[12] We should also note that psychologically second-guessing the character of and motivation for a position is a significant step. Every strongly held belief comes with psychological costs if it is rejected, and to cite social pressure seems to discriminate against more close-knit social groups.

These kinds of considerations can be turned also against instances of agreement; it might be plausible to suggest that a psychological desire to gain a 'western' or 'modern' lifestyle, or a self-interested material desire for western assistance, motivates progress towards human rights in less developed countries in the

[11] I use the word 'much' here, because Nagel recognises the possibility of some reasonable disagreement in ethics, at least in the political realm (Nagel, 1991, 160–1).

[12] Rather than holding, as Nagel incautiously appears to, that the Dreyfus case is one in which anti-semitism was entirely about strong interests, we might want to say instead that only some or many of those against Dreyfus were anti-Semites for material or other 'interests'. But then it should be recognised that Nagel's gesturing to this case (amongst others) as examples of perversion by strong interests is of limited force.

face of local pressures. Of course, beliefs generate interests, and interests are expressed in the forms of beliefs. In fact, we might argue that the more fundamental a belief to someone's belief system, the greater the costs of rejecting it. Thus, the more fundamental a belief, the more likely it is to fall foul of Nagel's 'strong interest' explanation. Nagel seems to accept an intimate relationship between beliefs and interests, referring to 'social prejudices transcended in the face of strong pressures' (Nagel, 1986, 148). Even were we to want to refer to a religious motivation, for example, as not interest-based, it might nevertheless still count as a 'social prejudice'. The use of distortion as a criterion to rule out moral disagreement is open to abuse. We can cogently question whether Nagel is being uncharitable in the view he is taking of the reasons why people morally disagree, and also whether he is applying the distortion standard with equal rigour to cases of agreement. The closer we examine the idea of distortion by interests or pressures, the more we can see that deciding what counts as a 'distorting' interest or pressure (and thus what invalidates an instance of moral disagreement) is problematic.

In this light, Nagel appears to be looking for psychological or causal explanations *first*. He is committed to rooting out distorting interests that stand in the way of impartiality and agreement. There is an odd tension here with a part of his position that I examined earlier. Nagel argues, as we have seen, that we should aim for normative rather than psychological accounts of moral judgements and reasons. He holds that we should look for a moral explanation of moral appearances, relying on the idea that our moral intuitions approximate the real substance of the moral realm. Nagel writes

> The initial data are reasons that appear from one's own point of view in acting. They usually present themselves with some pretensions of objectivity to begin with, just as perceptual appearances do. When two things look the same size to me, they look at least initially as if they are the same size (Nagel, 1986, 149).

I do not want to contend that the analogy with perceptual judgement is fundamentally important to the plausibility of Nagel's argument (Nagel can and does accept a number of disanalogies between the two types of judgements[13]). He *does* however rely on the idea that our moral intuitions have prima facie plausibility as universal claims, that this universality approximates the true nature of ethics. This constitutes a pre-

---

[13]   For example, he notes that ethical reasoning 'is not to be understood on the model of perception of features of the external world' (Nagel, 1986, 148).

sumption in favour of the normative, and of our moral experience. However, doesn't this sit ill at ease with the case-by-case evaluation of disagreement, and the presumption in favour of the psychological explanation of disagreement that goes along with it? Despite Nagel's strong opposition to the psychological reduction of moral phenomena, his suggestion that real moral disagreements are massively influenced by strong interests — present in morality 'to a uniquely high degree' — threatens to transform his position into something far more ambivalent. It also opens the door for a sceptic to reverse Nagel's strategy by performing a case-by-case analysis of how we psychologically *need* to think our judgements carry a degree of objectivity that they may not possess. Nagel's employment of the psychological analysis that he rejects as the best explanation of moral consensus allows the opportunity for the sceptic to deny that we ought to accept these 'pretensions of objectivity'. The sceptic has the possibility of providing instead either a blanket psychological explanation of why we always think in terms of moral objectivity or a case-by-case analysis of how, for all the cases of agreement that Nagel thinks support his argument, there is in fact a psychological explanation that we ought to prefer. I will not here attempt such an exercise on the sceptic's behalf, nor do I think that such an attempt would necessarily succeed. My point is rather that Nagel's adoption in some cases of a psychological explanation as the appropriate one gives the sceptic a foothold in Nagel's argument that she would otherwise lack.

Nagel's argument is right to the extent that if we removed from the set of moral disagreements in the world disagreements which generate and are associated on one side or another with strong interests, the set would be significantly emptier.[14] The idea of opposing massive redistribution of wealth could be shown to be a cover just for those who are greedy or lack liberal virtue. Alternatively, the desire for redistribution could just be envy on the part of the poor. What is left if we remove strong interests as factors in moral views? Remove all strong interests, and the only views left as admissible are objective, in the sense of being firstly disinterested and secondly impersonal ones.[15]

---

[14] although even in the space remaining, there would be room for significant disagreement as to exactly what constituted the right normative objective justification for various positions.

[15] Even Nagel's agent-relative reasons are impersonal in the sense that 'their value does not have to be seen through the particular values of the individual who has or lacks them, or through the particular preferences or projects he has formed' (Nagel, 1986, 171).

I am now in a position to tie some of these criticisms together. If the objective view is an impartial view (as Nagel appears to believe) and if Nagel only admits evidence of the appearance of objective values in our moral life, then it is unsurprising that his conclusion is that of the reality of objective value (however, disagreement will still persist between objective values over questions of weighting, as I note below). Perhaps this is what Nagel means when he says the objective standpoint is created 'by leaving a more subjective, individual or even just human perspective behind' (Nagel, 1986, 7). This perspective allows Nagel's assertion that subjectivism can only be rejected by first-order moral argument to be laid bare in all its necessity. His conclusion is his argument and both amount to this — that only the objective is truly moral.

Perhaps, however, this intimate two-way relationship between evidence, criteria and conclusion is desirable. Nagel's argument, he freely admits, 'accounts for our capacity to think these things in a way that presupposes their independent validity' (Nagel, 1997, 75).[16] On Nagel's behalf, it could be interjected that his view is simply coherentist — aiming at mutual support between all the elements — and this is surely desirable. Nagel writes, 'The only 'method' here or elsewhere is to try to generate hypotheses and then to consider which of them seems most reasonable, in light of everything else one is fairly confident of' (Nagel, 1986, 154). Coherence is an important value for a worldview; indeed, I will argue in chapter five that it is *fundamentally* important in moral justification. Nagel's position might just be coherence-based. However, I have stressed in my examination of Nagel his fundamental commitment to the 'self-evident' conclusion of universal, objective values, and the necessity of avoiding subjectivism. If this assumption of objective values constitutes the fixed foundation of his approach, then we can cogently question whether this *is* a coherence-*based* approach because it leaves no internal mechanism for questioning this fixed point. There are no resources, no evidence admissible within Nagel's account from which to revise the conclusion. Such revision would seem to be possible only from the wider perspective of considering the success or failure of Nagel's arguments against relativistic or subjectivist alternatives. Nagel's positive framework seems unassailable from within, though perhaps unattractive from without. Readers of Nagel

---

[16] Incidentally, if we take this validity to mean they are justified whether or not anyone has any reason from their particular perspective to endorse them, this validity seems perplexing. This is something that I take up in my discussion of objectivity in chapter four.

must judge for themselves whether they want to accept Nagel's framework or to think what for Nagel sometimes seems unthinkable, that a variant of subjectivism might survive Nagel's criticism. We can at least see now why Nagel's criticism of subjectivism assumes such importance.

In this section, then, I have attempted to critique Nagel's choice and interpretation of evidence for his conclusion of the presence and importance of objective reasoning. Nagel's argument appears too hasty in its description of agreement and disagreement and its invocation of 'strong interests' and 'evaluative faculties'. Recalling the limitations Nagel sets out on what he is aiming to achieve, he has two ways at his disposal of dismissing the questions I have raised. First, in conjunction with a fuller description of these elements, he could maintain that he recognises that his argument will not sway subjectivists like myself, but that he still finds the argument compelling. Perhaps we have a basic disagreement as to how to characterise moral agreement and disagreement. Second, he could argue that the burden of proof is on me to show that there are no objective values. At worst, I have merely weakened his argument for their existence; nothing that I have said here refutes the belief that some values are objective (in the sense of being agent-neutral). To look more at Nagel's claim for objective value, I turn next to the question of the *ways* in which values are objective and universal for Nagel.

(2) *Does the Objective Leave the Subjective Behind?*

Nagel claims, as we have just seen, that the character of his objectivity involves leaving the subjective or human perspective behind. What I want to note in this section are some of the ways in which Nagel fails to meet this standard. First, I suggest that sometimes objectivity is closely related to commonality of experiences among humans. I will then argue that the character of Nagel's objectivity is more first-personal than it initially appears.

As mentioned in the previous section, Nagel's argument for objectivity is based in evidence of our moral life. It appears (at least in part) that we are led to the reality of objectivity from the reality of *intersubjective* agreement as evidence for a *common* evaluative faculty (Nagel, 1986, 148). For all that objectivity leaves the human perspective behind, it seems conspicuously reliant on human evidence, though there is a question over whether this appearance is misleading.[17] This is even clearer when Nagel is

---

[17] Dancy puts this in terms of a conflict between two concepts of objectivity and their relations to the world (Dancy, 1993, 147–8).

talking about pleasure and pain, which he regards as clear-cut cases of objective reasons. In section three I argue that Nagel's simultaneous employment and avoidance of subjectivity with regard to pain is somewhat puzzling.

Of course, this reliance on our subjective experiences is by no means a barrier to forming objective conclusions. However, I do think it points the way towards an important problem for Nagel. I want to argue that either objectivity involves radical identification with individual, particular subjects and cases — and hence rests in a sense on *subjectivity* — or that objective explanations are not really action-guiding in the strong sense of being action-determining, and do not have the strength that he appears to claim for them.

First, I want to outline the problem, beginning with the implications of Nagelian objectivity. Nagel expresses the desire for objectivity thus,

> we wish to formulate our reasons in general terms that relativize them to interests and desires so that they can be recognized and accepted from outside, either by someone else or by us when we regard the situation objectively, independent of the preferences and desires we actually have (Nagel, 1986, 150).

But for our reasons to *determine* choice of the same action for any agent in my position, any individual reason must be one that holds the same weighting for anyone. Everyone must not only think that pain is bad in this situation, but also put the same priority on relieving it. This is because,

> One is trying to decide what, given the inner and outer circumstances, one should do — and that means not just what I should do, but what this person should do. The same answer should be given to that question by anyone to whom the data are presented, whether or not he is in your circumstances and shares your desires. That is what gives practical reason its generality (Nagel, 1997, 110).

The role of objective reasons in these particular cases is ambiguous. Nagel may believe that we can determine from an objective standpoint what anyone in a particular set of circumstances *should* do, where this constitutes a uniquely correct *answer*. However, this is different from saying that the same set of reasons are important considerations in determining action. Everyone weighing reasons A, B, and C must decide that these determine the same course of action, rather than A, B, C merely being the things we weigh up in deciding which action is appropriate. If the objective standpoint tells us what this person should do, this means that the same set of reasons must be weighted identically by whoever is in those circumstances. The key lies in how exacting the description of these circumstances must be.

Relativising reasons to interests and desires seems to produce reasons that are hypothetical commands — *if* you dislike pain and like pleasure (as Nagel thinks we commonly or perhaps necessarily do) *then* seek to minimise it. If we are looking for determinate answers to the question 'what ought one to do?' then we must factor in all the circumstances and priorities of the agent in that position. This enables the agent to stand back and ask objectively what any agent in his circumstances would do. The rules thought about from the objective standpoint must be relativised to the particulars of the situation, to the weighting attached to agent's projects, to their understanding of the situation — they must include every 'if'. If these accounts are to determine which action is correct, then in one sense they must be entirely particular to that case. If I am questioning what I should do from an objective standpoint then the position I must put myself in is in fact my own. Objectivity, on this account, is empathetic and the objective standpoint is radically particular rather than general. Of course, such a view is still universal, in the sense that it specifies what any agent in these radically particular and individuated circumstances ought to do. For any person in exactly these circumstances, a certain conclusion follows.

However, the kind of universality that universalists, including Nagel, seem to be aiming at, includes *generality* (as Nagel mentions above). I take generality to be the capability of a principle to be applied across many different questions and situations — Nagel terms this the 'breadth' of the principle (Nagel, 1986, 152). As an example, let us take a general rule to keep one's promise. This rule will apply to everyone who has made a promise — a fairly wide constituency. However, the number of cases covered by any straightforward moral rule or reason alone shrinks as it becomes more adapted to particular circumstances, or admits of particular exceptions. For example, suppose a man has the dilemma of keeping a promise or saving a life. Our perception of this case could be altered by circumstances such as the magnitude of the promise, the content of the promise, and the life in question. We can factor these circumstances and exceptions into the rule when deciding from an objective standpoint what any agent in those circumstances would do. Thus, we can conceive of the rule for this kind of case as being of the form 'do X except in circumstances A, B, C, or when X is outweighed by Y unless consideration Z is also present' and so on.

As we add qualifications so the *generality* of the rule is diminished, and I would contend that generality is desirable from a universalist standpoint. Nagel states that 'the search for generality is one of the main impulses in the construction of an objective view' (Nagel, 1986, 152). However, an objective moral principle cannot achieve this whilst also making the objective standpoint action-*determining* by taking all particular circumstances into account. If Nagel wants to hold that objective moral reasons ought to be strictly action-determining, then this can only be done at the cost of harm to the generality of these objective, universal reasons.

On the other hand, we might form rules of reason which will be applied differently in different cases, but then these rules are not as action-guiding. There will be a question over whether they admit of exception or modification depending on circumstance. They will say nothing about the way in which agents weight these rules; for example, though objectively all agents will be required to recognise that pain is intrinsically bad, nothing is said about the weight they must attach to that when it conflicts with self-interest or other objectively recognised values. On this account, the objective standpoint yields what *could* be seen as vague, unhelpful truisms such as 'pain is bad' without the practical import that we must always try to prevent pain, because it is open to people to rank the prevention of pain way below personal gain. Nor, without considerations of weighting, do objective reasons provide criteria against which to judge whether the actions are correct. The same answer will not be given by everyone presented with the data, but will depend on their interpretation of the data.

We are now in a position to summarise two possible accounts of Nagel's position. On the first account, we say that our moral decisions should be determined by reasons that would be shared by others in exactly the same situation. But this amounts to saying that were another person to be me, then they would act this way. Whilst in one sense objectivity requires that the analysis becomes more third-personal, the individual perspective is needed to make sense of the normativity of objective judgements. Thus, objectivity does not escape the merely personal — it relies on common judgements about personal circumstances. This is an important correction to the view that objectivity is equivalent to a pure 'view from nowhere' which transcends the perspective of individuals. Instead, giving objective reasons is very much taking a view from *somewhere* — that particular person's shoes. On the second account, and we are talking at the objective level merely about the principles that should have some role in our decisions. It is quite open to agents to admit their relevance whilst making that role practically insignificant.[18] The actual outcome of a decision factoring in these moral reasons could vary enormously from agent to agent in a situation, making the reasons of very little action-guiding import if nothing is said from the objective level about the priority we should attach to these judgements. On the first account, we are not thinning the self at all, nor are we *general*, and these are two qualities which Nagel wants to attach to objectivity. On the second, reasons are much less action-guiding.

If Nagel were to accord the same determinate weighting to all 'agent-relative' considerations, or unconditional weight to 'agent-neutral' considerations, this would stop the slide into radical association whilst maintaining the action-guiding character of the objective standpoint. However, there is a real question as to whether this is a plausible move. Surely, intuitively, some agent-relative considerations outweigh others? All values and projects are not of equal worth. Some personal desires will be adjudged unsuitable to form the basis of agent-relative reasons. A judgement must be made, though it is not clear by whom, as to whether someone's considerations fall into the 'agent-relative' category, or should be ignored altogether from the objective standpoint. I have thus argued that Nagel's position is presented with a dilemma; a choice between maintaining either the action-guiding quality or the generality of his universal moral reasons. This, then, is one way in which Nagel's approach fails to leave the human behind and is instead dependent on the human perspective. I turn now to consider pleasure and pain, another area in which Nagel thinks we can move beyond the particular to the pan-human in order to establish moral universals. I will contend again, though for different reasons, that this attempt raises questions and problems.

(3) *Pleasure and Pain*

The issue of pleasure and pain, for Nagel, constitutes both an argument for his theory and an example of how it might work. Nagel uses pleasure and pain as important examples of the way in which something being agent-relative — my pain being a reason with regard to *me* from the objective standpoint — implies agent-neutrality, or a reason *whoever* is suffering the pain. So far, I have discussed Nagel's position largely in the abstract. Pain pro-

---

[18] I say *practically* insignificant because the universal values must of course be significant in the sense that they must be taken into account by the agent. However, because the agent can rank them in places 1000 and 1001 on the list of things which she must consider, they may have almost no influence on the outcome of her decision.

vides an illustration of how and why some values are universal, and looking at this most clear-cut case brings out ambiguities and problems in his account.

In order to see clearly both the reasoning of Nagel's argument and the contribution it makes to his position as a whole, I want to look at his view in some detail. As a test of whether there are objective, agent-neutral reasons, Nagel sets out the issue thus:

> We have to decide whether the kind of reason people have to avoid pain for themselves can be plausibly combined with impersonal indifference to it . . . if we assign impersonal value to pleasure and pain, then each person can think about his own suffering not just that he has reason to want it gone, but that it's bad and should be got rid of. If on the other hand, we limit ourselves to relative reasons, he will have to say that though he has a reason to want an analgesic, there is no reason for him to have one, or for anyone else who happens to be around to give him one (Nagel, 1986, 160).

Nagel thinks that we can grant objective reality to the agent-neutrality of pain, because we cannot stop at recognising it as a valid reason for someone without acknowledging 'an impersonal reason to want it to go away' (Nagel, 1986, 161). The objective standpoint takes the sufferer's epistemic authority that he is suffering — that he is suffering something bad — as the 'clearest authority present in the situation' (Nagel, 1986, 161). It generalises this into the idea that there is an objective objection to suffering, no matter whose. This is Nagel's paradigmatic case of the reasoning behind something having the status of a reason for everyone; pain is bad *in itself*. This important example is, however, problematic in various ways. The first potential problem for Nagel is that it establishes the principle that the 'evaluative authority' of particular agents is fundamentally important in forming an objective standpoint. Why not grant this *prima facie* evaluative authority to people in situations of disagreement rather than providing a theory of how their views are distorted? Why invoke this evaluative authority only in some cases, but not in others?[19] Thus, though I will not take this further here, the way his example proceeds might undermine his treatment of moral disagreement that I discussed in section one.

We can, moreover, query the ambiguous idea of the 'objective self' which Nagel introduces here. Nagel writes 'the pain, though it comes attached to a person and his individual perspective, is just as clearly hateful to the objective self as to the subjective indi-

---

[19]   Nagel's apparent answer, that in some cases it will be appropriate whilst in other cases it will not be, does not seem to me to supply sufficient clarity on this point (Nagel, 1986, 169–72).

vidual' (Nagel, 1986, 160). One might begin by asking what this objective self *is*, given that objectivity involves a move away from particular or even human perspectives. Thus, we can ask whether the idea of an objective self makes sense. Second, we can query the role of the objective self in the enlargement of pleasure and pain into objective, agent-neutral reasons. Nagel maintains, for example, that,

> If I lacked or lost the conception of myself as distinct from other possible or actual persons, I could still apprehend the badness of pain immediately. So when I consider it from an objective standpoint, the ego doesn't get between the pain and the objective self . . . In its most primitive form, the fact that it is mine — the concept of myself — doesn't come into my perception of the badness of my pain (Nagel, 1986, 161).

I do not fully understand Nagel's position here. How can the concept of *my*self not come into *my* perception of the badness of *my* pain? Both the perception and the pain, to be mine, must belong to myself.[20] This is perhaps being too hard on Nagel. We can interpret his view as saying that I shouldn't think about pain purely in terms of it being mine. The intuition is that in a position where I am not individuated at all, I can still appreciate that pain is bad, even where there is no possibility of anything but agent-neutrality. If we take Nagel's point here to be that when I experience pain, I feel 'ow! pain is bad' not 'ow, pain is bad for me', a cogent reply seems to ask how there is any difference between these two statements from the perspective of the sufferer since both seem to amount to 'Ow! *this* pain hurts'. The view of the sufferer on this account should not be taken to mean that 'ow! pain is bad whoever has it' (objectivity-affirming) or that 'ow! pain is bad for me, but might not be for others' (subjectivity-affirming). It seems to me that if I think either of these two expanded 'ow! claims' when (even after a drugs and alcohol binge during which I have lost some of the conception of myself) someone hits me with a snooker cue then I am, in the words of Bernard Williams, having 'one thought too many' (Williams, 1981, 18). *Contra* Nagel, I believe that 'pain is bad', uttered by a sufferer, does not immediately translate into a report on the objective badness of pain. As an argument for this position I can only suggest that readers ask themselves what they have thought when they were in pain. Of course, such a counter-assertion does not constitute a reason for Nagel to revise or retract his position. I would contend, however, that pain could be the way that I

---

[20] I think there's a straightforward logical impossibility here. I must be involved in *my* perception of my pain.

describe it rather than the way Nagel describes it. I believe that the opaque nature of Nagel's position on this complex question strips it of unproblematic plausibility. Here the burden of proof lies with Nagel. For Nagel's argument to succeed, he must show how his conception is more correct than the alternative I have proposed.

After Nagel's earlier remarks that the drive for objectivity is always imperfect, limited by ourselves as finite, subjective beings, how can Nagel's account take on such a transcendental, mystical character? Nagel says that his conclusion 'seems to me self-evident, and in trying to explain why it's true, and why the alternatives are less plausible, I may not have gone far beyond this' (Nagel, 1986, 162). It is indeed hard to argue for something we believe to be self-evident, but at the same time I think that Nagel has gone a fair way beyond the simplest explanation required. Whilst Nagel maintains that there must be an agent-neutral objection to suffering, I think in one sense this is untrue. Pain, as Nagel acknowledges, is an *experience* had by a *sufferer*. Thus the desire to be rid of pain does not have only the pain as its object but the pain as an experience had by someone, whose authority we can take for them suffering. We can readily admit that pain is a bad thing when it happens to me. We could reason that pain is a bad thing when it happens to anyone, and we might foster a desire to ease pain by recognising that it is something that all human beings have in common. There is no need for Nagel's argument to go beyond this and maintain that pain has an objective reality as something I can recognise when radically disassociated from any self. Why not maintain that we see pain as a bad thing when we radically *associate* with everyone else, or with the sufferer in particular? The subjectivist, it seems to me, can happily maintain something like this, that pain is taken to be a bad for any human on an approach that emphasises empathy rather than transcendence.[21] If this is what is meant by being objective, then some subjectivists are happily in agreement with Nagel here.

I am left unclear as to how far Nagel's position goes beyond this and how much (if it does go beyond) it must or does add to this, since Nagel has chosen as his case of something having objective and universal force something which is at least contingently com-

---

[21] This approach seems to echo Nagel's conclusion. However, it illustrates that one can accept Nagel's conclusion that pain is a bad thing without accepting that morality must be objective in any kind of mystical sense. If part of Nagel's argument is that we must be objectivists in order to say that pain is a bad thing, then the presence of subjectivists who can also affirm this conclusion tends to undermine Nagel's argument.

mon to everyone. The limitations of Nagel's case are that whilst it is very hard to deny that pain is a bad for anyone, Nagel's position seems to rely on a blurred distinction between pain being bad for any individual and pain being bad from the standpoint of an unindividuated 'objective self'. I think there is a real question over whether this latter notion makes sense. I have questioned both whether pain without a self is a coherent idea and whether Nagel's understanding of our thoughts on pain as reports of objective badness is plausible.

Lastly, I have raised questions about how far Nagel has gone, or needs to go, beyond human solidarity in his argument for moral universals. We can see an example of Nagel's reliance on the idea of a human community for whom pain is bad in the following situation. A consequence of Nagel's argument seems to be that pain is bad not only whoever but whatever is suffering; the fact of pain, and the amount of pain are surely the relevant considerations. But then how can Nagel account for the entirely different scheme we have for judging the suffering of animals — we do not have state-funded veterinary practice on the same scale as the NHS, for example, nor did BSE become something of great import until the risks to humans' livelihood and well-being were outlined. In the recent foot-and-mouth crisis, slaughter, rather than vaccination or treatment, was the preferred solution. Nagel's account of such differences, it seems to me, must point not to differences in the amount of suffering but to a commonality of experience with other humans which we do not share to the same degree with animals — the fact that we exist as 'one person among others' (Nagel, 1996, 120).[22] If this is the case, why not let this underpinning commonality do all the work, without introducing the more mystical aspect of objectivity?

Summary

Nagel's position is a complex one, and in this section I have had the chance to do little more than sketch some of its features. Nevertheless, I hope I have illustrated some ways in which it may be problematic. In particular, we can see why Nagel believes that his position will not convince the anti-objectivist. Nagel's argument is self-reinforcing, but he accepts that if we do not accept his starting point, we will not be compelled to accept his conclusion. Thus, it is left open to the subjectivist to agree with Rorty that Nagel has

---

[22] This argument, I admit, is not watertight. Nagel could respond, for example, by saying that we ought, morally, to treat animal pain in the same way though countervailing considerations prevent us from doing so, or deny that animals suffer pain in the same way.

'articulated his moral sensibility', but recognise that 'philosophical argument will sooner or later run up against the limits set by such sensibility' (Rorty, 1998, 121).[23] I hope I have demonstrated here exactly what this might mean. Of course, as this section has indicated, we cannot assess Nagel's positive project in isolation. It should be viewed instead as intimately tied to his criticism of subjectivism. I complete this picture in the next chapter by briefly looking at the arguments he produces against the subjectivist or relativist.

Habermas' Transcendental-Pragmatic Argument

Nagel's approach attempted to draw universal conclusions from the nature of our moral experience. Habermas, whose views I will now turn to examine, is engaged in the same exercise — albeit from a different perspective. In works such as *The Theory of Communicative Action* and more recently *Moral Consciousness and Communicative Action*, Jürgen Habermas provides a distinct and promising approach to grounding universal norms that derives from, and forms part of, a wide-ranging analysis of language and our use of it. Habermas proposes a test of universalisation as the criterion for establishing the validity of a moral principle. This test requires that for any principle, 'all affected can accept the consequences and the side effects its general observance can be anticipated to have for the satisfaction of everyone's interests' (Habermas, 1990, 65).[24] As a test of validity, this proposes an idea of reversibility or exchange of roles, and seems close in spirit to Kant's idea of the categorical imperative.[25] Like Nagel, Habermas will insist that universal values are the unavoidable conclusion of looking at our moral experience. The dissimilarity between the two perhaps lies in the way that for Habermas, these values are embedded in our discourse rather than discovered by taking an objective perspective. Before moving on to examine the principle

---

[23] Indeed, it could be suggested mischievously that the inability of Nagel (as he himself admits) to produce an argument for moral universalism which *ought* to convince the relativist rather proves the relativist's point that the realm of morality is not one dominated by compelling, universal reason, but rather reasons relative to frameworks of belief.

[24] There is an ambiguity over how we determine the constituency of people 'affected' by a norm — perhaps 'affected' here should be interpreted in the largest possible sense.

[25] Habermas and numerous commentators have drawn out the similarities and differences between his proposal and that of Kant, though this lies beyond the scope of this short section. For example, Habermas, 1990, 194–215; McCarthy 1978, 325–30.

Habermas offers and the justification he gives for it, some brief effort must be made to place his proposal within the context of his wider thought.

Habermas offers an account of language as action. The idea is that speaking constitutes an action in itself, a 'speech-act'. Whilst some speech acts are strategic in purpose, true communicative action aims at understanding and rationally motivated agreement (Habermas, 1990, 58). Habermas thinks that there are rules implicit in this use of speech-acts, and part of his argument will proceed by making these rules explicit. The specifics of these rules will be analysed shortly. The most basic guiding principle, however, is that we must understand speech-acts as raising claims of validity, aiming either at truth, normative legitimacy or truthfulness/authenticity, and that they must be assessed on these terms.[26] The competence of people in these uses of language is something that develops through child- and adulthood.

Some rules, therefore, are immanent in all our exercises in communicative action. Habermas refers to the logical reconstruction of these rules as 'transcendental-pragmatics', and it is a 'transcendental-pragmatic' argument that Habermas offers for the principle I gave at the beginning of this section. In subsequent sections I will sketch the important features of this argument, and then look more closely at a number of areas where I feel Habermas' argument is incomplete or limited in its raw material, and thus in the strength and plausibility of the conclusions that can issue from it.

The 'Transcendental-Pragmatic' Argument

The transcendental-pragmatic argument's function is 'to show that the principle of universalization, which acts as a rule of argumentation, is implied by the presuppositions of argumentations in general' (Habermas, 1990, 86). Parallels can be drawn with Gewirth's argument that agents cannot without contradiction deny agenthood, and the rights that go with it, to others (Gewirth, 1978), and also to Nagel's position that morality is necessarily objective. Habermas says that this justification succeeds if 'every person who accepts the universal and necessary communicative presuppositions of argumentative speech and who knows what it means presupposes as valid the principle of universalization' (Habermas, 1990, 86). Before setting out how the argument operates, and the details of the conclusions it reaches, I want to set out by way of clarification three key features of the argument.

---

[26] Furthermore, Habermas believes that different vocabularies — notably different verbs — express attempts to reach each of these goals.

First, it should at least be established that argumentation about the validity of norms for Habermas is reflective and rational, involving considerations of generalisability (Habermas, 1990, 108). As such, it asks people to place their particular cultural/social/political frameworks 'at a distance' (Habermas, 1990, 107)[27] in order to go beyond the bounds placed on thought by particular conventions. As the form of discourse that allows us to gain reflective distance from our culturally situated position, it is concerned with questions of justice or the right rather than what Habermas terms 'evaluative questions' concerning the good life. Thus, he writes:

> Moral questions can in principle be decided rationally, i.e. in terms of justice or generalizability. Evaluative questions present themselves at the most general level as issues of the good life (or of self-realization); they are accessible to rational discussion only within the unproblematic horizon of a concrete historical form of life (Habermas, 1990, 108).

For Habermas there is a clear distinction between the right and the good, and his transcendental-pragmatic argument deals with the right only.

Second, and relatedly, it is important to stress that not all discourse or communicative action is pure argumentation or indeed argumentation at all. For Habermas, some discourse is properly influenced by strategic concerns which make it a success- rather than understanding-oriented exercise (Habermas, 1990, 140). Also, as I mentioned in the introduction to this section, communicative action raises three types of validity claim, each expressed in a different mode of language. These are cognitive (aiming at truth, objective) interactive (normative) and expressive (subjective) modes (Habermas, 1990, 137). For the purposes of my discussion here, I concentrate on the cognitive mode. This is because questions of justice or the right, for Habermas, are ones which aim at objectivity. The question of how much of the realm of moral debate belongs to the sphere of cognitive, reflective argumentation is one of the key issues that I will raise.

Third, before I move on to set out the content of the universal norms that Habermas' argument establishes, something must also be said about the relationship between universal norms and universal truths. Given the importance of reaching consensus for Habermas, we can ask whether his account should be seen as

---

[27]   Habermas uses the term 'lifeworld' to denote such frameworks, though his term has a richer and more nuanced meaning. Rather than engage in a lengthy explanation of the connotations and context of the term, for purposes of brevity I avoid using it altogether.

grounding not just universal norms, but also universal truths — i.e. whether his account constitutes a consensus theory of truth. If the latter is the case, then this will put a different perspective on his theory. On the consensus account of truth, truth would mean simply winning the argument in an ideal situation of reflective argumentation or 'ideal speech situation'. We can note that Habermas is at least committed to the idea that the *claim* of truth anyone makes in argumentation is linked to reaching agreement upon it. Whether he needs to go further than this and identify the predicate 'true' as being equivalent to 'object of a rational consensus' is unclear. Certainly doing so carries costs; for example, Habermas would have to answer two charges outlined by McCarthy in his discussion of the transcendental-pragmatic argument. These are first, that it rests on a category mistake — mistaking the meaning of truth for the methods we use to arrive at it — and second, that 'truth is a normative concept and thus cannot be tied to the de facto achievement of consensus: not just any agreement that comes to pass can serve as a warrant for truth' (McCarthy, 1978, 304). The debate about whether Habermas is committed to this strong claim lies outside the scope of this section, as does the debate over whether the consensus theory of truth is a consistent or plausible account of truth. I presume here only Habermas' commitment to a weaker claim about claims to validity implying the possibility of consensus.

Habermas' approach proceeds by identifying the rules present in argumentation about the right. Argumentation, says Habermas, is a process of reflective communication, the goal of which is 'reaching a rationally motivated agreement' (Habermas, 1990, 88). Thus, 'arguments are processes of reaching understanding that are ordered in such a way that proponents and opponents, having assumed a hypothetical attitude and being relieved of the pressures of action and experience, can test validity claims that have become problematic' (Habermas, 1990, 87). It is this goal and procedure of argumentation that entails for Habermas the pragmatic presuppositions 'necessary for a search for truth organised in the form of a competition' (Habermas, 1990, 87).

These pragmatic presuppositions take the form of a commitment to justification that he terms a 'speech-act immanent obligation to provide justification' (Habermas, 1984, 64). This commitment to justification, says Habermas, demands 'a principle of freedom of opinion' (Habermas, 1990, 85). This principle is spelt out in the following rules for reflective argumentation.

3.1 Every subject with the competence to speak and act is allowed to take part in a discourse.

3.2   a.   everyone is allowed to question any assertion whatever

b.   everyone is allowed to introduce any assertion whatever into the discourse.

c.   everyone is allowed to express his attitudes, desires and needs.

3.3   No speaker may be prevented, by internal or external coercion, from exercising his rights as laid down in (3.1) and (3.2) (Habermas, 1990, 89).

These rules are 'hypothetical reconstructions' of the presuppositions of argumentation. By their very nature, they constitute a commitment to the principle of universalisation. Habermas holds that anyone who denies these hypothetical reconstructions of the rules of argumentation whilst engaging in argumentation necessarily (inescapably) contradicts themselves. Thus the sceptic cannot avoid a 'performative contradiction' between his refusal to adopt the rules of discourse and 'the intuitive preunderstanding that every subject competent in speech and action brings to a process of argumentation' (Habermas, 1990, 89).[28] Habermas contends that due to the very nature of these rules, there are no alternatives available which will allow the same kind of argumentation to continue; they are always necessary (Habermas, 1990, 97).

Habermas, as we shall see, draws upon the work of developmental psychologists such as Kohlberg in connection with this argument to discuss its basis in evidence. As I have briefly indicated, Habermas is concerned to provide a philosophy of communicative action, not merely to ground moral universals. In so doing, his work is closely linked to psychological issues concerning the development of competence in communicative action, and this relationship is something that I will discuss later in this section.

I believe that limitations highlighted by Habermas himself will serve to illustrate alternatives to Habermas' conception of argumentation about the right. In response to Habermas' claim that there are universal presuppositions to discourse about justice and the right, I argue that such presuppositions are not inescapable.

---

[28]   There is an ambiguity here between any competent speaker, and what Habermas refers to as 'competent members of modern societies' (Habermas 1983, 94). The issue of argumentation being a particular or a dominant feature of our modern culture rather than universal — or whether it can be both — is something I touch on later in my criticisms of Habermas.

My critique aims to demonstrate that we can be committed to justifying what we say without this justification necessarily taking the form that Habermas stipulates. I begin by suggesting that there is a plausible alternative to giving everyone an equal right to speak so that sometimes, *contra* Habermas (Habermas, 1990, 91), it will be rational to effectively exclude persons from the discussion. This initial objection leads to the examination of related issues regarding both the evidence which Habermas provides for his position and the relation of the proposal to traditional ethical philosophies. My response to Habermas is two-fold. I contend first that his rules of discourse are not inescapable, even if we are to engage in the kind of argumentation about the right that he envisages. Second, I develop the position that there are live alternatives to the entire exercise of rule-bound argumentation.

Argumentation and Competence

The first part of my critique, then, aims to establish the plausibility of rules which are not Habermas'. Habermas claims that when we engage in argumentation our use of language necessarily commits us to justifying our claims in an attempt to reach rational consensus. I intend to argue that given that we wish to engage in truth-bound argumentation, our intuitive presuppositions need not be that we give everyone equality of opportunity to participate in the discussion. Thus, the particular rules that Habermas arrives at are not inescapable — there are viable alternatives. My position here, it should be said, is not that I personally believe that we should discriminate amongst participants, but rather that this presumption of equality in debate need not be an 'inescapable presupposition' of argument. To be sure, when I participate in an argument, I am perhaps committed to demanding that I get a fair hearing. However, my reason for demanding a fair hearing could surely be my belief that what I am saying is worth saying, i.e. it has a strong claim to validity. If I believe that I have a greater competence in the field of debate than others, this confidence can ground my claim that I am worth hearing. If we distinguish between degrees of competence and discriminate between those who possess different levels, are we hampering the ability of the argument to seek truth? Am I being inconsistent in claiming a right for myself that I am denying to others? If I hold that what gives me the right is a degree of competence that others lack, then it seems I am not necessarily guilty of this, for I can hold:

> 3.4 Only those subjects that possess a certain standard of competence in the field of debate, and perhaps a sin-

cere interest, should be accorded the full rights of discourse.[29]

I want to suggest that a rule like this is intuitively plausible for some and perhaps even prevalent in our modern culture. Consider scientific knowledge. This is perhaps as close as we come to the idea of a 'cooperative search for truth' (Habermas, 1990, 89). However, perhaps more in the realm of science than anywhere else, there is the feeling that expertise qualifies people to state opinions. Were Stephen Hawking and David Beckham to debate the origin of the universe, there is a case for saying that we would come to that situation with a predisposition to accord Hawking's position more respect than Beckham's. Similarly, the average scientist would surely agree to debate quantum mechanics with Beckham or myself only out of perverse curiosity, or the desire to inform *us* rather than the idea that such a debate would contribute significantly to their own understanding or 'the truth'. This hints at a disjuncture between the aim of securing rational agreement, which is surely of importance in legitimizing proposals, and the aim of testing claims to truth by subjecting them to debate. Whilst Habermas seems to combine these two motives for argumentation, they are surely in principle separable.[30]

If the case for competence applies to those who lack specialist knowledge, it applies even further to those who have been discredited as incompetent. For example, why ought we to include David Irving in a debate aiming to establish the truth about the Holocaust, after a court has found that he manipulates and misinterprets history?[31] Mill, despite his support of free speech and of 'giving truth a chance' nevertheless suggests that 'when two persons who have a joint interest in any business differ in opinion, does justice require that both opinions should be held of exactly equal value? . . . the opinion, the judgment, of the higher moral or intellectual being is worth more than that of the inferior . . . One of the two, as the wiser or better man, has a claim to superior weight' (Mill, 1991, 334).

Our modern social framework is surely one that makes a great deal of presumption in favour of *expertise* (the idea that some people are better qualified to contribute to a debate than others) and

---

[29] The obvious reply to this line of argument, is that Habermas can agree that during the course of debate some people will say things which are more rationally acceptable, but that this doesn't undermine the rules of discourse. Everyone has a right to be heard, but not necessarily to be agreed with. I discuss this defence shortly.

[30] This is something I return to later in this section.

[31] See for example Busfield, 2000.

representation (that there is no need for everyone to be involved provided someone is there to represent the interests of those not involved). Whilst in some ways moral debate is disanalogous to scientific discourse, I do not believe that this undercuts the objection. We can give a sense to competence in morality or justice; for example, we might dismiss the claims of an egoist as irrelevant whilst employing philosophers in the discussion of important moral or political problems precisely because of their expertise.[32] Thus, the central claim of this argument is that we should not accord everyone's views the same space in discourse — for example that we should accord different rules of discourse to people whom we hold as incompetent in the area under discussion.[33]

A defender of Habermas can, it seems to me, make two important counter-claims. He might well point out that judgments of competence can only be made at all after giving everyone a fair initial hearing in some respect. So even if we need not accord everyone equal respect in every debate, we must nevertheless have gone through some such 'ideal speech' procedure once, or else be using a proxy such as IQ tests. Otherwise, the judgments we have made are (even more) unfair. However, even if this were correct, the universal application of the rules of discourse need not be inescapably presupposed in *every* case, merely in some initial ones. Once we have a reliable verdict on, or proxy for, the competence of speakers, future discourses need not include those judged as incompetent.[34] Because the rules dictating equal opportunity to speak need not be applied after those initial cases, part of their inescapable character vanishes.

A second and more potent reply is that we are able to accord everyone an equal opportunity to speak, without being committed to finding his or her words of equal worth. Habermas' theory allows for granting people an equal opportunity to speak whilst simultaneously allowing unequal worth to be attached to these opinions; we can give everyone an equal chance to speak without an equal obligation to *listen*, and we can have an obligation to listen equally to all without being obliged to find their words of equal worth. This is surely correct, but the sceptic can contend

---

[32] For example, the appearance of Bernard Williams on the Wolfenden Committee, or of Bruce Ackerman in the Clinton impeachment debate. As I will discuss in chapter four, we may be able to dismiss the view of an egoist because it falls entirely outside the sphere of morality.

[33] Habermas does mention the possibility of participating in moral discourse 'as an expert' (Habermas, 1990, 94) but does not seems to elaborate on any implications this might have.

[34] Although of course people might gain in competence over time.

that, in effect, this would still be violating the *spirit* of his rules. This counter-objection can be put in the terms of Habermas' own theory. Rule 3.2b, for example, prescribes that everyone must be able to introduce any assertion whatsoever into the discourse — if I am speaking, and people are technically listening but no-one is taking me seriously, then in what sense am I part of the discourse? Habermas' rules seem to require giving someone a *fair hearing* rather than merely giving them a chance to speak. If Habermas is indeed committed to 'fair hearing', then this line appears demanding, given the possibility of 'cutting corners' by trusting people's expertise instead. It would radically lengthen the process for the sake of very little, if any, contribution to the search for truth. There also remains a question mark over the practicality of giving everyone a fair hearing. Can a discourse ever really be that open, or aspire to that openness, given time and space constraints?[35]

Thus, the line of criticism I am advancing here holds that rationally motivated agreement need not entail, or come about only through, presuming that everyone need have a maximally equal say. I now want to examine some other components that both support this picture of competence-based inequality and also constitute objections in their own right. Indeed, I want to suggest that an analysis of these factors, in addition to establishing the presence of an alternative approach, shows a potential conflict in Habermas' ideas between such an approach and his stress on ideas of equal freedom in discourse. To look more at this question of competence, and to develop a complementary objection, I turn to examine the way in which Habermas invokes the work of developmental psychologists.

Psychology and Presuppositions

Habermas contends that his theory 'is open to, indeed dependent upon, *indirect* validation by other theories that are consonant with it' (Habermas, 1990, 117). One such theory, says Habermas, is 'the theory of the development of moral consciousness advanced by Lawrence Kohlberg and his co-workers' (Habermas, 1990, 117). Kohlberg's research points to the establishment of six levels of moral judgement, from the first in which 'right is literal obedience to rules and authority, avoiding punishment, and not doing physical harm', to the last which 'assumes guidance by universal ethical principles that all humanity should follow' (Habermas, 1990,

---

[35]   The more global we wish the discussion to be, the more the question of the practicality of such a wide and open discourse raises its head.

123). Habermas thinks that these stages approximately relate 'in the dimensions of reversibility, universality, and reciprocity to the structures of impartial or just judgements' (Habermas, 1990, 123), which his principle of universality and the argument for that principle have identified. My reason for introducing Kohlberg is that Habermas' discussion of his work provides support for the idea of levels of competence in ethical debate. It reinforces the strength of my objection, and perhaps suggests that Habermas himself has some commitment to a competence approach. This examination leads me to question also whether there is an alternative not just to the presuppositions of argumentation, but also to that kind of rule-bound argumentation.

Moral Development and Competence

I argued above that an alternative to equality in discourse is merit-based inequality. Habermas argues that argumentation governed by the rules of discourse fits firmly into the 'post-conventional' level of moral judgement identified by Kohlberg, in which we appreciate the rational validity of universal principles and become committed to them for that reason. One potential problem arises for Habermas because it seems clear that post-conventional discourse is a *higher* or *better* stage of moral *development.* Not all levels of moral judgement are created equal. If I am operating at the post-conventional level, why should I not view the arguments of those who have not reached that level as inadequate, based as they definitionally are on societally bound 'conventional' or self-interested discourse?[36] Of course, we may need to test people in order to find out which stage they have reached, but this test need not take the form of including them in dialogue. Their pre-conventional reasoning will present itself, for example, in a multiple choice test. Once we have determined which people are only conventional reasoners, then I have good reason to leave them out of truth-seeking debate about justice. I need not listen to such people because as conventionally bound, they are incapable of engaging in post-conventional debate — in the kind of debate that can produce the kind of universally valid norms that we seek.

[36] It could be objected that ascertaining which level of discourse they have reached requires discussing the issues with them. However, such discussion could be minimal. We could, for example, devise a psychological test — perhaps multiple-choice — in order to find out which level they are at. After that, the debate could take on the character less of a test of truth, and more of expanding their minds. Thus, I believe people's 'level' could be determined prior to any dialogue bound by Habermas' rules.

Instead, I should merely engage in the exercise of convincing them to reject their parochialism and endorse universal principles. Letting them raise their tired and inadequate conventional responses will merely cost time rather than make any difference to the outcome of the debate.

So, why not be bound by the full rules of discourse only in argumentation with other post-conventional thinkers? It might be both possible and practically desirable to escape our presuppositions of equality when dealing with positions that are definitionally underdeveloped or inferior. There are perhaps two lines of response to this. One possibility is that treating holders of conventional or preconventional mind-sets as equals in discourse is a good way to develop their reasoning to the post-conventional stage. However, we should note that the participation of conventional reasoners in argumentation is then not about seeking truth or reaching agreement, but instead an instrument to teach them the error of their ways. A second response is that we should understand Habermas as claiming that all conventional reasoners are in fact committed not just to justifying their positions (in their conventional way), but in fact to all the rules of argumentation; however, they are ignorant that they are committed to these rules.

The main problem with the second response, to my mind, is that giving the rules of discourse such a necessary and universal character seems to conflict with Habermas' assertions at various stages that they are characteristic only of our modern world. Indeed, this reply seems to require a commitment to a theory demonstrating how even though throughout human history people have argued using non-conventional forms of discourse, they nevertheless were necessarily committed to freedom of speech. This is an ambitious project — perhaps a universalisation too far. Habermas accepts that a person is 'a product of the traditions surrounding him, of groups whose cohesion is based on solidarity to which he belongs, and of processes of socialization in which he is reared' (Habermas, 1990, 135), and recognises the danger of simply reproducing the content of western modernity as universal theory. He notes that 'the ethnocentric fallacy looms large. I must prove that my moral principle is not just a reflection of the prejudices of adult, white, well-educated Western males of today' (Habermas, 1990, 198).[37] The idea that people were at all times committed to post-conventional reasoning appears especially

---

[37] It should also be noted that on such an approach Kohlberg's work loses any relevance, since whatever the stage the reasoner thinks they have reached, they are always imperfectly aiming at reflective rational consensus in full and free discussion.

problematic in the light of Habermas' view that rendering the principle of universalisation plausible requires 'genealogical arguments which rest on assumptions of modernization theory' (Habermas, 1996, 357). Furthermore, Habermas specifies that the principle of universalisation functions to 'reassure ourselves in a reflexive manner of a remnant of normative substance which is preserved in *post-traditional* societies' (Habermas, 1996, 357, my italics).

Whilst this first objection questions the inescapability of rules for argumentation, a different problem might lie in a recognition of the limited sphere of argumentation in which these rules apply. There is a case for saying that those operating at a conventional level are in fact not really engaged in argumentation at all, at least when argumentation is defined as reflective, truth- and rational assent-seeking discourse. Instead, they are engaged in something else — perhaps emotive persuasion, or prudential evaluation — and the rules of argumentation only govern post-conventional debate. This might be a positive and desirable step for Habermas to take. After all, Habermas wants to suggest that post-conventional discourse is the form adopted by competent members of our modern culture; it is to his advantage if conventional discourse is engaged in by children, who gradually develop into post-conventional moral thinkers. Paralleling this, Habermas offers in *The Theory of Communicative Action* an account of how modern cultures are superior to traditional cultures in respect of their 'cognitive adequacy', and how evolution occurs in societies through history. (Giddens, 1994, 101)

However, Habermas does not query Gilligan's finding that on Kohlberg's criteria, over half the population of the United States would fail to meet the level of post-conventional moral discourse (Habermas, 1990, 175; Gilligan, 1982).[38] If our modern society is populated by plenty of adults engaged in conventional moral discourse, then this weakens Habermas' case, because plenty of the moral thinking done by people is not really post-conventional moral thinking. Hence, the claim of post-conventional discourse to be the dominant mode of our society is suspect, or else moral discourse is ungoverned by these presuppositions, in which case claims of universal inescapability appear problematic. This argument is reinforced, as I will discuss shortly, by the recognition that some ethical systems are incompatible with Habermas' universal discourse ethics. This line of argument que-

---

[38] Though he might, as above, say that all these conventional reasoners were in fact failed post-conventional reasoners.

ries whether this rule-governed argumentation is the best, a good, or merely one amongst a number of ways of understanding how we, in our moral world, debate questions of the right. A similar conclusion is reached by White, who suggests that 'in the face of the second stage of the transcendental-pragmatic argument, the sceptic could avoid a performative contradiction simply by refusing to engage in normative argument in its specifically modern, 'post-conventional' form. He has an escape route in the form of a choice of taking up an argumentation in its less reflective, conventionally bound sense' (White, 1988, 57). Such a form of argumentation, for White, would fulfil the same function as Habermas' reflective argumentation, but without the same set of rules.

The particular problem for Habermas here is that he himself proposes an alternative to post-conventional discourse. In his survey of Kohlberg's work, Habermas proposes that an adolescent can

> dissociate himself from the conventional mode of thought without making the transition to the post-conventional one. In this case he views the collapse of the world of conventions as a debunking of false cognitive claims with which conventional norms and prescriptive statements have hitherto been lined and prescriptive statements have hitherto been linked (Habermas, 1990, 187).

There *is* a live alternative to post-conventional discourse, albeit one in which the adolescent must come to terms with his continuing engagement in moral debate whilst still recognising such debate has been discredited by his reflection. This is an intriguing prospect which Habermas fails to develop. As it stands, this seems to play right into the sceptic's hands by claiming that there is an alternative to rule-bound moral discourse, and that sophisticated reflective people thinking about the right have the plausible option of rejecting argumentation as illusory or simply based on strategic interests. If there is an alternative to these presuppositions, they are no longer inescapable, or else we are no longer doing reflective argumentation. Either way, the link between reflection-based moral argument and rule-bound universalist discourse is weakened or perhaps severed.

Habermas and Traditional Ethical Philosophies

So far, I have questioned (1) whether Habermas' egalitarian presuppositions of argument are indeed inescapable and (2) whether as much of our moral debate is made up of rational-assent seeking argument as Habermas would like. These two elements are combined when we turn to consider the apparent conflict, indicated by Habermas himself, with what he calls 'traditional ethics'.

Habermas thinks that his goal of rational assent is incompatible with traditional ethical philosophies — those for whom 'a dogmatized core of basic convictions' are protected from 'all criticism' (Habermas, 1990, 88). White notes that this 'sweeping' statement seems to cut out several ethical approaches (White, 1988, 54). We can conceive of the constituency of 'traditional ethics' as being based on religious faith, for example, or unchallengeable conviction. Such traditional ethics might actually acknowledge some version of the competence position, perhaps in respecting the positions of elders, leaders, or interpreters. One immediate question is how we characterise what those who propose traditional ethics — for brevity, I will refer to them as traditionalists — do when they talk to other people about morality. I presume they must be at least capable of arguing with others with the aim of 'converting' or rationally convincing others. So, these people could engage in moral debate aimed at securing agreement whilst escaping Habermas' presuppositions.

What seems to be different in such a case is that the possibility of finding a truth which impugns their own most deeply held convictions is ruled out. Thus, we might contend that traditionalists do not really or fully engage in Habermas' kind of reflective argumentation. They are engaging in a process aimed at moral agreement (but not at any cost) from a situation of certainty, and need not be characterised as irrational, solipsistic or egoistical, unlike a sceptic who rejects the whole project of morality (White, 1988, 54). The traditionalist has surely separated the two functions of moral argumentation, so that she is motivated by the desire for agreement rather than interested in the testing of her validity claims, which she remains confident of. Habermas may have problems convincing such traditionalists that they must commit themselves to his rules of discourse in order to get rationally motivated agreement. Instead, the traditionalist might maintain that she engages in debate to make other people agree with *her*, and can produce rational arguments for her position; for example, Jehovah's Witnesses rehearse the argument that the world exhibits design, and design requires a designer. Post-conventional argument against her, conversely, will be deflected by the certainty of her central convictions. At this point, it may seem unclear how this is a problem for Habermas. After all, he need not maintain that such traditionalists escape his inescapable presuppositions. He can interpret them instead as engaging in an entirely different activity.

Unfortunately, I think that this reply provokes a number of further questions or problems. First, it establishes that some can and do talk about morals with the end of securing rational agreement without doing 'reflective argumentation'. Especially in cases where we are convinced that our view is largely correct, how is this in any way an inferior model of moral argumentation? This is especially problematic given that much moral debate in the modern world does proceed from such central, difficult to shift, convictions. The answer would presumably be that reflective argumentation has a better chance of tracking truth (Nozick, 1981), and/or that it has a better chance of attaining rational agreement. However, this is only a powerful reason if we are willing to countenance the idea that our most deeply held convictions are false, or that agreement is worth compromising our inviolable convictions for. Habermas' argument that we do make universal presuppositions in argumentation will not suffice to overturn these barriers, because *ex hypothesi* we are not doing the kind of argumentation that is grounded in these rules. As an example of how deeply the opposites of 'fair hearing' in the service of 'truth seeking' can sometimes be deeply embedded even in 'Western liberal' culture, consider the following case. The German government fines and imprisons Holocaust deniers — it does this presumably (a) because it feels the 'official' account of the holocaust is pretty much completely true and (b) the debate is itself offensive and comes with socially disutile consequences. Ought Habermas' rules of fair hearing to underpin debate about whether the Holocaust happened? Considerations of truth-seeking, or reaching rational agreement, don't seem to be paramount in this case.

Therefore, if we enter a kind of debate aimed purely at the success of our proposal, Habermas is in a position to say that we are not engaged in understanding- or agreement- oriented action. However, in this circumstance the sceptic can maintain that argument about the right is partly of this strategic nature — in the sense that we are motivated to limit the potential for agreement by personal factors such as the immanent truth (to us) of the core tenets of our beliefs. The sceptic can say that moral argument, even in our modern culture, is more often like this. As evidence she could point to the intractability of some disputes where both sides, despite an intimate familiarity with the strengths or weaknesses of the others' position, refuse to engage in reasoned appraisal.

Conclusion

This brief section has inevitably concentrated on some areas of Habermas' argument at the expense of others. The most notable omission concerns the idea of the 'cultural specificity' of the rules Habermas provides and the kind of universality which can result from such a foundation — can it escape the culture in which it originates? This constitutes a very different line of criticism from the ones I have pressed here. This critic could, following Gadamer, protest:

> How can we prove our communicative competence to reflect a higher stage in a species-wide developmental process if all the research that we undertake in order to show that it is a higher stage already assumes what is to be proven? How do we escape the vicious circle in which we accept as the principle of research . . . precisely that which is at issue; namely the greater cognitive adequacy of the latter? (Warnke, 1987, 135).

However, perhaps this is to impute too universalistic a view to Habermas; after all, he accepts that the transcendental-pragmatic argument 'cannot claim the status of an ultimate justification . . . such a strong claim should not even be raised' (Habermas, 1990, 44). The universalism at which he aims can instead be understood as closely related to and redeemed only through discourse, and is perhaps procedural, rather than substantive and hence action-determining, in character (White, 1988, 50). In addition, I have not examined in any depth how and why the transcendental-pragmatic argument yields universals only for morality rather than ethics, for the right rather than the good.

Nevertheless, I believe this section has brought out some important limitations of Habermas' approach. I am not questioning the intuition perhaps underpinning Habermas' position, that if we are engaged in discourse with a certain end (in this case, testing validity claims), we would be badly advised to undertake things which damage or eliminate our chances of reaching that end. However, I believe that the scope of his proposal and the character of the rules which we ought to set for argumentation fall short of inescapable universality. Habermas does not successfully establish that moral argument must take the form he describes and thus he fails to refute the sceptic. It is open to the sceptic to accept that our use of moral language implies a demand for justification or validity, but to deny that this must take Habermas' form. The sceptic can do this, I have argued, by questioning either the inescapability of Habermas' presuppositions if we wish to engage in reflective discourse, or by denying that reflective discourse is the correct way to engage in debate about, and establish the validity of, moral claims.

The Universalism of Stuart Hampshire

Stuart Hampshire takes the defence of universalism in a different direction. Nagel looked for necessity in universal moral reasons, whilst Habermas contended that universal moral reasons are inescapable presuppositions of our moral discourse. Hampshire aims to take a more minimalist and contingent approach, decrying any abstract or ahistorical 'monomoralism' which claims 'a supernatural authority in ethics' (Hampshire, 1999, 56). In this respect Hampshire takes a naturalist approach, looking for universals in human nature and history.[39] However, Hampshire's work also shares elements with the work of the other thinkers I have discussed. Like Habermas, many of the norms grounded by Hampshire's approach will be procedural ones. As with Nagel, reason will play an important role in their derivation. Whilst most values are not universally held, Hampshire will argue that some constitute a common moral core. In this, Hampshire is not alone. For example, Michael Walzer has argued that minimalist moral rules against 'murder, deceit, torture, oppression, and tyranny' are embedded in the 'maximal morality' of different cultures (Walzer, 1994, 10).[40] Martha Nussbaum similarly holds that a common list of human virtues can be drawn up (Nussbaum, 1993, 196). Hampshire's universal values, however, are largely procedural, and concern the regulation and settlement of disagreement and conflict. Here I want to set out what these universal values are and the different justifications he offers for them. Hampshire, in many ways, offers us a halfway house between transcendental or necessary universalism and a more contingent form.

For Hampshire, our moral experience is characterised by deep disagreement between 'polymorphous ideals' and 'diverse conceptions of the good' (Hampshire, 1999, 56). In fact, conflict is endemic to his conception of human experience. Speaking of reconciling conflicting forces within society and ourselves, he holds that 'there will never be such a harmony' (Hampshire, 1999, 18). However, despite Hampshire's claim that moral conflicts do not permit easy resolution because they are between reasonable conflicting ideas of the good, he nevertheless thinks that a certain uni-

---

[39] Naturalism, in the broad sense I use it here, simply consists in a conviction that human psychology, biology and, more generally, *life* are relevant to questions of morality.

[40] I mentioned earlier that I did not believe Walzer can be satisfactorily classified as a relativist. The reason for this is his acceptance of 'moral minimalism' (Walzer, 1994, 10). However, as I note in the section on contingent universalism, some descriptions of a single universal core are compatible with relativism, so I do not want to close the door entirely.

versal procedural core of justice exists independently of any particular idea of what is good. This procedural justice is 'an absolute duty independent of all conceptions of the good' (Hampshire, 1989, 168). It consists in the values of 'argument on two sides, respected procedures of gathering evidence, impartial adjudication, the avoidance of violence, distribution of rewards and penalties in accordance with rationally defensible and well-established criteria' (Hampshire, 1989, 69).

Hampshire indicates that whilst some moral norms are contingent or particular, others are not and can be uncovered as being universal via a process of 'stripping down'. He writes 'the stripping down removes a supposed overlay or dressing of local custom, of distinctive cultural factors, and removes the moral idiosyncrasies of individuals, which have their local explanations and temporary causes' (Hampshire, 1983, 129). As indicated, Hampshire thinks this stripping down uncovers a core of procedures that must be followed in disputes about the good.

How, then, and to what degree does Hampshire oppose the relativist? Whilst Hampshire believes that there are many different reasonable conceptions of the good which can be successfully defended (Hampshire, 1989, 169), there nevertheless exists a minimum of decent fairness, and judgments grounded in this moral core are universal and objective. Thus Hampshire writes:

> I am arguing that moral judgements . . . are no less determinate and no less 'objective' than empirical judgements involving 'ought' and 'must' and related modal notions: no less determinate, in that they are equally susceptible of being true or false, or of being founded on evidence and reasons (Hampshire, 1989, 91).

Hampshire, with regard to core procedural justice, affirms everything that the relativist denies. Moral disagreements over the core are simple to characterise; if one party transgresses this core, then they are simply wrong. Moral truth is universal and objective, and the values in the core purport to be justified to all human beings. Indeed, the theory is almost constructed so we can say to the Nazi or other persecutor, 'you are absolutely evil'.

Hampshire justifies this moral core by contending that 'if the underlying structure of moral distinctions has no supernatural source, it must be recognised by rational enquiry as having its origin in nature and, specifically, in human nature; that is, common human needs and interests, and in canons of rational calculation' (Hampshire, 1983, 128). Justice, argues Hampshire, has a structure 'that is defensible by rational argument and by common observation of human desires' (Hampshire, 1983, 128). In this position we can identify two separable considerations in favour of his position, one laying the stress on rational enquiry, the other on common human needs. I think it is worth examining these two separately. They are advanced at least once in a combined form in *Morality and Conflict*, yet in *Innocence and Experience*, where the idea of justice is outlined as procedural and given a more determinate content, the combination of the two approaches is much less obvious. In *Justice and Conflict*, the emphasis is squarely on the rationality of certain procedures, most obviously the norm of adversary reasoning (e.g. Hampshire, 1999, 22–8).

The Rational Justification of the Moral Core

What I will term the rational justification for this basic morality is one which appeals to the rationality of every human being, regardless of his or her current contingent situation. The acceptance of a core of procedural justice is, on this interpretation, a 'rational calculation' (Hampshire, 1983, 128). Notably, it is rational for each to want to restrain a 'drive to domination' which would lead to misery for everyone (Hampshire, 1989, 77). Restraint is institutionalised in a set of basic principles that underpin negotiation between proponents of different ideas of the good. The core notion of procedural justice is justified by a *modus vivendi* appeal to the rationality of conflicting parties in civil society. Hampshire writes, 'a bare minimum concept of justice is indispensable if there is to be a peaceful and coherent society' (Hampshire, 1989, 73). It is also supported by the idea that the core notion of justice is a *part* of rationality, in the form of an account of practical reasoning. Thus Hampshire maintains also that 'the canons of rationality are here the canons of fairness . . . justice and fairness, at their most abstract level, are specifications of the notion of practical reasoning' (Hampshire, 1989, 53). An appeal to rationality surfaces again in Hampshire's discussion between the liberal and fundamentalists. He argues that it is irrational, and hence unfair, for each to insist on having their own way (Hampshire, 1989, 155). In his most recent work Hampshire gestures towards a Habermasian approach, suggesting that rationality 'transcendentally' or necessarily involves ideas of hearing both sides — what Hampshire calls 'adversary argument' (Hampshire, 1999, 45). Thus, one strand of Hampshire's argument proposes that morality is rational.

Universal Values Arising from Human Nature

There is, however, a second distinct line of reasoning present in his work. Hampshire also makes reference to the 'species-wide' nature of these basic moral injunctions. He talks of procedural justice as 'uniting all humanity, from the cradle to the grave' (Hampshire, 1989, 53). He writes:

> It makes sense to speak of happiness, freedom, and pleasure as good things, as contrasted with unhappiness, imprisonment, enslavement, and pain as bad things; states to be pursued for their own sake, and states to be prevented and avoided for their own sake. For such states, there is no need to appeal to any distinctive conception of the human good (Hampshire, 1989, 128).[41]

On this interpretation, Hampshire appeals to a universal concept of what humans value and dislike. This common recognition by humans of the bad things in life, coupled with everyone's experience of living in civil society and dealing with moral disagreement, means that core procedural justice has always been the response. For Hampshire, procedural justice

> is a duty that arises directly from a combination of two virtually universal conditions of human life: first, that men and women need to live together in societies and states of some kind, and, second, that all men and women both do, and ought to, encounter persons with contrary moral concerns and with incompatible conceptions of the good, both beyond the actual frontiers of their societies and within them (Hampshire, 1989, 140).

This second argument may go so far as to say that core procedural justice ought to be universally present wherever there is civil society, and hence its universal authority is authorised by the 'view from everywhere'. Or it might combine elements of the rationalist approach and say that these common desires and needs also contribute to making core procedural justice rationally binding. As Hampshire writes in *Morality and Conflict*, 'the most general facts about human needs and interests are put together with a model of rationality to derive the idea of the principles of justice' (Hampshire, 1983, 128).[42] However, this should not be confused with the claim that we can 'infer what is universally the best way of life from propositions about human nature' (Hamp-

---

[41] In *Morality and Conflict*, Hampshire uses the example of good health. 'Because bad health causes pain and death, it is natural that people in all places at all time should attach at least some considerable value to good health, and that good health should count as a fundamental and constant need and not only as a contingent interest' (Hampshire, 1983, 128). Martha Nussbaum makes a similar claim that we can identify common elements of human flourishing which ought to form a common moral core (Nussbaum, 1996) .

[42] This passage occurs in the context of a description of Rawls' argument. This is one reason why I do not necessarily ascribe the 'mixed' view to Hampshire, though it is undoubtedly one possible interpretation.

shire, 1983, 155). Hampshire is fundamentally opposed to this monomoralist position.

Hampshire believes that rationality of a certain kind is part of human nature, and to that extent unavoidable. Despite the combination of rationality and human nature, I believe these two approaches to Hampshire can be distinct. One is a direct appeal to rationality, i.e. 'rational people ought to believe this because they are *rational*'; the other is an appeal to human nature or personhood, i.e. 'rational people ought to believe this because they are *people*'.[43]

I want to raise some potential problems for these two approaches and their conjunction. My attempted critique begins with an important feature of Hampshire's own account. Hampshire alludes to procedural justice being necessary to avoid humanity's 'drive to domination'. This seems to indicate that he acknowledges this as another important part of human nature, albeit one that needs restraining. However, the presence of this natural but evil characteristic of humankind seems to illustrate a problem for the second 'human nature' strand of the argument. The drive to domination is a part of human nature. So is a tendency to core procedural justice. One is bad, the other good. Therefore, human nature cannot itself serve to justify moral universals without a further independent criterion telling us which parts of our human nature we should and should not accept as the core of morality.

Hampshire perhaps addresses a similar kind of question when he discusses 'Hume's Ghost' in *Innocence and Experience*. In response to Hume's assertion that 'It is not contrary to reason to prefer the destruction of the whole world to the smallest injury to my finger', he argues that the presuppositions behind such a statement remove it from the moral sphere (Hampshire, 1989, 87). This kind of statement, says Hampshire, 'leaves us at a loss' (Hampshire, 1989, 87). However, given that the evil of domination has, according to Hampshire, manifested itself throughout human history (in *Innocence and Experience* he gives both an analysis of it and a view of *why* it is evil), it is plainly not *too* far beyond our comprehension, nor does its abhorrence lie beyond explanation. It is one thing to be evil, and another for something to lie outside the moral sphere. We might ask similar questions about ideas like vengeance or competition, which have been argued by various thinkers to be 'natural' sentiments and plainly concern the

---

[43]   Of course, this second requires rationality — it simply does not make it the focus of the argument.

way we ought to behave towards others, yet perhaps are not the kinds of things we would like to enshrine as part of a moral core.[44] There must be a criterion independent of human nature that allows us to screen out such undesirable elements. Hampshire simply does not seem to provide an answer.

Let us turn now to the first consideration. Someone wanting to defend this account could rightly object that the presence of this drive to domination is what necessitates core procedural justice — what makes it so *rational*. Thus, the two arguments are conjoined. The arguments could also be linked because we might rationally consider the common assessment of goods and evils as a good basis for morality. However, the problem seems to replicate itself at this level. Why is the drive to domination, or intolerance, irrational? Perhaps the question needs to be reinterpreted as one about the *conception* of rationality by which this is judged irrational. We can clearly see how it could be *instrumentally* rational, in the sense of being a fitting means to my desired end, for me to engage in deception, warfare, intolerance or more generally any negation of the norms that Hampshire wishes to establish. Despite his talk of rational *calculation*, which might sound akin to rational choice theory, Hampshire can be seen as committed to a 'thick' idea of rationality. For example, Hampshire holds that rationality is identified with adversarial reasoning, 'as argument and counterargument, with the just and fair weighting of conflicts of evidence and conflicts of desire' (Hampshire, 1999, 45). For Hampshire rationality has an affinity with practical reason of an Aristotelian kind; it is a faculty that reasons about the good.[45] It is clear, on this approach, how the norms of the moral core come about, but their foundation is itself controversial. The thicker the conception of practical rationality becomes, the more problematic the claim that all rational persons should arrive at a consensus about justice. The claim is problematic because it excludes all

---

[44] I take Mark Lilla to be making a related psychological point in a recent review of *Justice is Conflict*. Speaking of the rules of procedural justice, he notes that 'people accustomed to conflict would grow to resent the constraints imposed on them by the rules of the game and would cast them off at the first opportunity' (Lilla, 2000, 49).

[45] I am unclear as to the exact nature of the concept of rationality employed by Hampshire. It seems to relate to the evaluation of 'moral claims, and even a whole way of life, by reference to human welfare and to justice as fairness' (Hampshire, 1983, 165) and involves a weighting of universal and conventional considerations (Hampshire, 1983, 166). I remain unsure that it is not thereby 'thickened' by ideas of human flourishing or the good. Even Hampshire's stress on adversarial reasoning as the norm in *Justice is Conflict* is controversial; for example, see Smith, 1994.

those people who do not converge on that consensus. This might lead us to question the distinction between rationality or genuinely common needs on the one hand and 'local prejudices and superstitions' on the other.

Two aspects of Hampshire's position here seem to pull in different directions. On the one hand, Hampshire specifies that justice and fairness are part of practical reasoning (Hampshire, 1989, 53). In this case, his argument clearly goes through. If we are concerned only with just and fair reasoning, then we will naturally be able to identify a core of justice and fairness in that reasoning. On the other hand, if the 'essence' of practical reasoning is 'promoting arguments for and against a proposal' (Hampshire, 1989, 53) then there is clearly room for strategic, self-interested or means-end arguments to be considered. On the first account, his argument is transfigured. It now states that we should adopt a core morality of fairness because we *ought* to be fair. However, this raises problems for Hampshire's claim to be doing something different from the monomoralism he criticises, and makes the argument to a large extent independent of any contingencies, circumstances or commonalities.

In summary, Hampshire offers rationality and commonality as the foundation of a common core of procedural justice. Neither of these, I have argued, can straightforwardly bear this weight. On the second 'human nature' account, just because we are made some way does not mean we should enshrine this in our morality. We might take the view[46] that we uniquely have the ability to overturn or refuse evolutionary imperatives. Hampshire notes that 'the dependence of very young children on adult nurture, the onset of sexual maturity, the instinctual desires associated with motherhood . . . may be appealed to as imposing some limits on moral requirements at all times and in all places' (1983, 142). Going too far down this road, however, soon becomes problematic. What exactly ought to follow from these biological imperatives? Some people would, perhaps rightly, now resist the idea that anything about a woman's role within a family and society follows from the presence of maternal instincts.

With regard to the first consideration, it is not clear that rationality determines that we should tend to negotiate or be impartial. The rationality of procedural justice will only offer a compelling justification to those who accept that conception of rationality. Procedural justice might only be as universal as the conception of rationality that provides reason to adopt it. My

[46]   With Richard Dawkins for example (1989, e.g. 200–1).

thought here is that when we are engaged (as Hampshire is) in justifying the universality of moral principles, an appeal to a conception of rationality which everyone *ought* (morally) to accept does not necessarily advance the argument. Hampshire must engage in the justification of a universal rational core before this can justify the acceptance of a universal moral one. The justification Hampshire offers is, it seems to me, inconclusive; hence his claim to provide a cross cultural or universal justification of universal moral norms is problematic.[47]

Hampshire's universalism is *contingent*, in the sense that it relies either on an account of human nature and human history, or the rationality of procedural justice, or a combination of both. His claim that conflict is endemic or necessary to human experience — his rejection of a single unitary approach to morality — also raises the question of the stability of his own position. Can ideas like rationality or human nature really be independent enough of this conflict to yield supra-cultural universals? Can he maintain that morality is continual conflict, but that the procedures of justice are stable? To point out these potential problems, however, is not necessarily to refute Hampshire's position. Whilst I have raised objections in this section, replies are available to Hampshire. The claim that some moral norms are universal because they are commonly affirmed by people is an idea that merits further examination. Thus, the possible relations between non-moral facts and universally justified and true moral principles is the subject matter for my next discussion, of what I will term contingent universalism.

Contingent Universalism

We have seen that one element of Hampshire's approach looks for universality in common norms. The final version of universalism that I will discuss here takes this search as one of its central concerns. I shall term this approach contingent, or convergence, universalism. I want to use this term to consider a number of disparate positions that nevertheless have something in common. Elements of this approach surface in some human rights literature. Alison Renteln, for example, argues, 'preliminary evidence suggests that there is, in fact, a convergence on moral values' (Renteln, 1990, 81), and that 'just because there are discrete, separate and competing moral systems does not necessarily mean that they do not overlap' (Renteln, 1990, 79). Milne provides a list of

---

[47] I examine in more detail the idea of common principles justifying universal ones in my next section on what I term 'contingent universalism.'

nine socially focussed values which 'every community must possess . . . if it is to be a community properly so-called at all' (Milne, 1986, 46). These are beneficence, respect for human life, justice, fellowship, social responsibility, freedom from arbitrary inference, honourable conduct, civility, and child welfare (Milne, 1986, 46). Michael Walzer, as I have already noted, has talked about basic prohibitions on 'murder, deception, betrayal, gross cruelty' which 'constitute a kind of minimal and universal moral code' (Walzer, 1987, 24). Simon Caney, arguing that common defences of universalism are unsatisfactory, proposes that universalism can instead be defended from a common or convergence position (Caney, 1999, 22–4).[48] In this section I discuss some of these proposals, and some potential problems with them, in order to draw out exactly what contingent universalism is — what is *contingent* about it, and how it constitutes a variety of *universalism*.

Contingent universalism as I understand it makes two essential claims. The first is what Caney has termed the 'convergence claim'. The contingent universalist 'maintains that individuals from distinct societies will be able to accept some common moral principles and values' (Caney, 1999, 26).[49] The second is that we can understand these common moral principles as universal, in that they provide rules of binding force for everyone. I want to examine, discuss and raise problems with these two claims; whilst I believe that there are considerations which erode the strength of the first, the second is the source of the most serious problems.

The Convergence Claim

Contingent universalists can point to reasons and considerations supporting their claim that cultures do converge on certain moral values. There are perhaps three such considerations. The first is that all cultures seem to accept certain things as bad, notably disease and natural disaster. The second is that these common bads arise from the lack of fulfilment of common needs, such as that for 'water and nutrition'. . . These needs, it should be stressed, may

---

[48] I believe the foundations of such an approach can also be found in Bok, 1993.

[49] For Caney, an essential corollary of this claim is that these principles and judgements are subject to painstaking critical evaluation. He terms this component of the argument the 'methodological claim' (Caney, 1999, 24). As I will argue later in this section, Caney's proposal constitutes an example of contingent universalism guarded by strong constraints on what counts as a 'considered judgement'. Nevertheless, not all those I term contingent universalists endorse this level of critical reflection.

not be merely physical — they can incorporate self-respect and affection as well as food and shelter.[50] These shared needs and problems could form the cornerstone of a justification for universally binding principles. The third is that given interaction between cultures, specifically the way some are shaped by others, we should expect some convergence. However, this last claim says nothing about the *desirability* of such convergence. We might hold, as I noted with regard to Nagel, that this interaction was manipulative in character, and the resulting commonality thus undesirable. It might be the result of homogenisation, of a dominant single culture imposed on others.

This approach utilises our moral judgements and principles, searching for commonality amongst people's moral intuitions. In doing so it raises questions about how we come to affirm these moral principles and to what extent we should rely on our first thoughts about right and wrong. One natural way to elucidate the convergence claim is by using the method of reflective equilibrium, first set out by Rawls in *A Theory of Justice*. According to the most straightforward interpretation of the method, justification is reached by making our considered moral judgements and theories, and the deep theories which underpin them, cohere so as to provide mutual support. Thus, justified moralities will form seamless webs, where beliefs which do not fit are re-examined in the light of theories, and vice-versa. Reflective equilibrium allows for the use of critically examined moral convictions. Contingent universalism can employ this methodology to maintain that these critically assessed convictions are the raw material of convergence, and that we should aim for a world-wide equilibrium. For example, Caney makes the methodological claim that 'all moral argument must make use of people's moral convictions but . . . such moral judgements should be critically appraised' (Caney, 1999, 25).

I do not want to discuss reflective equilibrium in great detail here. Interpretations and implications of this methodology will form the bulk of the subject matter for chapter four. Reflective equilibrium seems an attractive methodology for it allows our intuitions some weight and importance without making unchallenged intuitions the foundation for justification. What should be noted is that for the purposes of contingent universalism, as I shall attempt to show, the stipulation about *critical examination* of our moral beliefs is crucial. Because our moral beliefs can be mistaken, they require examination to see whether they are in error. As I dis-

---

[50] See, for example, Part 1 of Coate, Rosati eds. 1988).

cuss below, this stipulation solves one of the most obvious problems with the convergence claim, but generates others depending on the criteria upon which we are to judge a moral belief erroneous. Different contingent universalists can advocate more or less stringent examinations of our moral beliefs; thus, I distinguish in the next chapter between what I term 'strong' and 'weak' criteria that determine what counts as a considered moral judgement. Their decision on how strong a test to adopt, as an important component of determining *which* intuitions and theories are good starting points for cross-cultural universals, will influence the character of the theory that results.

I want to look at two general lines of criticism of the approach in order to present its important features more fully. The first of these two angles of attack on the convergence claim asks how it is to be decided which principles are 'common' enough, or moral enough, to feature as the starting point for 'common moral principles'. The second criticism questions the content and the character of the principles that will result from the search for convergence.

(1) Whose Principles, Which Justification?

The first line of criticism examines an ambiguity in the convergence claim: how many people need converge upon a principle for it to be significantly common? Consider a principle that demands respect for others: some people will place strict limits upon the constituency that it applies to. For example, neo-nazis will be unlikely to accord the same respect to Jews as to Aryans, perhaps because they do not consider Jews to be persons. Some Serbian nationalists will assert respect for other moral human beings, but deny this status to Bosnians.[51] If we are aiming for substantive convergence, we must be in a position to count out such views which undermine a common assessment of goods and bads. One way to do this is to dismiss these judgements and others like them as the result of distorting factors or faulty reasoning. As I will argue in chapter five, it might be possible to demonstrate to Nazis, by the use of reasoning which they are committed to accepting, that their approach rests on false factual premises. Some universalists will have a freer hand in this, because they believe that something can be a reason for an actor even if it can find no foothold in her reasoning.[52] In a similar way, the arguments of individuals who argue for unlimited capitalist accumu-

---

[51] Similarly, some radical animal rights activists will sincerely affirm respect for animals, but not for those who keep or kill them.

[52] I discuss this claim and its opposite in chapter five and seven.

lation may be problematic if their position is based purely on self-interest. Egoistic hedonism, it could be argued, has no place within the determining of moral principles.[53] I think something like this will go on in *any* moral theory that takes into account people's intuitions. However, there are problems with the use of such disqualifying factors when we are looking for common values. Richard Rorty notes a crucial variance in the constitutency to which moral norms apply. To the Kantian claim 'notice what you have in common, your humanity' he holds that people *without irrationality* can reply that they are morally offended 'by the suggestion that they should treat someone who is not kin as if he were a brother, or a nigger as if he were white' (Rorty, 1998, 178).[54]

Is not just self-interest, but also partiality to some over others, invalidating? If many people's moral judgements establish different requirements with regard to those outside their immediate community, are we going to judge them an unfit subject for convergence? If someone believes a moral position is partly justified by the way it benefits him/her and their fellow countrymen, and is limited to these constituencies, should we be in the business of proving this false, morally inadequate, or flawed in process, in order to discover convergence?[55] The standard impartialist response is to hold that, as a part of impartial morality, everyone has a right to favour some over others. Nevertheless, at the level of justification, the justifying reasons should be impartial ones. I will discuss this response in more detail in chapter four. Here, how the contingent universalist responds will depend on the balance she strike between the intuitive appeal of universal beliefs as those that are common to all (minimally rational) humans, and a set of stricter tests as to which moral views we should consider as the raw materials for moral universals. There are two ways contingent universalists can go. Some may opt to rely on the use of *common* judgements. They might do this because beliefs which are

---

[53] For example, Harman concludes his discussion of egoism in *The Nature of Morality* with this idea, that 'it would follow almost by definition that moral reasons are based on concern for others and not on self-interest' (Harman, 1977, 151).

[54] Contingent universalists who want to maintain a commonality here will have to disagree with Rorty and instead find such positions irrational. This illustrates the problem; almost any standard of rationality used to adjudicate between adequate and inadequate beliefs runs the risk of turning a set of particular principles into universal ones and of loading the dice in favour of the desired conclusion.

[55] Here, as elsewhere in the chapter, the question arises of whether we should treat morality as necessarily impartial. I discuss this question in more detail in the next chapter.

common could point to constancies of human nature, for example. It is an important corrective to this approach to say that some (perhaps widely held) judgements will be excluded from consideration. The smaller the constituency of people who actually hold these common moral norms, the less this intuitive appeal seems to be — in fact, the smaller the constituency, the *less common* a belief is. If the contingent universalist's position aims to establish a link between the common and the universal, then the less common these principles are, the more the intuitive power of this side of the argument is weakened. In the absence of significant overlap, contingent universalism seems indistinct from other kinds of universalism.

However, the contingent universalist can put less emphasis on the convergence claim, and move instead in the direction of high critical standards for deciding which moral beliefs are to be accepted or rejected as possible foundations for convergence. In such a case, the burden in examining and defending the proposal shifts away from the intuitive appeal of common moral judgements to the content of these critical standards. The convergence claim is modified so it claims that distinct societies will be able to accept some common moral principles and values *if* their views were filtered to remove invalidating factors. As long as there *would be* convergence, were distorting factors removed, whether there is or is not convergence might be almost incidental. The contingent universalist might hold that *if* we took away all the distorting factors — perhaps in the form of an appeal to a Habermasian 'ideal speech situation' for example — the result would be a common core. The appeal made by such a contingent universalist is to moral judgements common amongst those we find to be sound moral agents. The nature of these invalidating factors can vary enormously, from ones such as drunkenness which are relatively uncontroversial, to ones such as bias which are incredibly so, as I will examine in chapter four. There I sketch the differences between a weak and a strong model of invalidating factors. My purpose here, less ambitiously, is to indicate that the contingent universalist can be pushed in either of these directions. Whilst I think there are other potential issues regarding the use of filtered moral judgements in this approach, I do not intend to take this issue any further here; instead, I take them up in the next chapter.

Before moving on to the second criticism of the convergence claim, I want to discuss a different approach to finding convergence amongst apparently diverse norms. As an alternative (or in addition) to extensive filtering of moral views, the contingent universalist can employ *environmental relativity* to rule out some conflicting views. This is the idea that circumstances should influence the interpretation of universal moral norms. Thus, in cases where people do things very differently, there might nevertheless be the same principle at work, merely *interpreted* differently. Obviously, this would aid the universalist's defence of common norms. Apparently bad moral norms, like complete egoism and disregard for others, might just be an interpretation of the right to self-preservation in a very difficult 'lifeboat' environment. Environmental relativity 'implies only that some practices which are in fact evil under particular social-historical conditions may not be so under others' without implying that 'each society has its own moral truth' (Stout, 1990, 86).[56] Undoubtedly, in some cases this might be a plausible interpretation of a situation; however, it should be noted that large-scale employment of environmental relativity risks turning talk of moral universals into sophistry. This is not to say that there are not instances where environmental relativity can be a useful explanatory tool, but simply to warn against over-zealous application.

(2) Which Principles, Whose Morality?

If the first criticism demonstrates the difficulties in deciding on principles, the second questions the extent, content, and authority of those principles. Presuming that the process does issue in some moral principles, what are they likely to look like? The kind of principles that could come out of a convergence methodology are, I would suggest, ones such as

(1) Pain is a bad thing.

(2) Treat equal cases equally.

(3) People should get what they deserve.

(4) We should not murder innocents.

(5) Punishment should be proportional to the crime.

However, it is worth pointing out that these examples — even the most simple — are not straightforward when it comes to their content, and when they come to guide action. Why is this a problem? Remember that the universalist is committed to the convergence claim, which holds that 'individuals from distinct societies will be able to accept some common moral principles and values' (Caney, 1999, 26). There are two considerations which can be put

---

[56] David Brink similarly employs environmental relativity as part of his realist approach (Brink, 1989, 91).

forward against any claim to have discovered a common moral principle, such as the five above. Whilst they do not contradict the convergence claim, they nevertheless point to significant limitations. First, the terms used in these principles will be interpreted by different people in different ways, depending on the content of the rest of their moral system. Second, whilst there might be convergence on these principles, there will not be convergence on the weight different people attach to them. If contingent universalists want to attain at least a list of common moral principles, they may have to sacrifice any determinate ranking of principles.

The first consideration is that people will not agree on one understanding of 'treating people equally', 'deserts', 'innocence' or 'proportionality to the crime'. With regard to deserts; if you believe people have equal moral worth then they will deserve, *ceteris paribus*, equal shares. If you believe what clever, talented people deserve is success, and what lazy people deserve is failure, then inequality will be justified. Sinners might deserve divine retribution, or help. In other words, the content of these principles will differ so widely between moralities that the single universal morality may be so general that its prescriptions will lack substance.[57] I think this objection applies to principles increasingly the more complex they become — 'pain is bad' is less vulnerable to this objection than 'we have a duty to relieve the pain of others throughout the world'. There is still scope for disagreement as to the moral course of action between advocates of different conceptions of the same common value, because some conceptions will seem to be so far apart as to not *be* the same value.[58]

Contingent universalists, of course, might dispute this claim. For example, Renteln conducts an ethnographic analysis of retribution, proposing it as a commonly held view about negative reciprocity (often given the form of *lex talionis*) positing the rejection of 'arbitrary, indiscriminate killing' (Renteln, 1990, 132). Contingent universalists could perform something like this activity for a number of different principles, arguing that there are common cores to moral norms. However, Renteln recognises some relativistic limits to this particular common norm, noting for example

[57]   As it exists here, this is merely an unsubstantiated objection. I cannot give an ethnographic analysis here sufficient to ground a strong conclusion that the core morality of contingent universalism will be too vague. Nevertheless, I think that some of the force can be felt here in its unsubstantiated form. My point also indicates the way that relativists can respond to claims of common moral norms.

[58]   For example, consider Rorty's reasoners (Rorty 199, 178). Both believe that all persons are equal. However, one believes that large sections of humanity are not persons. Do they really have this value in common?

that 'it will not resolve the arguments about infanticide and abortion, for some societies view these acts as arbitrary, unjustified killings while others take the opposite view' (Renteln, 1990, 135). An appropriate relativist response is to query, on a case-by-case basis, this idea of norms having common cores.[59] To take this example, Renteln admits indeterminacy in the norm of negative reciprocity with regard to hard cases. I think this problem is not just confined to difficult issues like abortion, but to negative reciprocity generally. If indeterminacy extends not just to hard cases but to the bulk of the analysis, then that principle cannot claim to be held in common.

In the case of reciprocity, what one society might consider just retribution, to another will seem massively disproportionate. Consider the following colourful example from the *Hagakure* of Yamamoto Tsunetomo:

> Horie San'emon's misdeed was robbing the Nabeshima warehouse in Edo of its money and fleeing to another province. He was caught and confessed. Thus it was pronounced 'Because this is a grave crime he should be tortured to death' . . . At first all the hairs on his body were burned off and his fingernails were pulled out. His tendons were then cut, he was bored with drills . . . in the end his back was split, he was boiled in soy sauce, and his body was bent back in two (Yamamoto, 1979, 120).

Closer to home, the Taliban regime in Afghanistan could order the public execution of a man for participating in consensual homosexual sex.[60] Clearly, at least for the law, the punishment is proportional to the crime in these cases. Proportionality may be a universal, but interpretations of what is punishment for a particular crime vary so dramatically that it may be impossible to pick out any meaningful moral core. Something like this activity could go on, I would suggest, for many specific moral principles.[61]

---

[59] This approach will not work as straightforwardly for those contingent universalists who endorse a demanding set of critical standards, as I discuss below.

[60] 'Afghanistan: Cruel, Inhuman or Degrading Treatment or Punishment' Amnesty International Report — ASA 11/15/99 November 1999.

[61] To illustrate my point I have drawn on examples where the punishment seems too harsh for the crime, or in the second case where no crime that we should recognise has been committed. My point here is not to imply any moral criticism of the contingent universalist because these examples are acceptable cases of proportionality. Instead, I use these graphic examples to illustrate the diverse range of understandings of proportionality. I am not sure that cases of leniency would have illustrated this diversity equally well. Of course, the contingent universalist could filter prior to the ethnographic analysis, only surveying those approaches not

Because the relativist response here moves to actual views, without a consideration of whether these views would pass stringent filtering tests, this kind of argument will not work against all contingent universalists. For those contingent universalists that endorse high constraints, such conflicting examples might not be admitted on the grounds that the judgements of the magistrate or the Taliban are formed erroneously. The relativist would have to supplement her argument by holding that the Taliban or Feudal Japan were instances of 'sound moral reasoners' who nevertheless hold morally iniquitous views. This kind of universalist looks at actual convergence, but *removes* from the instances of it those cases where convergence fails the tests. However, she also *adds* those cases where convergence is only prevented by unsound moral reasoning — and this is the kind of case exemplified by the Taliban or the Hagakure above. This raises the question of what evidence could falsify a contingent universalist position of this kind. At first sight, the only evidence admissible would seem to be that of sound moral reasoners who were committed to disagreeing on all the components of a core morality.

However, there is slightly more scope for the relativist than this, since the position of the universalist has to be that some principles are common to *all* sound moral reasoners. There are two aspects here which bear examination. First, we can see that a great deal depends here on what it is to be a sound moral reasoner. If for example, being a sound moral reasoner requires that one must hold all the tenets of the core morality, then this kind of contingent universalism is necessarily true, and cannot be falsified. Such a contingent universalism might, like Nagel's argument perhaps, be too true to be good. If, on the other hand, being a sound moral reasoner means something more like reflecting in good faith on one's moral convictions and removing those which one was not willing to see applied by everyone then there seems to me no reason in principle why such evidence could not be provided.[62]

Second, we can also see here that commonality is still important to the strong constraints theorist. A principle would ideally be common amongst *all* sound moral reasoners. It is unclear how many sound moral reasoners would have to object in order to sink the project; nevertheless, sufficient sound-minded dissenters would invalidate a high constraints convergence claim. Now, the

considered 'distorted'. In this case there would be no unacceptable diversity in the resulting sample.
[62] I look at 'weak' and 'strong' constraints on what counts as a 'considered moral judgement' in the next chapter.

more demanding the filters, the more likely we are to get convergence. However, if those reasoners found to be sound constituted only a tiny proportion of the world's population, the moral core would be in trouble. We would be justified in asking if the tests were too demanding, or too rigged, and the moral core might have little practical impact. But the lower the constraints, the more chance there seems that examples could be found of a sound moral reasoner who did not affirm a common moral principle. Thus, commonality remains an important consideration even for the high constraints universalist. Any example I give here of moral reasoners who do not affirm a common moral principle might fail because it violated one or another possible set of high constraints. Paradoxically, however, if the people I chose seemed reasonable, then with each example rejected as unsound, the intuitive appeal of high-constraints universalism would diminish.

To come to the second point, the contingent universalist proposal leaves the different universal moral values unranked both amongst themselves and vis-à-vis other moral values that different moralities will believe are universally valuable. Thus, even between people who hold the same conception of a moral principle, this does not suffice to guide the choice of moral action for any particular agent. Differences in ranking between moral systems means that action is radically underdetermined by the list of moral goods and bads, because the *place* assigned to these values in individuals' moral frameworks will be hugely significant. Is a belief deeply held, or weakly held? Is it to take absolute precedence over others or engage with them as part of a calculus? A related problem, about in what sense this list of common moral principles exist, is also pressing. It is likely that few, if any, people will have a morality which actually maps on to the common morality. Partly because of its necessarily vague and common nature, the particularities of people's moral views — which they will nevertheless believe have universal application — will not be captured. What is intended to be the 'view from everywhere' (Galston, 1991, 49) might actually become, practically, the 'view of no-one.'[63] The intuition behind this point is that in some cases

[63] As an addendum to this discussion, it could also be noted that an empirically fairly common belief about moral justification might take the form that moral judgements are justified to the extent that they reflect the will of the perfectly good supreme being(s) through the holy book(s). This view is common to many followers of major world religions; Judaism, Islam, Christianity, and perhaps Hinduism. As a test for the contingent universalist's method, this seems to pose a potential problem. A sub-

we can claim commonality which is nevertheless flawed or illusory.

Take a case in which there are two moral reasoners. A believes (1) never kill another living thing and (2) proportional punishment will be distributed in the afterlife so it is not man's business to punish. B believes (1) killing is only justified in self-defence or in defence of the law and (2) any crime warrants lengthy incarceration. We might be tempted to look for common moral principles by saying that both affirm that killing is morally bad and crime should receive punishment. And whilst I do think the views have something in common, it also seems to me unsatisfactory to think that morality is like maths, so that we can determine the highest factor common to the two. The common morality ends up capturing the essence of neither of their views, and also fails to provide any kind of motivation to either agent, both of whom continue to be motivated by their particular views. To miss the absolute character of A's prohibition (1), or the difference between their views on the agency responsible for the punishing and the character of that punishment (2), badly neglects some of the content of these moral views. In this way it is misleading, or an over-simplification at best, to say that A and B have these principles in common.[64] It is false in this case to say that the same principle guides the moral life of both A and B, though it is true that both believe killing to be a bad thing. Of course, many things can be true but not very helpful. Why would either A or B assent to, or be motivated by, the common element of their views when they both have far richer understandings?

The Universality Claim

As the above discussion indicates, the convergence claim contains scope for significant ambiguities. Finding principles that are truly common to all (sound) moral reasoners will be a difficult busi-

---

stantial proportion of the world's population believes something along these lines. Does this make it *common*, and hence universal? After all, some theologians have argued that we can find the same god in many different religions. Or does the fact that the people believe in differing instantiations of this deity, or indeed in what they would maintain is the *single true* deity, undermine this commonality? Alternatively, do such sincere religious believers fail the requirements for being sound moral reasoners? I will argue in chapters four and five that the relativist will disagree with this characterisation of moral justification. However, it does not seem to pose the *same* problem for a relativist view of justification, because this does not rest on a convergence claim.

[64] Of course, both one or other of the reasoners could fail the tests of being a sound moral reasoner.

ness. However, I believe that the most important problem for the universalist's argument concerns the second premise. Let us restate the position I have outlined as forming the core of contingent universalism;

(1) (Sound-thinking) individuals from distinct societies will be able to accept some common moral principles and values.

(2) Hence comparing (critically assessed) judgements and theories across cultures will issue in some universal moral principles, where universal moral principles are moral principles that apply to everyone.[65]

So far, my criticisms have concerned the problem of determining the common moral principles in (1), but we can also ask cogently about the link between (1) and (2). For the argument above to work, commonality must *constitute* or be *linked to* universality, and as it stands, it is not clear what would constitute such a connection. For the strong 'hence' claim to work, an additional premise has to be inserted: (1a) all (critically assessed) common values are universal values. A weaker claim could be (1b) *some* (critically assessed) common values are universal values.

The point of this incompleteness is that contingent universalism in the form I am considering it does not give us a full explanation of *why* any or all common values are universal values. Its plausibility as a theory will depend largely on the story it tells about this link.[66] At first glance, the fact of commonality does not provide this universal validity. Suppose, for example, that the entire world adopted a single morality. The 'social criticism' argument that I mentioned in chapter two could be employed here against the contingent universalist — on what grounds could we criticise this common morality? Most universalists I have discussed in this chapter believe that just because most people hold something to be the case, does not mean that it *is* the case. Contingent or convergence universalism would seem to suffer from a problem about the possibility of social criticism. People who spoke out against common moral values would necessarily

---

[65] I include this stipulation about what 'universal' implies because I take this to be the substance of the universalist's claim. As I will argue in chapter seven, I think we can split the notions of universality of application (as used here) and universality of justification.

[66] Even its most systematic account, that given by Simon Caney, does not pin down this link or equivalence (Caney, 1999).

be universally wrong.[67] Thus, drawing a link between a principle being commonly held and it being *universally* correct leaves the contingent universalist in a relativist dilemma. Either the contingent universalist bites the bullet, or else she must affirm that the answer has to lie in whatever *justifies* the values being held by so many people. I want to suggest four possibilities.

The *first* is that everyone is bound by universal moral rules because, contingently, everyone happens to affirm these moral rules, so everyone is bound (recalling Rousseau) only to rules that they themselves propose. The *second* is that everyone is bound by such moral rules because convergence reveals them to be common features of our universal human nature. The *third* is that the fact that everyone is bound by such moral rules because their commonality is evidence of moral universality. On the *fourth* account, consensus or convergence is what *constitutes* moral truth. I want to briefly set out each of these approaches in turn, and examine some of their implications.

(1) 'Some moral principles are affirmed by everyone and hence valid for everyone'

The first account might be criticised — by universalists — for being not universal enough. This is because in emphasising *contingency* — that this is just what people happen to agree on — it gives little independent life or reality to universal moral truths.[68] Indeed, it is strictly compatible with the relativist claim that there need be no single true morality — it just so happens that people agree about some things, and for those people it is binding. Relativism and this view can happily coexist.[69] This approach seems vulnerable to objections as to whether people really do agree on

---

[67]   This morality could be a good one or a bad one by our current standards, as long as it were not perfect. For if it were perfect there is perhaps a case for saying no-one would need grounds to criticise it. If the adoption of such a morality passed any filters provided by the contingent universalist, then it seems this case has relevance even for the 'strong constraints' theorists. Of course, the strong-constraints theorist can deny the possibility of any morality, other than the minimal moral core they endorse, ever passing such constraints. In this instance the example could not come to pass.

[68]   It is unclear, for example, whether this approach could speak of moral facts or moral truths in the way that many realist universalists would want to.

[69]   As an example of this kind of synthesis, we can perhaps consider Herskovits' claim that 'universals . . . are those least common denominators to be extracted from the range of variation' (Herskovits, 1972, 31–2).

common values, or on how many — amplified versions of the criticisms I have already outlined.[70]

(2) 'Convergence demonstrates that these principles are part of our common moral nature'

The second account is problematic because it faces a dilemma. Somewhere it must either yield an 'ought' from an 'is' (a claim about morality from a claim about human nature) or else it proceeds by justifying a claim about how we *determine* universal moral principles on the *basis of* universal moral principles (i.e. what human nature *ought* to be). If we can identify universal needs which are part of our nature, then this still says very little about the priority we should attach to them vis-à-vis personal or non-human nature-based goals. Furthermore, common desires or common human activities may be a dangerous grounding for universality, partly because of age-old debates about nature and nurture, and partly because they seem to sanction other widespread desires such as revenge, self-interest, competition and violence to the same extent as 'soft' needs such as love. The contingent universalist may not want to countenance legitimising these desires.

(3) 'Convergence is our best evidence for universal moral principles'

I would contend that this third approach *assumes* universalism, and perhaps realism: that there are in some sense real objective values which convergence points towards. This is not by itself to devalue the convergence approach. It serves as an additional consideration helping to justify the acceptance of a universalist phenomenology (Caney, 1999). Convergence serves an epistemic function, telling us how we might start looking for these moral truths. I discuss a variety of this proposal in more detail in the next chapter. I have argued in section one of this chapter that the ubiquity of pain and pleasure does not prove that it constitutes a transcendentally objective reason. Similarly, convergence, as I shall demonstrate, does not by itself prove the presence of real objective values. The question of the *interpretation* of the evidence in crucial. A debate follows from this proposal about whether convergence is really the best way of ascertaining such truths, and whether it can be separated from *constituting* such moral truths — i.e. whether it confirms the existence of truths we already thought were out there, or whether convergence itself leads us to

---

[70] Perhaps also to a post-modern claim that contingent universalism celebrates homogeneity rather than difference.

posit the possibility of moral truths. Some of these questions will be answered in the next chapter when I talk about different interpretations of reflective equilibrium.

(4) 'For a moral principle to be universally binding and valid is just for it to be held in common.'

This claim, stronger than (1) which proposed a contingent link, holds an equivalence between the concepts of 'universality' and 'commonality'. This looks very much like the consensus theory of truth. For a moral principle to be universal is for it to be the object of consensus. I noted in my discussion of Habermas some objections against such a position. As we have seen such a proposal must answer criticisms charging that it mistakes the meaning of truth for the methods we use to arrive at it, and that truth can exist even in the absence of consensus. Again, as a clarificatory remark, it should also be noted that an approach which identifies universality with intersubjective agreement has moved much closer to Rorty. On such an account moral universals do not have any transcendentally objective status. From the relativist perspective, this may constitute a positive strength of the argument. Certainly, I will suggest in chapter five that it may be desirable to move away from what I term an idea of 'objectivity as transcendence'.

Some of these approaches render contingent universalism compatible with relativism. Clearly, whilst for many thinkers relativism and universalism must be mutually exclusive, this need not be the case. This is a question I pick up in more detail in later chapters. For now, we can see the roles that convergence could play in justifying universalism. Convergence or commonality may be *practically* important in adding real force to theoretical moral notions. I will contend in chapters four and five that commonality is fertile ground for making arguments compelling to others. However, I believe there are real problems with trying to make convergence a *justification* of *universal* moral principles.

Conclusion

Universalism

This chapter has outlined four distinct universalist approaches to our moral experience. Whilst I do not have space for a complete attempt to refute these positions, I have nevertheless indicated ways in which I think these approaches are problematic. We are also in a position to note similarities and differences in the approaches. The main problem with approaches such as Nagel's is their circularity; the desired conclusion provides the basis on which we are to interpret the evidence for possible conclusions. This circle need not be vicious; indeed, one might maintain, with Stout, that with regard to notions of morality, moral judgements and objectivity, 'one cannot acquire them all singly. Fully understanding any involves fully understanding them all' (Stout, 1990, 53). However, this is exactly what the relativist, or for Nagel the reductionist or subjectivist, will contest. The positive argument that Nagel constructs, as he himself notes, in no way impugns the position taken by the relativist. Nagel's analysis is heavily dependent on his ability to undermine the rival subjectivist proposals. Thus, I believe Korsgaard is correct when she says:

> Like his rationalist predecessors, Nagel asserts that all we can do is rebut the sceptical arguments against the reality of reasons and values. Once we have done that, there is no special reason to doubt that they exist.... And there's nothing wrong with that. But it is an expression of confidence and nothing more (Korsgaard, 1996, 41).

Habermas proceeds rather differently, from the nature of communication rather than the nature of morality. Whilst the idea that making claims implies an obligation or ability to attempt to justify those claims is a sound one, I have argued that such a justification need not take the form that Habermas envisages. Thus, the use of moral language need not commit the speaker to substantive principles of equality in discourse.

Turning now to Hampshire, I have argued that there are two strands to Hampshire's argument for a core of procedural justice. He holds (1) that practical rationality dictates these norms and (2) that commonalities in our nature and experience prompt them. Either way, a justificatory burden falls on these notions that I do not think they can easily bear.

Contingent universalism likewise permits of different interpretations as to what is bearing the justificatory force in the argument — whether it be a human nature claim or the idea that convergence is evidence for moral truths. But whether it constitutes proof of moral universals depends on our assumptions and the interpretation we place on convergence, so that convergence is not really independent evidence.

Universalism and Relativism

Whilst I started this chapter by looking at Nagel's proposal which he portrays as directly opposed to the relativism 'epidemic in the weaker regions of our culture' (Nagel, 1997, 4), the closer we look at the proposals of Hampshire and the contingent universalists, the less helpful an exacting distinction between relativism and universalism becomes. The difference concerns the *character of universality or objectivity*[71] rather than the presence or absence of it. For example, I have suggested that the kinds of universality offered by some understandings of contingent universalism seem compatible with relativism. This appearance will be confirmed in my discussion of coherence relativism in the next two chapters. There I discuss the possibility of different kinds of objectivity, and distinctions between universal validity and universal application. The purpose of this chapter is to demonstrate the variety of universalist positions and to suggest that whilst recent formulations of relativism are problematic, so are recent formulations of universalism. The success of some of the universalist justifications I have examined depends greatly on whether one adopts their preconceptions or assumptions, and I believe there are good reasons to deny these foundational elements. This feature of the discourse could be explained by relativism in terms of the framework-relativity of even those approaches that claim to prove universalism to be true.[72]

Central to all these universalist approaches has been the idea of our moral judgements, and in particular the role they are to play in moral justification. To an extent, they form the raw materials or evidence which any theory must cope with or be based upon. Towards the end of this chapter I also asked how we are to filter them for errors, and what relation moral judgements have with moral principles. These are the questions I now turn to in my examination of the method of reflective equilibrium.

---

[71] Placing these two terms together, here as elsewhere, should not be taken as implying that they share the same meaning.

[72] This of course begs a question, for if universality is proven, then it is not framework-relative. However, as we shall see briefly in chapter four, universalism also begs a relativist question. I am simply establishing a level playing field. The discussion of this area forms part of my analysis of the critical component of Nagel's approach, where he levels the charge of inconsistency or irrelevancy against those who do not affirm universalism.

Chapter 4

Reflective Equilibrium and Relativism

Introduction

The previous two chapters have evaluated contemporary relativist and universalist approaches to morality. This chapter aims to discuss reflective equilibrium, and in doing so addresses two important questions from the preceding chapters. First, I indicated in chapter three that controversy surrounds the issue of what counts as a sound moral judgement. Because these judgements are the raw material for the reflective equilibrium process, I address this question in some detail below. This discussion is thus relevant to the characterisation of contingent universalism with which I ended the preceding chapter. Second, and most importantly, I argued in chapter two that contemporary relativist approaches possess significant problems. Reflective equilibrium points to a way to resolve these problems, and provides the background for an improved relativist account.

Theories of moral justification are often split roughly into two camps, foundationalist and coherentist.[1] Reflective equilibrium is regarded as the most important contemporary coherentist method. This chapter will map out a relativist interpretation of reflective equilibrium that I term *coherence relativism*. It will also develop a link between such an interpretation and the contemporary defences of relativism discussed in chapter two. I will contend that coherence relativism, by drawing on the reflective

---

[1]   For example, see Jamieson 1991, Brink 1991.

equilibrium framework, can answer the main charges levelled at other contemporary variants of relativism.

This chapter comprises five main sections. Section one introduces the concept of reflective equilibrium and situates it within the debate between moral methodologies, and between views about the nature of ethics. Section two examines different conceptions of the considered moral judgements that play an important role in reflective equilibrium. It examines more and less stringent interpretations of the concept of a 'considered moral judgement', and argues for the less stringent model. Section three explores the special role of considered judgements in the reflective equilibrium process. Section four introduces the idea of coherence relativism — relativism interpreted through reflective equilibrium — and examines some initial problems with it. These include Nielsen's charge that reflective equilibrium is not open to a relativistic interpretation, and the objection that in any case, the outcome of a relativist equilibrium could not claim any objectivity for its conclusion. A discussion of these issues clarifies the link between relativism and reflective equilibrium. Section five aims to demonstrate how employing the ideas of reflective equilibrium can solve the problem of underdetermined theory choice. In chapter two I argued that contemporary relativist approaches do not supply an explanation of moral choice. Here I argue that reflective equilibrium appears to share this problem, but that it can be resolved through the role of considered moral judgements.

Thus, sections one to three examine reflective equilibrium, whilst sections four and five indicate how the interpretation of reflective equilibrium shares objectives, problems and resolutions akin to those of relativism. Finally, my conclusion summarises the work of the chapter and concretises the model of coherence relativism. I argue that a relativism utilising a coherence standard overcomes the problems found with previous relativist accounts. My aim in this chapter and the next is to establish coherence relativism as a plausible account of moral justification. As a major component of this exercise, I intend to discuss the way in which coherence relativism explains our moral experience. In chapter two, I concluded by identifying five elements of our moral experience which relativism must account for satisfactorily. In my discussion here, I address two of these elements: the problem of theory choice indeterminacy and the demand, underlying the issue of moral truth, that moral judgement must not be arbitrary — i.e. that relativist views can claim some kind of objectivity. Chapter five continues this work by discussing the issues surrounding moral criticism, moral horror, and moral disagreement.

Reflective Equilibrium as a Method of Moral Justification

Since it was brought to the attention of the philosophical world by John Rawls in *A Theory of Justice*, reflective equilibrium has seemingly come to dominate the landscape of moral theory — at least within the Anglo-American analytical tradition. Its adherents include Joel Feinberg, Will Kymlicka, Norman Daniels and Kai Nielsen.[2] Since Rawls' initial formulation,[3] the method and its implications has been the subject of a large amount of scholarly scrutiny and expansion. Much of this has been carried out by Norman Daniels, and in this chapter I will often focus on Daniels' interpretation.

Central to the concept of reflective equilibrium is the idea of coherence between our moral views and the theories that support them. Coherence here is taken to imply more than mere consistency, but instead some notion of mutual support between beliefs and theories. The process of reflective equilibrium is the process of revising both our particular moral judgements and our more general theories which underpin them (not all of these theories need be moral ones), moving back and forth between them until they reach this state of mutual support. Daniels writes

> The method of wide reflective equilibrium is an attempt to produce coherence in an ordered triple sets of beliefs held by a particular person, namely (a) a set of considered moral judgements (b) a set of moral principles, and (c) a set of relevant background theories. (Daniels, 1996, 22)

The quotation from Daniels introduces a further distinction between wide and narrow reflective equilibrium (WRE and NRE for short). Narrow reflective equilibrium consists in best fit only between (a) and (b), that is, our judgements and our principles. Wide reflective equilibrium brings in (c), the background theories, as a basis on which to assess our principles on the grounds of more than just their fit with our judgements. By allowing independent support for the various sets of principles and a wider circle of justification, WRE aims to allow for more extensive theory-based reflection and revision. Rawls characterises the distinction between WRE and NRE thus:

> The notion [of reflective equilibrium] depends upon whether one is to be presented with only those descriptions which more or less match

[2] See Feinberg 1973; Nielsen 1993; Kymlicka 1990, 5–8; Daniels, 1996.
[3] Rawls 1972 19–21, 46–53; also 1951.

one's existing judgements except for minor discrepancies, or whether one is to be presented with all possible descriptions to which one might plausibly conform one's judgements together with all relevant philosophical arguments for them (Rawls, 1972, 49).

The first alternative described by Rawls is narrow reflective equilibrium, the second is the 'wide' variant. As the fuller version of the methodology (and the more attractive), I am concerned almost exclusively in this chapter with reflective equilibrium in its second, wide, sense.

I take a coherentist theory of moral justification to be one which claims 'A's moral belief p is justified insofar as (a) p is part of a coherent system of moral and non-moral beliefs, and (b) p's coherence at least partially explains why A holds p' (Brink, 1991, 198). For reflective equilibrium, coherence is the test of a justified view. It therefore appears an exemplar of a coherentist method[4] and as such it is properly contrasted with foundationalist methods. Whilst foundationalism is a complex body of thought, I take its central meaning to lie in 'the view that systems of belief are justified in virtue of the logical relations that obtain between beliefs that require justification, and other beliefs that themselves are in no need of justification' (Jamieson, 1993, 480). Thus foundationalism claims some beliefs are either self-justifying or not in need of justification.

However, to a certain extent this picture is incomplete. The concept of reflective equilibrium, as this chapter will show, is open to a number of different interpretations. Just as I will argue that one interpretation is essentially relativistic in spirit, other interpretations have argued that reflective equilibrium enables us to obtain objective moral truth through the clarification of our intuitions.[5] As the names of the thinkers I cited earlier might have suggested, reliance on reflective equilibrium is commonplace amongst egalitarian liberals. It is my firm conviction that liberals have not clearly realised the implications of their support for this method. The questions of interpretation that I engage with in the following sections are ones which require resolution. Whilst reflective equilibrium is vague enough to allow several opposing interpretations, the studied agnosticism of liberals — notably Rawls himself — on which of these they endorse is not a satisfactory position. This is illustrated by the scope and significance of the voids in the method, and the way in which these can be filled by competing interpretations. I now turn to the issues that have been subject to

---

[4]   I leave for the moment the question of whether coherence is *sufficient* for justification on a coherentist account.

[5]   For example, see Holmgren 1989, DePaul, 1986.

these divergent interpretations. I am especially interested to sketch two lenses through which we can see certain crucial areas of the method. As elsewhere, these are relativism and universalism. Each of these approaches will view parts of the methodology in different ways. There are three key areas where dispute is likely. These are (1) the nature of considered moral judgements (2) the role of considered moral judgements (3) the likely outcome of reflective equilibrium and its significance. The first of these is discussed in section two, and the second forms the main subject matter in section three. In section four, the third area is discussed as part of my clarification of coherence relativism.

A relativist analysis holds that reflective equilibrium methodology is relativistic because it does not determine the *content* of those moralities that pass the reflective equilibrium test. Instead, reflective equilibrium is held to provide standards of justification which more than one morality could meet, thus expressing the relativist idea that there need be no single justified morality. This relativist interpretation, I argue in the following sections, is likely to have a certain position on these three key points of reflective equilibrium methodology. They will also have certain ways of responding to the key criticisms of reflective equilibrium that I consider later in this chapter.

In this chapter I will consider at various points three different universalist approaches, each of which offers a different perspective on reflective equilibrium. Intuitionism, which takes intuitions as foundations for moral theory, will give considered moral judgements a pivotal role in the process of reflective equilibrium — i.e. provide a distinctive analysis of areas (1) and (2). Rationalist theories have a largely negative view of reflective equilibrium, as they will object to the use to which considered judgements are put in the process. Varieties of contingent universalism will place a great deal of emphasis on (3), the outcome of equilibrium and its significance.[6] Thus, at various points in the chapter I will indicate where conflicts between these interpretations may arise.

Before I begin my substantive analysis of reflective equilibrium, I want to deal with an initial challenge to whole idea of

[6] I take figures such as Price, Moore and Prichard as pillars of an intuitionist tradition, though here I will discuss only the more recent intuitionist interpretations offered in Holmgren (1989) and DePaul (1987). Rationalists, such as Brandt, take principles found by reason to be the starting point of morality (Brandt, 1979, 187). I discussed contingent universalism in chapter three. There I indicated four possible links that could be posited between the convergence claim and the universality claim; as I will discuss below, some of these can be realised through the apparatus of reflective equilibrium.

reflective equilibrium as a method of moral justification. Some theorists have argued that reflective equilibrium fails to acknowledge the nature of our moral sense. We do not strive for coherence; instead, our moral sense is characterised by conflict. For example, Raz notes 'our views on some occasions are at odds with our views on other occasions. We may also note that our views on most occasions are adequately represented by a certain moral theory, whereas on a small number of occasions our views differ from those represented by that theory' (Raz, 1991, 125). Reflective equilibrium requires us to jettison some of our moral judgements (the ill-considered ones) in order for the rest to be rendered coherent. However, we may just be wrong in trying to impose coherence on our moral life. Or, at a more basic level, we might be wrong to search for a moral theory in the sense of seeking principles that justify individual judgements, and then justification in turn for those principles.

Nevertheless, I take the intuition behind looking for support for moral views to be that we feel the need to justify our moral beliefs to others. This is done by pointing to reasons for holding the position we do. Such reasons can and do take the form of appeals to principles, and beyond them to deeper moral and non-moral theories. Whilst it might be incorrect to say that on a day-to-day level we always seek reflective equilibrium in our moral practice, it also appears incorrect to say that people do not seek, or should not seek, to justify their moral judgements. On a relatively common-sense account of our reasoning, our reasons must be consistent with our judgements and provide support for them. Space precludes a fuller discussion of this objection; nevertheless, I would argue that there are good reasons to be concerned with the coherence and consistency of our moral views. If morality is to guide our actions, incoherence is undesirable because it undermines the possibility of guidance.

'Considered' Judgements

Having considered one basic objection to the methodology, let us now turn to the three aspects of reflective equilibrium where there is scope for differing interpretations. The first issue to be tackled, and one where there is considerable scope for disagreement in interpretation, concerns the notion of a 'considered moral judgement'. This issue surfaced at the end of the preceding chapter with regard to the judgements used by varieties of contingent universalism. Here I want to look in more detail at the definition of considered moral judgements. This section aims to answer two questions: (1) why should we use considered moral judgements rather than *any* moral judgements? And (2) what criteria must a judgement meet before it can be termed a *considered* moral judgement? I want here to outline two different definitions, a more demanding model of 'strong criteria' and a less demanding 'weaker criteria' model. Each of these, I will suggest, can change the character of reflective equilibrium. The more demanding model introduces more substantive moral content into the definition of considered judgement. This will support an interpretation of reflective equilibrium that issues in universally valid values. Thus, it is linked, though quite loosely, to a universalist interpretation of reflective equilibrium. By specifying quite closely which judgements are initially suspect, the more demanding account underpins a greater likelihood of finding either convergence or a rationally compelling moral truth.[7] Conversely, less demanding tests on considered moral judgements can support a relativist interpretation.

The question of what constitutes a considered judgement thus has a direct impact for both of these views on moral justification. It will also have an impact on the role that considered judgements play in the reflection process. Before examining these conflicting interpretations however, it is necessary to give some idea what considered judgements are, and why reflective equilibrium concerns itself only with considered judgements.

We can begin with Rawls' notion of 'considered judgements' as 'those judgements in which our moral capacities are most likely to be displayed without distortion' (Rawls, 1972, 47). The idea of consideration is relatively uncontroversial; it involves nothing more than thinking about our judgements. The area where interpretations will disagree is the question of exactly what constitutes being 'without distortion'. There are two important reasons why we should concern ourselves with only *considered* judgements. One is that intuitively it makes more sense to undertake the lengthy and difficult process of reflective equilibrium only with those judgements in which we have confidence. Another reason stems from the significant role that judgements will play in the reflective equilibrium. For reasons that will become clearer in section three of this chapter, for judgements to play the role of 'provisional fixed points' in the process we must have tested them for

---

[7]   As my remarks later in this section indicate, I think this could be achieved by filtering considered judgements so that only ones consistent with the eventual moral truth were allowed into the process. For the moment I lay aside the question of the relationship between convergence and the moral truth.

obvious sources of error. I will also argue in section five that we should appeal to considered moral judgements to help decide between equally justified moralities. Because of this, it is even more crucial that we place such value and responsibility only on such judgements as can bear it. Having set out in general terms what considered judgements are like and why they will prove important, we are now in a position to begin the examinations of the two accounts of what is to count as a considered moral judgement.

Weak Criteria − The Less Demanding Interpretation

The less demanding interpretation says that we should examine the *circumstances* in which we make moral judgements, and apply a set of criteria to them in order to uncover those judgements where our moral sense is likely to be distorted. Rawls' weak constraints approach holds that 'considered judgements are simply those rendered under conditions favourable to the exercise of the sense of justice, and therefore in circumstances where the most common excuses and explanations for making a mistake do not obtain' (Rawls, 1972, 47–8). The list of conditions or criteria Rawls provides is not necessarily intended as complete, but includes 'those judgements in which we have little confidence' and those judgements given when 'we are upset or frightened, or when we stand to gain one way or the other' (Rawls, 1972, 48).

These criteria will determine which moral judgements get used as the 'raw material' for the process of reflective equilibrium. They represent a process of rational decision-making, freed from immediate disrupting influences. Factors like being upset and unable to think clearly are something that we generally accept skew both our moral and non-moral judgements. Rawls also indicates that self-interest − standing to gain one way or the other − will tend to make a judgement unreliable. I think the best interpretation of this idea would see Rawls as referring to immediate gain. For example, suppose I am in a situation where I am offered £10,000 to kill someone. In that situation, my moral judgement that killing was permissible would be ruled out as being liable to error. This, note, does not mean that the moral judgement I would make would *necessarily* be flawed. Were I sitting in a philosophy seminar discussing the same question (the permissibility of killing for gain) with the ability and desire to make the right choice, my conclusion could count as a considered moral judgement. This account is one interpretation of circumstances conducive to making considered moral judgements. However, we can think of a different interpretation of 'standing to gain one way or another', which would see it in a much broader way. Whenever I make a judgement about an arrangement of distributive justice, or a moral judgement on my actions or those affecting me, I may gain or lose in some sense. A radical interpretation of Rawls' view of self-interest would not classify such judgements as considered. I think there are two reasons for rejecting such a radical interpretation. First, almost every moral judgement could be construed as having consequences for us and thus very few moral judgements would count as considered. Second, Rawls is concerned to provide criteria which are not arbitrary, and which are 'similar to those that single out considered judgements of any kind' (Rawls, 1972, 48). We have to consider whether such a radical ban on 'standing to gain or lose' is present on other considered judgements.[8] In the light of these reasons, I believe that we should give only a straightforward and moderate limit on self-interested circumstances. This account would rule out cases where the immediate circumstances meant we stood to gain or lose.[9]

The Rawlsian model demands that we judge in good faith in circumstances where most excuses for making poor judgements do not apply. What we are not required to do is critically examine our judgement; instead, we should critically examine the *circumstances*. The aim of this test is not to tell us which judgements are actually faulty, just which *classes* of judgements are reliable enough to use in reflective equilibrium.

Strong Criteria — The More Demanding Interpretation

Having analysed the weak criteria model, and argued for a certain interpretation of 'standing to gain or lose', we can now contrast this with the strong criteria account. On the second, more demanding interpretation, a considered judgement is a critically analysed judgement. Considering a moral judgement requires critical analysis to determine whether judgements are *faulty* rather than whether they are *liable* to error. Circumstances do not suffice as a proxy for 'consideration' in this account. Thus, the focus moves to the criteria that must be met to render a judgement faulty or correct. Simon Caney has identified one such list of criteria for critically analysed judgements. Caney does not argue that these criteria should constitute the test of considered moral judgement. Nevertheless, such standards might be invoked as an

---

[8] For example, it would seem impossible for a judgement of economic preference to ever be 'considered'.

[9] Again, the emphasis is on the circumstances in which a judgement is made rather than the sense in which the justification for the judgement appealed to either short-, mid- or long-term gain.

account of strong criteria for considered judgement.[10] Caney writes,

> It is commonly argued, for example, that moral judgements are faulty if they depend on any of the following; (i) self-interest, (ii) incorrect factual claims, (iii) self-deception, (iv) wishful thinking, (v) logical errors, (vi) adaptive judgement formation or (vii) manipulated judgement formation (Caney, 1999, 26).

On this view, we should see a considered judgement as the outcome of a critically appraised *process*. Faulty judgements are ones in which the correct procedure was not followed. For example, my judgment that we ought to lynch paedophiles might stem simply from emotive coverage in the media, and so be ineligible. In summary, Caney says we should use moral convictions, but exclude biased ones (1999, 26-7). We can see some of the problems of this more demanding approach by looking in more detail at these factors. On my interpretation, Caney's categories of error can be broadly divided into three.

(a)   Inconsistency in the process, in terms of either inconsistency with known facts or with rules of logic.

(b)   Ways in which the rational decision-making process can be subverted by non-rational elements, such as wishful thinking, adaptive judgement formation, etc.

(c)   A notion of the presence of bias or self-interest.

Before moving on to discuss a methodological problem for the approach as a whole, each of these elements requires some critical examination.

(a) The first is, seemingly, the least problematic. Internally inconsistent or factually doubtful judgements are distorted in a way that would remove them from reflective equilibrium. However, it should be noted that disagreement can rest on differing factual claims — regarding God's existence, for example — and disagreements also exist about the interpretation of facts and modes of reasoning. In other words, the perception of what constitutes a fact, what the fact of any matter actually is, and what counts as a correct inference from that fact, is something that will vary between cultures and individuals.[11]

---

[10]   Caney is concerned only to offer criteria for 'critically analysed judgements'. Whilst I think that identifying critical analysis as crucial to 'considered judgements' is a plausible extension of Caney's proposal, Caney need not take this approach.

[11]   I discuss the question of when and how facts constitute or prompt compelling reasons in chapter five, and pick up on some of these issues.

(b) Brainwashing, or unconscious adaptation of the desirable to the possible, will cast doubt on judgements because they have not been thought through properly. Jon Elster cites several examples of what he terms 'the subversion of rationality', including adaptive preference formation, wishful thinking, manipulation and conformism (Elster, 1985). This second criterion shows clearly a distinction between stronger and weaker approaches. First, this puts these stronger 'considered judgements' in a different relationship to the reflective equilibrium process. On the less demanding account, the process of reflective equilibrium is one of assembling the raw materials — considered judgements — and then submitting them to reflection. Thus, manipulation will more likely be discovered during the process of reflective equilibrium rather than prior to it. The more demanding account of considered judgements requires us to perform critical analysis of our judgements (rather than their circumstances) prior to reflective equilibrium. Critical analysis becomes something we do all the time, and the purpose of reflective equilibrium is to add coherence between our judgements and theories (though this does not rule out consideration of theories during our analysis of judgements). As I will discuss later, I believe this model of the relation between critical analysis and equilibrium is problematic.

According to a 'weak constraints' approach, flaws in our judgements are best discovered during a sustained process of reflection involving other moral and non-moral theories. Thus, with regard to adaptive judgement or preference formation, it is only by entering a wide equilibrium and examining other theories of what is possible that we may realise how our judgements are falsely constrained. The 'strong criteria' theorist will argue that because manipulation is a procedural problem, it is discovered by looking back on the *formation* of the judgement at the 'critical analysis' stage prior to reflective equilibrium. Because reflective equilibrium is concerned only with coherence, any light it sheds on the formation of judgement will be accidental. In response to this, we can note that if I am thoroughly manipulated, my manipulation will present itself not only in a judgement, but also in supporting evidence and reasoning for that judgement. The consideration of alternative theories, evidence and judgements would provide a stimulus to look closer at our own beliefs and why we hold them.

Eliminating subconscious manipulation in the filtering of beliefs would be a demanding process in itself.[12] We would have

[12] The distinction between the filtering of considered moral judgements prior to reflective equilibrium and the process of reflective equilibrium

to ask ourselves about every one of our moral judgements 'how did I come to hold this view?' However, if our judgement has been successfully manipulated, then by definition it will not seem to us 'liable to error' or ill-considered.[13] The presence of theories and background theories gives us more resources to use in discovering errors that might be hidden from view were we simply to look over our judgements. Thus, the type of distortions that motivate the strong constraints model are best dealt with *not* by adopting tighter constraints on what counts as a considered moral judgement but instead by adopting a weak constraints model and then determining flaws in considered moral judgements during the process of reflective equilibrium.

We can note here that the strong criteria account comes much closer to specifying the *process* that must be followed if we are to term a judgement considered and moral. It incorporates an analysis of the kind of justification that should be offered. I think one implication of this is that it becomes more controversial. For example, calling into question beliefs acquired in these kinds of 'non-autonomous' ways (through forms of indoctrination, for example) operates in favour of those moral views operating by 'our' rules of rationality. The desire to exclude all these external, irrational factors will raise objections that it smuggles in a conception of autonomy or self-mastery. Those who acquire moral views in non-autonomous or non-rational ways, yet hold them with equal or greater fervour and with some supporting reasoning, could surely complain that the process is biased against them.[14] Are we to judge these commitments ill-considered or flawed, or

itself can be over-emphasised. I do not want to deny that reflection on moral judgements is continuous. We might examine theories before the process to see whether they, too, were liable to error. However, I believe at the conceptual level there is a distinction between the two stages or elements.

[13]   One problem is that the relationship between *how* I came to hold a view and *why* I came to hold a view is unclear. There is presumably a psychological, causal answer to the latter question as well as a justificatory one. Suppose my parents taught me what was right and wrong in my formative years, and then I largely accepted what they thought was correct because it was apparently confirmed by my own experience. Psychologically, I hold this view because my parents held it and they 'influenced' me into holding it (perhaps not intentionally). In this case my judgement has been manipulated but I also support it with good reasons. Is this view manipulated, and hence in violation of the strong criteria, or do my good reasons do the real work, so that we can say the judgement 'depends' on them? In other words, what is the link between the formation and justification of belief on the strong criteria account?

[14]   I think that the notion of reflexivity provides some kind of defence to this charge, as I discuss later in this chapter and in chapter five.

expect the people who hold them to change their beliefs? Deciding which judgements have or have not conformed to the procedure required of moral judgements raises questions of authority. Who is to decide, and can we expect people to be judges in their own case? On the less-demanding interpretation, a rough and ready judgement is made only about the *circumstances*.

(c) The most important problem with this list of constraints concerns the last element — the suggestion that self-interest or bias makes judgements liable to error. In challenging this idea, I will offer an account of the different senses in which a 'considered moral judgement' can be 'considered' and 'moral'. I want to use the notion of bias here to discuss how the two approaches to considered moral judgements fit into two different interpretations of reflective equilibrium. As we have seen, Rawls argues that those judgements in which we 'stand to gain one way or another' are 'liable to error'. This more demanding approach argues that moral views that 'depend' on self-interest are flawed and should be excluded. I accept that this view is correct in holding that ethical egoism — the idea that things are right or wrong to the extent that they promote my self-interest — is a difficult position at best. However, the case of bias still raises interesting questions, and points to important problems in the thought of strong criteria theorists.

Important personal interests do have a place in morality. On the question of whether I should risk my life to save another or not, considerations of my well-being are obviously relevant. Bias towards my family might also be morally permissible, within limits. Only a radically impartialist conception of morality will argue that my future well-being and the people or things who I value are totally irrelevant in moral judgements. However, such judgements might seem to involve bias or self-interests, the things that render judgements faulty. So, how can the 'more demanding' theorist incorporate these features?

One response on behalf of the 'strong constraints' model is that personal interests are morally legitimate to the extent that they can be universalised. Universalisability requires that particular moral judgements always imply universal ones; i.e., they can be expressed as a judgement not only on one specific case, but also on other people in other places and times but the same circumstances. For many theorists, any judgement that cannot be universalised should not be termed a moral judgement at all (Hare 1952,

Frankena 1958, 1976).[15] Invoking universalisability thus might allow us to rule out those judgements that do not rely on 'self-interests' important to everyone. In section one of chapter three, I discussed something like this in my analysis of Nagel and his agent-neutral reasons. Here, as there, a problem arises in our analysis of 'circumstances'. If we mean that 'any agent who is exactly like me ought to do in circumstance X exactly what I would do in circumstance X', then virtually anything can be universalised, including self-interest or bias — 'any agent who is self-interested ought to be self-interested'.[16] Somehow we will have to draw a line between unacceptable and acceptable bias or partiality. I am not at all convinced that a test of universalisability will suffice to draw that line, at least not until we look closer at the idea.

The problem for universalisability as a criterion for terming a judgement 'moral' lies in setting the specification of the test. How can we specify it so that the things that intuitively do not belong in the moral realm are left outside, without keeping out judgements that, intuitively, *are* moral ones? The approach here runs into difficulties because some of these intuitions about what is, and what is not, moral, will be to do with the *immorality* of certain activities. I assume that any approach that aims to speak about how we justify moral judgements must try to import as little substantive moral content as possible, in order to avoid charges that it loads the dice so only certain moral conceptions are justified. Introducing substantive moral views when deciding which substantive morality is justified seems viciously circular.

Nevertheless, any conception of a 'considered moral judgement' must specify what it is for a judgement to be 'considered' and 'moral'. How, other than universalisability, are we to define a 'moral' judgement on the less demanding approach? I want to suggest that there is perhaps no need to search for a formulation of universalisability which satisfies our intuitions whilst not pre-

---

[15] In particular, Frankena has distinguished between a formal concept of morality and a material and social one (Frankena, 1976, 125–6). The formal concept demands that a morality, to be moral, must be universalisable, prescriptive and supremely authoritative. The material concept can be interpreted as 'an action-guide with a subject matter that pertains to interpersonal relations' (Wong, 1986, 216). The weak criteria theorist can perhaps operate on the latter (I propose something like this later in this section), whilst the strong criteria approach can be identified with the former.

[16] I think that self-interest can be given this universal form. The problem with it however, is whether we can give any 'moral' sense to the self-interested injunction to promote self-interest.

judging the outcome of equilibrium in favour of impartiality. Such a search is complex, and fraught with ambiguity: Kagan cites eight different kinds of universalisability test (Kagan, 1997, 256–71) and real issues concern first, whether such a test *is* the essence of morality (e.g. MacIntyre, 1970, 26-39) and second, whether the universalisability test can or should accommodate our partial concerns. Perhaps the 'weak criteria' answer lies in making the definition agent-centred, and then allowing for different agents to make different judgements for themselves as to what counts as a moral judgement. This would not do if we were aiming to establish a sharp, canonical statement of what is sufficient or necessary for a view to be moral. My tentative suggestion is that this could be sharpened up during the course of, or after, reflective equilibrium rather than *prior* to it. Perhaps all we should require at this early stage for a 'moral' judgement is a conscientious belief about how I ought to live.

Having looked in detail at the particular content of the constraints, and in particular the idea of filtering out bias, I now want to examine a separate *methodological* problem for the 'strong criteria' approach. We can see this in the way that Caney describes what could be considered as such a methodology. He writes

> Moral argument, it is maintained, involves trying to render consistent our moral judgements with our general moral theories (that is, what Rawls describes as 'reflective equilibrium'). Our moral judgements should, in addition, be subjected to critical analysis (Caney, 1999, 25).

We are justified in asking, on this conception, what reflective equilibrium adds over critical analysis. This is because, as we have seen, the critical analysis is concerned with the *reasons* that justify our judgements through its concern with the process of formation. Critical analysis operates on the basis of a theory about which factors *cannot* justify moral beliefs and so make the process faulty. For our judgement to be considered is for it not to rest on an impermissible kind of reason. Furthermore, I have indicated that it may be difficult to specify an adequate universalisability test which does not build in views about what ought morally to constitute morality (for at least some thinkers, this will be impartiality). The 'critical analysis' component thus already concerns itself with the consistency of moral judgements and theories. It requires scrutiny of the reasons offered for a moral judgement. Isn't it already telling us whether a judgement is minimally consistent with theories of impartiality and sound moral reasoning, and whether it is justified? If so, then critical analysis is the locus of moral justification on this approach. The process of moving backwards and forwards between our judgements and theories is of secondary importance. Thus, the more demanding approach might sit in a different relationship to the equilibrium process itself. We lose any sense of considered judgements being the 'raw material' or starting points for the process of moral justification. Instead, they are the *result* of a demanding process of critical evaluation themselves, and because of that they already have independent force.

In summary, I have suggested that the strong criteria approach possesses a number of problems. Most importantly, it incorporates a limited theory of impartiality at the stage of deciding which judgements we ought to try to cohere with moral theories. In its strongest form, the charge is that it thus 'loads the dice'. It also shifts the justificatory burden from *equilibrium* to the strong criteria. Because of this, it may be that this approach might not be described properly as employing a reflective equilibrium methodology. By contrast, Rawls' less demanding approach leaves questions of what counts as a permissible or impermissible justification more open. Apart from a description of 'liable to error' that should be common to moral and non-moral judgements, it performs little substantive filtering prior to the process itself. The underlying point of this discussion is that beneath these two competing understandings of considered moral judgements are competing understandings of the process itself. Reflective equilibrium will be interpreted in wholly distinct ways as part of differing proposals.

The Positions of Relativism and Universalism

Having analysed two competing accounts of the nature of considered moral judgements, we can now examine the implication of these accounts for relativism and universalism. The less-demanding account perhaps offers support for a relativism committed to the view that there is more than one justified morality. A more demanding account, by contrast, is more likely to yield universal judgements. It places stringent limits on acceptable considered judgements, and thus acceptable outcomes. If 'coherence' becomes 'coherence with a thin theory of impartiality' then single moral universals are very possible. The method of reflective equilibrium itself will always require justification of some kind. However, the more concrete moral considerations are built in, the harder it becomes to defend the method against charges of loading the dice and against the objection that these moral beliefs — rather than coherence — are doing the real work.

We can offer a different interpretation of reflective equilibrium for which this would not be a problem. If reflective equilibrium were viewed as a method of refining a truth which was already 'out there', either as a rationally commanding position, a fact about human nature, or in our intuitions themselves, then the above criticisms would have no force. Indeed, as I will discuss shortly, some universalists will view the method in exactly this way.

The Status of Considered Moral Judgements

So far, I have examined the debate concerning what was meant by a considered moral judgement. In this section, I examine different interpretations of the role played by considered moral judgements in the process of reflective equilibrium. Reflective equilibrium, as we have seen, is an attempt to attain a coherent equilibrium position between our considered moral judgements and our moral theories, and in turn the deep or background theories that support them. The issues I will discuss in this section concern the extent to which our considered judgements should be adjusted in the light of theories. In other words what, if any, kind of particular importance is attached to them in the reflective equilibrium process. In this section I will lay out three alternative perspectives on the role and weight of considered moral judgements. The first account accords them a great amount of initial plausibility, and sees them as basically fixed. This approach could be associated with some intuitionists.[17] Reflective equilibrium would then be about refining our intuitions and improving our confidence in them. A second, contrary, approach accords considered moral judgements no special status whatsoever in the process. This might be attractive to those universalists who wish to start with rationally justified theories, which our considered judgements would simply have to adapt to. Third, and the option that I will endorse as the best analysis of justificatory reflective equilibrium, is a hybrid of the first two, which uses considered judgements as *starting points*. In examining the hybrid model, I will concentrate on the account set out by Norman Daniels.

Considered Moral Judgements as Fixed Points

One interpretation of reflective equilibrium sees it as a form of sophisticated moral intuitionism.[18] Our considered moral judge-

---

[17] In my discussion I will concentrate on Holmgren's work. Of course, some relativists who view shared societal views as having moral value in themselves (e.g. Walzer) might also adopt this approach.

[18] Holmgren, 1989. DePaul is another theorist who makes a similar suggestion (DePaul, 1986).

ments constitute our moral intuitions on various moral topics. Our intuitions are tested to remove those liable to be faulty, and then possible moral theories are tested for coherence against our intuitions. Some revisions might be made to our intuitions, but for the most part it is the theories which will be adjusted. Holmgren summarises the 'basic tenets of sophisticated moral intuitionism' (Holmgren, 1989, 60) thus: '(i) that our considered moral judgements possess a *prima facie* credibility and (ii) that most theories derive their credibility from the fact that they adequately systematise these judgements' (Holmgren, 1989, 60). This *'prima facie* credibility' consists in a belief that intuitions apprehend the moral truth directly, or that (less outlandishly) our gut feelings, particularly ones that we are deeply attached to, are likely to be right.

Two things are worth noting about such an account. First, on this account Wide Reflective Equilibrium would add little justificatory weight over Narrow Reflective Equilibrium. Holmgren, for example, contends that NRE fulfils the justificatory role as well as WRE, and ultimately we have no reason to prefer wide over narrow equilibrium (Holmgren, 1989, 60). If intuitions are relatively fixed, there will be no need for the extensive theory-based revisions made possible by WRE. Second, it is easy to see how a 'strong criteria' model of what counts as a considered moral judgement or intuition bolsters such an account. I will examine problems with this 'fixed point' model shortly, but it is worth noting that claims that considered moral judgements are unreliable will be made less damaging the tighter constraints are, and hence the more judgements are excluded.

The most potent criticism of a 'fixed point' view argues that intuitions are in fact doubtful as sources of moral justification. As Daniels expresses the point,

> Since such opinions are often the result of self-interest, self-deception, historical and cultural accident, hidden class bias, and so on, just systematising some of them hardly seems a promising way to provide justification for them or for the principles that order them (Daniels, 1996, 83).

Remember that Daniels is working on a relatively weak set of criteria for considered moral judgements. The initial screening element of 'consideration' will, on Daniels' account, not weed out such problems. Instead, these are considered in the process itself. For the process itself to screen out these elements, it must involve the possibility of wide-scale revisions of our intuitions, which the 'fixed point' theory does not allow for. In short, whilst the fixed point theory does not quite constitute what Caney describes as 'uncritical intuitionism' (Caney, 1999, 25), unless strong filters are also applied it comes with a risk that it will merely sanctify our existing view whether that be moral prejudice or perfection. Of course, criticisms of the unreliability of our moral judgements will not bite as hard if all possible sources of unreliability have been excluded in the course of determining what constitutes a considered moral judgement. There ought to be, intuitionists might argue, a correlation between the stringency of the tests applied to find 'considered' judgements, and the certainty we can attach to them as fixed points. Effective criticisms would instead have to encompass the debate between intuitionism and its opponents on a larger scale.

I do not want to attempt a resolution here of the debate between this kind of intuitionism and its opponents. This would involve a detailed critique both of intuitions and of the view that the initial weight belongs to moral theories rather than judgements. Such an analysis lies beyond the scope of this chapter or, indeed, this book. As Daniels notes, what is required for a complete account of intuitionism, and what cannot be provided in the space available here (even if such an account exists), is a 'little story . . . explaining why we should pay homage to those judgements and indirectly to the principles that systematise them' (Daniels, 1996, 83). The central task for me here is to set out the interpretations to which reflective equilibrium is open. An intuitionist account is no longer, it should be noted, about coherence. Instead, it is about coherence *with something fixed*.

The 'Zero Initial Plausibility' Model

We can conceive of an alternative to the 'fixed point' model which proposes the exact opposite. Instead of us considering all potential moral theories against a fixed set of intuitions, we should throw all considered moral judgements open for selection in the same way. There are two versions of this position. The first would say that the starting point, instead of considered moral judgements, would be a theory or theories of which we were confident (perhaps to the point of saying they were universally justified). So for example, if utilitarianism was justified by Brandt's reasoning, or if human rights were justified by Gewirth's argument, we would cast about for intuitions that cohered with this fixed starting point.[19] The second would say that all theories and all judgements should be initially open; that there should be *no* fixed starting point. We consider all theories for coherence, why not consider all moral judgements from the start also?

---

[19]   See Brandt 1979, Gewirth, 1978.

Both of these possibilities face problems. The former faces the problem that there are competing moral theories, each with their own adherents. It is tempting to view moral philosophy as an area in which almost every philosopher believes that one moral theory has been proved superior, but they are not agreed as to which theory this is. If the theory which is to form our starting point is merely one we are confident in, then the problem intuitionism has above — about why our judgements have substantial credibility — is also a problem for this account of why any particular moral *theory* has substantial credibility. Just like judgements, theories can be liable to error — they can reflect prejudice, ignore salient facts, or be otherwise flawed.

The second of the two possible 'zero plausibility' models — that we should not start from either our judgements or our theories — has what could be called a psychological and a philosophical problem. The psychological problem is that, hard as reflective equilibrium might be to carry out, it will be harder still if we have to 'forget' that our considered moral judgements are *our* considered moral judgements. We have to open all our moral selves to wholesale revision at once without *any* reference point, which might not be possible. In this chaotic situation, the philosophical problem — that if we have no semi-fixed starting point, how could we achieve any kind of fixed answer — seems to bite. Presented with a myriad of possible moral judgements and moral theories, how could we know which to choose? We are left with a method of moral justification that does not guide our choice of moral system.

This problem of underdetermined theory choice arose first in chapter two, where I contended that relativist accounts left it unsolved. I intend to offer a solution later in the chapter. Rather than discuss it here, I first want to examine the third 'starting point' model of the role of considered moral judgements.

Middle Ground — The 'Starting Point' Interpretation

The *locus classicus* for the starting point interpretation is Daniels' exposition of reflective equilibrium. As we have seen, Daniels rejects an intuitionist interpretation. He argues that Reflective Equilibrium is 'not a standard form of moral intuitionism because it is not foundationalist. Despite the care taken to filter initial judgements to avoid obvious sources of error, no special epistemological priority is granted to considered moral judgements' (Daniels, 1996, 83). However, he does acknowledge that considered moral judgements do have a certain special role, in that we treat them as a 'starting point in our theory construction'

(Daniels, 1996, 28). On this account, they are starting points only, and can be revised during the process.

The question I want to address here concerns how we understand this notion of considered moral judgements as starting points. Is the notion innocuous, the suggestion being that we have to start somewhere and we cannot avoid having these judgements at the beginning of the process? Or is it problematic, because it really does grant them a special priority? Daniels writes:

> No one type of considered moral judgement is held immune to revision. No doubt, we are not inclined to give up certain considered moral judgements unless an overwhelmingly better alternative moral conception is available and substantial dissatisfaction with our own conception at other points leads us to do so . . . It is in this way that we provide a sense to the notion of a 'provisional fixed point (Daniels, 1996, 28).

Thus, Daniels' starting-point theory allows considered moral judgements a special role, but one that is only provisional. Moral judgements are not immutable barriers to the adoption of theories. However, this might still appear to attach too much 'epistemic priority' to considered moral judgements. Daniels wants to hold that considered moral judgements are *'most definitely* open to revision' (Daniels, 1996, 28). Critics will argue in response that Daniels' position allows only that *most* considered moral judgements are *definitely* open to revision. The suggestion here is that certain deeply held convictions would practically serve as barriers, despite Daniels' denials. Daniels says that it might take a great deal — 'an overwhelmingly better moral conception' and 'substantial dissatisfaction' (Daniels, 1996, 28) — to move us from a deeply held moral conviction. In practice, might not people's most firmly held moral convictions be immune to revision *because they are so firmly held*?

Daniels' answer to this objection will have to draw upon the other aspect of his theory. This is the power of Wide over Narrow Reflective Equilibrium to provide theoretical leverage in an effort to overcome this kind of conservatism. He advocates the WRE model because he believes it allows 'far more drastic theory-based revisions of moral judgements' (Daniels, 1996, 27). On the other hand, it is appropriate within the context of Daniels' theory that our most firmly held convictions would be much harder to shift. Daniels could reply that it is not a flaw of his theory that it acknowledges the huge intuitive power of a few deeply held considered moral judgements, even if the scheme as a whole allows for 'substantial theory-based revisions'.

Even if Daniels' approach is not morally conservative, the role attached to considered moral judgements might mean that reflective equilibrium is better described as a variety of modest foundationalism rather than coherentism. Ebertz, for example, contends that considered moral judgements 'play a special justificatory role in the system in reflective equilibrium in virtue of support they receive from some feature other than coherence with other beliefs' (Ebertz, 1993, 203). For Ebertz, this feature suffices to render the methodology a variety of foundationalism, in which considered moral judgements are the foundations. Ebertz contends that, at least on Rawls' account of reflective equilibrium, in the final equilibrium, 'a set of principles could never be justified if they did not match the judgements we reach when we hold the beliefs in question and carefully and reflectively judge the justice or injustice . . . of particular actions or kinds of actions' (Ebertz, 1993, 203). Ebertz is correct to the extent that principles must cohere with the (critically assessed) judgments. However, as part of the process of reflective equilibrium, the judgments must also be revised so as to cohere with the theories (Daniels, 1996, 22). If we are to term the role of judgments a 'special priority', then we must attach a 'special priority' also to the principles or theories. If all the elements of the methodology play a 'special justificatory role', then in one sense at least, the role really isn't that special. Within reflective equilibrium, judgements play no more of a justificatory role than theories. Thus, Ebertz's charge of a special priority for judgements dissolves when we see that a similar priority is attached to all the other elements. It is precisely what we expect of a coherence methodology that all the elements are relevant in the justification of each other.[20]

In this section I have argued that the 'starting point' role accorded to considered moral judgements by Daniels does not make them foundations in a strong sense; thus, *contra* Ebertz, reflective equilibrium is not a form of foundationalism. Certainly, Daniel's proposal appears the most promising account of considered moral judgements. Because they are the raw material for reflective equilibrium, they will come with some initial plausibility attached. However, in the case of all but our most deeply held

[20]   Ebertz's position is stronger with respect to Rawls' theory. Rawls did indeed say that 'there is a definite if limited class of facts against which conjectured principles can be checked, namely, our considered judgments in reflective equilibrium' (Rawls, 1972, 51). However, if indeed Rawls does attach a special role to considered moral judgements, there is no reason why other interpretations must do the same. Ebertz's attempt to widen the argument is unsuccessful.

convictions, there are theoretical resources available to overturn those judgements. They need not play a special justificatory role any more than theories or deep theories. Nevertheless, it is perhaps realistic to admit that it might be difficult to shift our deepest convictions.

So far, I have examined some fairly specific issues with regard to possible interpretations of reflective equilibrium. In section five I examine a possible role for deeply held convictions in relativist accounts of equilibrium, drawing on their role as 'starting points'. First, I must set out some features of what such a relativist account of reflective equilibrium would look like. Thus, I turn now to examine the scope and outcome of reflective equilibrium, and through this the possibility of a link between reflective equilibrium and relativism.

The Nature of Coherence Relativism

We can begin looking for a relativist interpretation by examining the impact of reflective equilibrium on issues of relativity. One dimension concerns whether the outcome of reflective equilibrium would be convergence or divergence in moral outlooks, and what significance we would attach to this outcome. I briefly noted this question in my discussion of contingent universalism in chapter three. Here I want to discuss it in more detail, and in the process firm up what a relativist interpretation of reflective equilibrium would look like. We can begin here, as elsewhere, with Daniels' analysis of the issue. Daniels certainly believes that reflective equilibrium may produce greater convergence, by rendering moral disagreements more tractable (Daniels 1996, 34). However, Daniels does not believe convergence on values constitutes moral truth. He notes:

> To see that convergence in wide equilibrium is not a sufficient condition for claiming that we have found objective moral truths, suppose we actually produced convergence among diverse persons. Whether or not the principles or judgements they accept would count as such truths would depend on how we come to explain the convergence (Daniels, 1996, 35).

The key, on Daniels' account, is how convergence or divergence is *explained*. Convergence could constitute evidence for the presence or absence of moral truth, if it were not explained away by other influencing factors. The strongest version of this claim is that whatever principles were converged on would constitute the moral truth. Alternatively, the lack of common principles might *prove* that there was *no* single justified morality. My contention is that for the presence or absence of convergence to have meaning, it must be accompanied by a view of justification. Only in the light of this does the outcome take on relevance. To illustrate this, I want to discuss the way in which the outcome might be relevant (or irrelevant) for relativist accounts.

We have already seen in the previous chapter that distinctions can be drawn between contingent universalism and a universalism like Nagel or Habermas's that is *a priori* — independent of actual convergence. Similarly, we can think of relativism in a contingent way or as an *a priori* account that does not depend on actual divergence in the outcome of reflective equilibrium. While certain interpretations of reflective equilibrium are inherently universalist,[21] other interpretations, notably the one I will advance here, are inherently relativistic — they constitute an *a priori* model of relativism. The *a priori* relativist interpretation of reflective equilibrium allows for more than one justified morality, even though one morality might result (convergence) if the process were carried out hypothetically or for real.

This inherently relativistic interpretation of reflective equilibrium constitutes the core of what I will term *coherence relativism*. Because of the importance of coherence relativism to my argument, we must be clear on its nature and its relationship to reflective equilibrium. Relativism claims that there can be multiple justified moralities. One explanation or expanded version of this claim is that the standards of moral justification are ones that can be met by multiple moralities. The burden is then on the relativist who makes this claim to provide an account of the methodology of justification, an answer to the question 'what do these standards look like?' Reflective equilibrium, as I have discussed here, can provide such an account. The standards offered by the coherentist account of reflective equilibrium — the fundamental importance of coherence and consistency — constitute one specification of these relativist standards of justification. It provides an explanation of what these standards look like and how these standards form part of a process of justification. I am not claiming that every relativist approach makes a reflective equilibrium-type claim, or that every account of reflective equilibrium can function as a specification of relativist standards of justification. Rather, the relativist who believes that there are multiple justified moralities must back this claim up with an account of the nature of moral

---

[21]   E.g. 'sophisticated intuitionism' draws on narrow reflective equilibrium to support judgements about the credibility of our intuitions (Holmgren, 1989, 60).

justification. Some interpretations of reflective equilibrium provide just such an account.

I noted earlier in the chapter that there are several different interpretations of reflective equilibrium. Because of the multiple conflicting interpretations of reflective equilibrium, terming this account of relativism 'reflective equilibrium relativism' would be misleading. Instead, the term 'coherence relativism' captures the appeal to coherence standards of justification that function as part of some accounts of reflective equilibrium.[22] As I indicated above, some accounts of reflective equilibrium are intrinsically relativistic. If coherence and consistency are the standards for moral justification, and multiple moralities can meet these standards, then there can be multiple justified moralities. Because of this we can refer to these accounts of reflective equilibrium as relativist interpretations or construals of reflective equilibrium. These interpretations reflect an *a priori* relativism in the standards they specify. However, some features of the account of coherence relativism I offer take it beyond questions of its relationship with reflective equilibrium. These include such matters as its interpretation of moral criticism or its role in liberal arguments for neutrality or toleration, which I discuss in chapters five through seven. The way I build up a distinct coherence relativist proposal in future chapters means that it is more than *just* an *a priori* relativistic interpretation of reflective equilibrium as a method of moral justification. Nevertheless, such an interpretation lies at its core.

In terms of my analysis of reflective equilibrium in sections one, two and three, such a coherence relativist account of reflective equilibrium would most likely rest on a set of weak criteria for considered moral judgements. Strong criteria are problematic for a relativist account of reflective equilibrium because they make the process less open-ended. Coherence Relativism would also endorse a 'starting point' interpretation of the role of considered judgements. A fixed point interpretation would endow moral intuitions with enough weight to constitute a single moral truth. I will argue shortly that the starting-point interpretation also provides an appropriate response to the problem of theory choice indeterminacy.

A comparison with Wong's argument may help to clarify my approach. Wong argues that the criteria for something being an

---

[22] Why not 'coherence and consistency' relativism? Partly because this term is even more unwieldly, but partly also because consistency is not a distinctive feature of the approach. For almost any moral theory, asserting both p and not-p is a problem — the consistency component does nothing to mark my proposal off from other such views.

'adequate moral system' are such as to allow for multiple instantiations of an adequate moral system — what Wong terms multiple valid 'extensions' of the idea (Wong, 1986, 45). Likewise, a relativism drawing on reflective equilibrium argues that there can be different instantiations of a coherent and consistent, and hence justified, moral system arising from reflective equilibrium. In Wong's case, if people actually settled on a single idea of an adequate moral system, this would not affect his argument that there could be more than one such adequate system. In the same way, if people were to converge around a single moral system in reflective equilibrium, this does not affect the relativist position that more than one justified morality could emerge. In this sense, the account of 'coherence relativism' I am advocating will be of the *a priori* kind.[23]

By way of contrast with such an *a priori* relativist view of reflective equilibrium, the 'contingent' relativist prediction that different moralities will result from reflective equilibrium does not advance any kind of argument against the universalist. As we saw in chapter two, the fact of diversity does not by itself provide a justification for relativism. Daniels is right when he says that the burden will be carried by the *explanation* of convergence or divergence. Without such an explanation, the bare fact of convergence or divergence proves nothing by itself, though it might (or might not) be taken as evidence for a relativist or universalist view. As Wong says,

> while many have been moved by such examples [of diversity] to adopt moral relativism, the argument from diversity does not support relativism in any simple or direct way . . . the simple fact of diversity in belief is no disproof of the possibility that there are some beliefs better to have than the others because they are truer or more justified than the rest (Wong, 1995, 444).

Diversity has certainly been the impetus moving many to relativism. It might, by means of an argument showing that relativism can account for widespread diversity better than universalism, constitute evidence for relativism. However, without a justificatory strategy explaining how moral justification

---

[23] This section reinforces my discussion in the previous chapter concerning whether relativism could coexist alongside contingent universalism. The answer, as I indicated there, depends on the sense of 'contingency' in the universalist account. If the values were accepted as objectively valid purely because of the convergence, then I would suggest that the two accounts are not mutually exclusive. However, if the justification of the common values lay not in the fact of convergence but in features of human nature, say, for which convergence was *evidence*, then it would conflict with coherence relativism.

allows for there to be more than a single true morality, it does not constitute any non-vacuous form of relativism itself.

A priori coherence relativism raises a number of issues straight-away. Some of these can be put in terms of the problems for relativism that I outlined in chapter two, and I will address these questions in the remainder of this chapter and in chapter five. I want to begin by answering a criticism that might be thought to immediately refute an understanding of reflective equilibrium as a relativist account of justification. This is the claim, made by Kai Nielsen, that reflective equilibrium yields universal and objective principles. Looking at his conception of reflective equilibrium will demonstrate some of the features of reflective equilibrium that lend themselves to a relativist interpretation. I then move on to examine the claim of objectivity present in Nielsen's interpreta-tion. If many coherent equilibria will emerge, how can anyone claim that his or her equilibrium is *objectively* correct? The ques-tion of objectivity has dogged relativism throughout its history, and I believe coherence relativism can make a worthwhile response. In doing so, I will also answer the charge that relativism renders morality arbitrary. As indicated in chapter two, whilst I will not discuss my relativism in terms of *truth* I must at least pro-vide an account of the objectivity that can be claimed for it. Section five then addresses the problem of theory choice indeterminacy, a problem for relativism that was also raised in chapter two. Draw-ing on my discussion of considered moral judgements earlier in this chapter, I present a resolution to the question of how to decide between competing moral frameworks. My answers to these questions will lay the groundwork for a full discussion of the remaining elements of our moral experience which emerged from the work of chapter three. The discussion of these — moral disagreement, moral horror and moral criticism — follow in chapter five.

Are Relativism and Reflective Equilibrium Really Compatible?

I have suggested that one reasonable and consistent interpreta-tion of reflective equilibrium is relativist — i.e. it specifies stan-dards of justification that can be met by multiple moralities. Kai Nielsen, in his article 'Relativism and Wide Reflective Equilib-rium' (1993) challenges such a position head on, arguing that Wide Reflective Equilibrium carries no relativist implications. Obviously, if Nielsen is right, and my position is included in those described by Nielsen as relativist, then I am wrong. However, I do not believe that Nielsen's argument renders my position incoher-ent or even implausible. Here I will indicate why I believe this to be the case, by setting out Nielsen's argument and then my criticisms of it.

Nielsen distinguishes between the two forms of relativism that I set out in chapter two: ethical (normative) and metaethical. Ethical relativism, on Nielsen's account, claims that 'what is right or good for one individual or society need not be right or good for another' (Nielsen, 1993, 316). Metaethical relativism claims that 'there are no objectively sound procedures for justifying one moral code or one set of moral judgements as over against another' (Nielsen, 1993, 316). Nielsen's argument, simply put, is that what both of these relativist positions have in common is that they deny objectivity to moral belief. However, reflective equilibrium *does* provide objective grounds upon which to examine moral codes and actions, and decide which is best (Nielsen, 1993, 327). Therefore, reflective equilibrium is not relativistic. This argument is important, for if Nielsen is correct in his interpretation of reflective equilibrium, then the very idea of coherence relativism is rendered deeply problematic. In response, I contend first that Nielsen gives an implausible interpretation of wide reflective equilibrium. I also argue that the relativisms that he chooses to attack are not those which I wish to defend, a situation compounded by ambiguities in his use of key terms. I shall begin with the first of these points.

Nielsen characterises wide reflective equilibrium as a process of rationalisation, involving ' a shuttling back and forth between theories, principles and concrete moral judgements with a mutual correction between them until we have, for a time, considering them together, the best fit' (Nielsen, 1993, 323). Such a depiction is relatively uncontroversial. However, Nielsen attributes three other properties to reflective equilibria.

(1)   While there can be several distinct narrow equilibria, there can be only one wide equilibrium, where 'wide' means 'widest'.

(2)   The widest equilibrium is the most adequate reflective equilibrium.

(3)   The width of a wide reflective equilibrium constitutes an objectively sound criterion upon which to justify one moral code as being superior to another.[24]

These three properties seem to me to embody a number of assumptions that I wish to challenge here. First, Nielsen does not give us any basis upon which we can precisely measure the width

---

[24]   All of these claims are made on page 327 of the article (1993).

of reflective equilibrium. Are we to assume it is something to do with the amount of different background theories, or different principles, which any given equilibrium embodies or accounts for? Are we to count these, and award the title of 'widest' to the equilibrium that has the most? We should, of course, make a distinction between wide and narrow reflective equilibria. And reflective equilibrium methodology requires us to examine and distinguish between those moral frameworks which are coherent and those which are not. Rough and ready judgements on whether X coheres satisfactorily or not, or whether X incorporates or explains important theories and deep theories, are surely possible. However, Nielsen must have something more accurate in mind in order for him to be able to say that even if two moral frameworks were closely matched, we could judge one of them to be superior to another on grounds of width, and thus that there can only be one, maximally wide, 'true' reflective equilibrium.[25]

Second, reflective equilibrium links coherence and justification. Because Nielsen links width and justification, are we to take him as saying that width is linked to coherence? Nielsen's remarks imply that a wider wide reflective equilibrium is *necessarily* more coherent than a narrower one. Coherence is *prima facie* a *relational* property; width an absolute one. We are given no reason to suppose that if two moralities have an equal *quality* of coherence, and both deal with enough key moral issues, then we should prefer one on the basis of the *quantity* of judgements and theories cohered with, which is what I take width to be about. Suppose we have two equally internally coherent equilibriums. Should we consider the equilibrium that takes into account 1001 theories and background theories objectively superior to one that takes into account merely 1000 such theories? I am willing to accept that it might be more important to deal with some theories and deep theories than with others. For example, we might be more concerned that our view dealt satisfactorily with the idea that 'people are moral equals' rather than the view that 'people are mostly alien beings, having been substituted for real humans after abduction experiences'. But whether quality considerations

---

[25] It seems to me that this is a dangerous position for Nielsen to advocate. If there is only one, widest, truly justified equilibrium, then precisely because of its width, it is quite possible that the theory could be either hugely complicated, very general and abstract, or trivial in nature. Particularly for egalitarian liberals, or contemporary socialists, whilst it might be thought quite likely that adherents of such theories are in *wide* equilibrium, there is no guarantee that the *widest* — and hence most justified — equilibrium is not instantiated in some form of fundamentalism.

enter into the equation, and to what extent, are questions untouched by Nielsen. Beyond a certain point of acceptability, the width of a view — how many different theories, intuitions and deep theories it draws upon (i.e. the size of the framework) — is of distant secondary importance to the quality of the links and the mutual support within the framework.

To see the problem with width as a measure of adequacy, suppose that an atheist thought that all religions embodied the same psychological needs instantiated in entirely different codes of conduct. This might take into account or explain a much wider spectrum of moral views than a sincere believer in one of those codes of conduct could. However, I am resistant to the idea that this makes the atheist account more adequate. On the interpretation that values width first, this view should command the assent of all. It is objectively superior by virtue of its width. However, this outcome is surely counter-intuitive, at least without a much stronger look at the nature of the coherence the account offered us.[26]

Thus, I dispute Nielsen's points (1), (2), and (3). (1) and (2) require us to have an accurate metric of width, in order to be able to determine that only one maximally wide equilibrium exists. Against this, I have argued (1) that we do not have such a metric of width and (2) that even if we did, width is not necessarily related to the coherence of an equilibrium. Nielsen's implied view, that the wider a wide equilibrium the more coherent it must necessarily be, is implausible. A rejection of (3) follows from the rejection of (1) and (2). We have no well-defined metric and no direct assessment of coherence is involved. Therefore this approach cannot constitute an objective method of determining which moral theory is best, at least if objectivity involves notions of reliability, clarity and general acceptance.[27]

Nielsen also defines the relativism he is attacking in such a way as to rule out those theories I have discussed in chapter two, and the one I am advocating here. This is because, despite the comments I make above, Nielsen is right that reflective equilibrium methodology allows some judgements of superiority on criteria of coherence and consistency. This will clearly be problematic for

---

[26] Of course, Nielsen could invoke a stringent set of filters to rule out all 'ill-considered' moral views, then make width the benchmark for those that survived these filters. Even in this case, I'm unsure that width (quantity) rather than coherence (quality) ought to be the decider.

[27] Here I give three uncontroversial attributes often associated with objectivity. In the next section I move to a detailed discussion of objectivity and its relation with relativism.

relativists who deny the existence of *any* standards for morality, so that all moralities are on a par. However, as I have suggested earlier, such relativists have somewhat more significant worries than their relationship with reflective equilibrium. Relativists who believe that all moral frameworks are on a par fly in the face of our everyday experience that we want and need to be able to judge some moralities to be better than others. The relativism I am advocating, like Wong's, allows for a degree of assessment whilst denying that there is a single objectively true morality. Thus, even if Nielsen's criticisms are correct, they do not apply to this kind of relativist theory.

Lastly, a good deal hangs on exactly what Nielsen means by objectivity. If the essence of objectivity lies in reliability and broad intersubjective agreement, then even 'hardcore' relativists might not deny the possibility of assessment from a shared standpoint. However, if Nielsen means by the objective standpoint a 'view from nowhere', then he is right that relativism denies the existence of such a place. These questions are part of the second criticism that I now turn to examine. This charges that relativism in general, and coherence relativism in particular, leave insufficient room for objectivity. This, as I have already indicated, is related to the demand for an account of truth that I examined in chapter two. I suggested there that part of what lay beneath that concern was the idea that morality should not be rendered arbitrary. In the next section I discuss this issue, and in so doing counter a number of general and specific problems for relativism.

Relativism, Reflective Equilibrium and Objectivity

This sub-section will examine two problems for coherence relativism. First, I will show how and why the multiple justified moralities envisaged by coherence relativism are not merely arbitrary statements of personal preference — in other words, what kind of authority they can claim. Second, in responding to this issue I can also clarify how relativism, including coherence relativism, can avoid the common objection that relativism is either self-refuting or uninteresting. Critics such as Nagel see those who propose relativism as being in a dilemma. Either an 'everything is relative' claim 'can't be subjective, because then it would not rule out any objective claim, including the claim that it is objectively false', or a relativist 'who presents the claim as applying even to itself . . . does not call for reply, since it is just a report of what the subjectivist finds it agreeable to say. If he also invites us to join him, we need not offer any reason for declining, since he has offered us no reason to accept' (Nagel, 1997, 15). What both of these criticisms have in common is that they posit an opposition between relativism and objectivity. In response, I will argue here that there are at least two schools of thinking about objectivity and one of them is an ally, rather than an enemy, of relativism.[28] Fred D'Agostino has distinguished between two traditions of objectivity, which he terms *transcendence* and *conversation*.[29] The line D'Agostino draws is to my mind pretty much correct, and thus the line I will draw is very similar. I will talk here about objectivity as transcendence; the alternative I will term objectivity as a 'community of reasons'.[30] My central contention is that relativism can successfully claim the latter kind of objectivity.

Objectivity as Transcendence

D'Agostino summarises the 'objectivity as transcendence' position thus:

> Our beliefs or values are objectively valid when they are or would be endorsed from a perspective — sometimes picturesquely reified in the notion of an 'Archimedean point' (Rawls) or a 'God's-eye view' (Putnam) or the 'view from nowhere' (Nagel) or the 'class consciousness of the proletariat' (Lukacs) — which transcends the particularities, biases, and contingencies of our own egocentric perspectives (D'Agostino, 1993, 87).

I do not want to go into D'Agostino's arguments distinguishing varieties of such an account, and arguments against them, at any length here. My purpose here is not to defeat such ideas of objectivity, but rather draw out some of their features. Objectivity, on the transcendence account, is about attaining independence from particular perspectives — only universals can ultimately justify. We encountered this as an interpretation of Nagel's approach in chapter two. Similarly, Wiggins, talking about a robust ethical objectivism, characterises it as the view that 'we can put together considerations which leave nothing else to think' (Wiggins, 1996, 37) — a position which he stresses, 'does not mean that there is

---

[28] Nagel, of course, takes the opposite view. In presenting his problems for relativism, he holds that they suffice for a refutation; 'the familiar point that relativism is self-refuting remains valid in spite of its familiarity' (Nagel, 1997, 15). I will argue here, however, that these problems only present the relativist with a dilemma on *one particular* account of objectivity and universality.

[29] D'Agostino, 1993, 87–108.

[30] This change in terminology is partly justified by the more obvious relation that exists between the idea of a 'community of reasons' and relativism, my central concern here. It is also partly justified by my feeling that the idea of common reasons forms more a common denominator for approaches that might not be happy with the 'conversationalist' epithet.

nothing left *for us* to think' — justification must be universal and general rather than local. On such an account of objectivity, it is easy to see the relativist's problem. First, relativism does not allow this universal, general justification. Second, the relativist is caught in a potential self-contradiction in affirming that there is no single justified morality, but that this view should be taken as universally correct.

Objectivity as a 'Community of Reasons'

However, there are several alternative accounts of objectivity, most of which I believe are united by the link between the idea of objectivity and a community of reasons. Not all thinkers, of course, can be squeezed into either of the two camps I am presenting here. Norman Daniels, for example, attempts to remain neutral on controversial questions of objectivity by affirming objectivity in the sense of reliability — repeatability in the scientific realm — and agreement (Daniels, 1996, 33). Here I will outline the ideas of some thinkers whose work, I would argue, constitutes a move towards situating objectivity in a 'community of reasons'.

For example, Richard Rorty has argued that objectivity could be replaced by the idea of 'unforced intersubjective agreement',[31] and that any attempt at transcendence 'is a fantasy, as we cannot escape from our own circle of beliefs' (Gaus, 1996, 118, quoting Rorty 1991, 13). Gaus, whilst unhappy with linking intersubjective agreement and justified belief, admits

> In a way ... seeking objectivity in interpersonal agreement is an effort to get outside our own system of reasons and beliefs, looking for the objective in what is outside of ourselves. But surely our commitment to, and understanding of, objectivity is itself a cluster of beliefs and epistemic norms. It is no more outside our beliefs than are our inferential norms or other beliefs (Gaus, 1996, 118).

What these kinds of views have in common is an assumption that objectivity is about people as having, or conceiving of themselves having, beliefs and reasons in common. An appeal to objectivity is an appeal to, or an attempt to establish, common beliefs and reasons. Though relativists 'cannot simply presume that their evaluative concepts and beliefs are recommendable, unconditionally, to everyone' (Moser, 1993, 167), they can offer justifica-

---

[31] The constraint indicated by Rorty's specification that agreement should be 'unforced' is to my mind a fairly weak one. The weak account of the criteria for a considered moral judgement can easily accommodate situations where my judgement is subject to coercion as situations where that judgement is 'liable to error'.

tions based on reasons, concepts and purposes held in common.[32] Objectivity for the relativist, as for at least some thinkers who deny the transcendence idea of objectivity, can consist in appeals to the reasons people share. Thus, D'Agostino's conversational objectivity[33] maintains that a necessary feature of objectivity is 'to have confronted other perspectives and found common cause, in a variety of ways, with their advocates' (D'Agostino, 1993, 101). Conversational objectivity is linked to ideas of 'public justifiability'. D'Agostino argues 'those judgements are objective which could be justified to a suitably general potential audience' (D'Agostino, 1993, 101).[34] In science for example, there is a widely shared account of the conditions which invalidate or show the success of experiments, so that scientific objectivity is an ongoing *process* of testing and retesting hypotheses against the world (Brown, 1987, 200–2). It could be argued that such scientific observations can be objective relative to a shared set of criteria. Similarly, the community of people who accept the rules of mathematics can regard 2 + 2 = 4 as an objective judgement. I am suggesting that relativists can argue their position by an appeal to things they share with their opponents, an account of good and bad reasons common to the parties. Thus, the argument I am engaged in aims to show the plausibility of metaethical relativism for good reasons, such as its ability to explain our moral experience. The divergent but equally justified equilibria of coherence relativism can also strive for and claim this kind of objectivity.

Furthermore, I would argue that this is not just a popular account of objectivity but a defensible one. It should be noted that this account shares a concern for commonality with the transcendence position. The universal reason(s) of the transcendence accounts are also based on the assertion that these reasons are justifiable to everyone; this can be interpreted as the idea that they would be *common* to all in perfectly rational circumstances. We saw in chapter three that one possible interpretation of universalism relies on the fact that some values are contingently shared. Of

---

[32] 'As long as relativists have purposive normative reasons for certain evaluative concepts, and others share their purposes underlying those purposive reasons, they can reasonably recommend their concepts to those others' (Moser, 1993, 167).

[33] The emphasis on conversation seems partly to arise from Hilary Putnam: 'The important thing is to find a picture that enables us to make sense of the phenomena from within our world and out experience, rather than to seek a 'God's-Eye view' — and this we can best do, I think, conversationally' Putnam, 1988, 109).

[34] This link surfaces in chapter six, where I discuss the relationship between public justification and Rawls' conception of objectivity.

course, the advocate of a transcendentalist view of objectivity will ask why we should be prepared to settle for an account of objectivity which, unlike the 'transcendence' approach, could be prone to parochialism. In describing the 'conversational' alternative, D'Agostino asks;

> Why, it might be said, should we care about the things which have objective value for us if their objective value consists entirely in some quasi-conversational agreement that they are of value to 'us' — with the implied recognition that they might not be to others (D'Agostino, 1993, 103).

One reply available to theorists who view objectivity in terms of a community of reasons would refer to the impossibility of attaining a truly transcendental perspective — this is, in fact, all we can ever be left with. Furthermore, the danger can be minimised by advocating maximal reflexivity, so 'we must be prepared to deal when they arise with counter-arguments even to our specification of what constitutes a legitimate potential counter-argument' (D'Agostino, 1993, 102). The wider the 'us', the smaller the problem becomes.

Whilst it is not my intention here to leap into the deep end of the debate between these two accounts of objectivity I want to outline a bit further here what I see as the main contention of each of the two sides. The most important argument for the second, non-transcendental account of objectivity is that the first kind of objectivity is impossible to achieve. I take philosophers such as Wittgenstein, Putnam, and Rorty to be making this kind of point. Wittgenstein compares the problem of finding an objective standpoint from which to assess ethics as being like 'saying that it must be possible to decide which of two standards of accuracy is the correct one' (recorded in Rhees, 1982, 100 — cited in Johnston, 1989). Similarly, Putnam argues that 'the question: which is the rational conception of rationality itself is difficult in exactly the way that the justification of an ethical system is difficult. There is no neutral conception of rationality to which to appeal' (Putnam, 1981, 136).[35] Theorists of transcendental objectivity are thus looking for a chimera in taking objectivity to be in some sense a neutral position, standing outside our views.

---

[35] This should not to be taken to mean that Putnam, Rorty or Wittgenstein consider themselves relativists. As I discuss elsewhere, for Rorty the issue may be merely terminological. Putnam ultimately opposes relativism, and provides arguments which, he considers, refutes it. None of these arguments, in my opinion, are ultimately successful (a detailed discussion of them can be found in Preston, 1992).

Conversely, theorists of transcendental objectivity argue that non-transcendental accounts are unintelligible. Nagel suggests that an account of objectivity resting on a community of reasons 'directly contradicts the categorical statements it purports to be about — that there are infinitely many prime numbers, that racial description is unjust, that water is a compound, that Napoleon was less than six feet tall ... The contradiction comes from adding a qualification that is incompatible with the unqualified nature of the original' (Nagel, 1997, 30). What Nagel overlooks is the possibility that the content of (though not necessarily what we intend by) such statements is implicitly relativised, in the same way that Harman argues that judgements about motion or mass can *only* be made relative to a spatio-temporal framework (Harman, 1996, 3). Nagel's argument is that we cannot escape the possibility of reason and rationality. His opponents suggest that we recast the way in which we think of the domain of reason and rationality. For example, Nagel cites with incredulity Rorty's comment that 'what people like Kuhn, Derrida and I believe is that it is pointless to ask whether there really are mountains or whether it is merely convenient for us to talk about mountains' (Rorty, cited in Nagel, 1997, 29). I want to suggest that at least one sensible account can be given of Rorty's statement, and that this account will help explain the disagreement. If we are to talk about mountains in our discourse, then we use them as part of a web of perceptions, beliefs and reasoning; the fact of the presence of mountains is translated into beliefs about it. Rorty could be saying that it is these *beliefs* we hold about mountains that do the real work in our discourse rather than the mere presence of mountains. Nothing here moves Rorty's account out of the realm of talk about the content of cognitive systems. By contrast, Nagel wishes to allow for a more direct connection where facts constitute beliefs, so that 'if a belief is true, it would be true even if no one believed it' (Nagel, 1997, 30), because we cannot acknowledge a reason without acknowledging its factual or strongly objective status.

I have sketched two alternative views of objectivity. Whilst the first is rightly viewed as problematic for relativists, the second, I would argue, is not. This second kind of objectivity allows us to respond to the two criticisms of (1) arbitrariness and (2) self-contradiction or irrelevance I indicated earlier. In response to (1), relativism can obtain the second, 'local' kind of objectivity when it is successfully argued for amongst people to whom the reasons used to support relativism seem coherent and appealing. On this account of objectivity, the moral framework of the relativist is not rendered arbitrary or mere preference, but nor is it a self-refuting attempt at transcending framework-relativity. The coherence relativist can conceive of the justification for her proposal in these 'community of reasons' terms, utilising coherence and consistency as common reasons. The particular reflective equilibrium an individual holds can also claim the second kind of objectivity, only with regard to the (smaller) community of people who accept the reasons involved in her post-reflection moral view. In response to (2), such an account makes objectivity contingent on common reasons, rather than necessary or universal, and allows there to be more than one single valid moral (or perhaps conceptual) scheme, hence preventing self-contradiction on the part of the relativist. Furthermore, unless considerations of coherence and consistency and the desire to understand our moral experience are not shared, the relativist can (*contra* Nagel) attempt to give good reasons for others to change their views. Thus, the dilemma Nagel posits for the relativist is only a dilemma on the first account of objectivity. The second account renders the relativist neither self-refuting nor irrelevant.

Though the coherence relativist can claim objectivity for both her method and her particular results, there will be limits to the constituency of views, the 'community of reasons' against the background of which her view is objective. People who believe that coherence or consistency should instead be coherence or consistency with certain foundational truths constitute one such limit. Many people in the world accept a variant of the view that coherence with moral ideas of *any* kind will not do. Rather, coherence must obtain with certain moral and non-moral facts, for example the existence of God and God's law. Is there a way for the relativist who uses coherence and consistency as standards of justification to justify their approach to these objectors?

I think there are several considerations that could serve to justify a coherentist methodology to such people, even though there is no single knock-down answer. 'Coherence with' is still a variety of coherence. Whilst such views require more than coherence — specifically, coherence *with* a certain something — *at least* coherence is required. Furthermore, the relativist could argue that doctrines, religious or otherwise, are constantly being reinterpreted so as to reach some kind of equilibrium with other prevalent moral intuitions.[36] Examples of this phenomenon could be the change in attitude by the Church of England towards women

---

[36] MacIntyre's idea of epistemological crisis is relevant here. He argues that doctrines must adapt when they face incoherence or a lack of explanatory resources (MacIntyre, 1988). I examine this idea in more detail in chapter five.

priests; the embracing of competition, if not democracy, by Chinese communism; the attitude of many Roman Catholics towards contraception. Pressure to change can be supplied by people with particular moral views which conflict with doctrine, until a new equilibrium between doctrine and considered judgements is reached through reinterpretation.[37]

Of course, many of the 'indubitable' facts with which coherence might be required concern metaphysical issues that are hotly disputed. Reasonable believers of disputable facts might recognise others' doubts of their own fundamental truths, and allow for reflective equilibrium as a kind of common ground at the level of moral justification. On such common ground, something which counted as a good reason or a fundamental truth for them might not for others, but the need for coherence and consistency would be recognised as constant. Even if people were unwilling to recognise that controversial facts should be played down at a private level, they might admit that *public* justification should not presuppose any particular comprehensive doctrine.[38] We can conceive of these responses as an attempt to engage with such people and to show the relevance of reflective equilibrium as something more than merely 'subjective'.

We can accept the general point of this section despite recognising that coherence and consistency possess limits in their role as objective reasons. The multiple justified equilibria made possible by a relativistic interpretation of equilibrium can claim objectivity in the second 'community of reasons' sense, and this second sense is sufficient to prevent coherence relativism (and the multiple coherent equilibria that it allows for) becoming purely arbitrary, self-contradictory, or irrelevant to others. This section has not answered every possible question about the 'community of reasons' strategy. Nevertheless, it has indicated how responses to these 'objectivity objections' are possible.

---

[37] This point, about the scope for adaptation in moral systems, is illustrated by Rawls' explanation of the move from a mere *modus vivendi* to a constitutional consensus (Rawls, 1993, 158–62). Rawls suggests comprehensive doctrines will mould themselves to the political conception of justice; 'these adjustments or revisions we may suppose to take place slowly over time as the political conception shapes comprehensive views to cohere with it' (Rawls, 1993, 160, footnote 25). I discuss the transformative power of political liberalism in chapter seven.

[38] This is a possibility that I will examine in detail in part two of the book, where I examine the difference between individual and public justification as part of an argument for state neutrality, in particular John Rawls' account of political liberalism.

How We Choose Between Multiple Justified Moralities

In the previous section I discussed some prominent problems for a relativist interpretation of reflective equilibrium, and some potential responses. I have argued that such a coherence relativism is not implausible, either in its interpretation of reflective equilibrium or in claiming objectivity for itself. The primary task of this section is to address a further problem for any relativism or relativistic account of reflective equilibrium. I suggested in chapter two that some have objected to relativism on the ground that we should expect an account of moral justification to be able to guide our theory choice, and this is exactly what relativism fails to do. This is what I have termed the problem of theory choice indeterminacy. I want to argue here that the relativist can give a good reply to this objection. In such a reply, the notion of considered judgements will again prove significant. This section is thus crucial in establishing the plausibility of my nascent 'coherence relativism', but also serves to clarify the nature of my proposal and its links with reflective equilibrium.

Assuming that more than one morality survives the process of reflection — i.e. is a coherent, consistent structure of moral judgements and supporting theories — we are left with an important question. How can I explain my adherence to one, rather than another, moral system — what should guide my choice? (Why should I be X-moral rather than Y-moral?).[39] This question is not entirely unlike the question, 'why should I be moral at all?' Both ask about moral motivation and neither, in my view, admits of a simple, decisive answer. With regard to the latter question, considerations are advanced which convince all but the most die-hard, and psychologically improbable, egoist. An answer to the question of why I should be this-moral rather than that-moral runs a similar course. My answer is that we explain our choice using the psychological or emotional attachments we have to particular values, ideas, and modes of reasoning. I want to draw support for this claim from two further contentions. The first stresses the difficulty or *impossibility* of shedding our deep commitments, drawing on a communitarian understanding of the self. The second arises from a discussion of the views of Williams and Scheffler, who argue for the importance of such commitments, albeit in a different cause. Following their approach, I will contend that it is also *undesirable* to disregard our deep commitments.

---

[39] I discuss the related question concerning moral criticism, 'what kinds of judgements can I pass on another morality that shares the same kind and amount of justification?' in chapter five.

Our Selves and Our Ends

My first claim is that it is difficult — if not impossible — to divorce ourselves from our deep commitments; that is, to stand back from all of them and examine the impact they would have on our choice of moral systems. Like it or not, they will influence our choice. Support from this idea comes from within the communitarian tradition, from prominent figures such as Sandel and MacIntyre. Sandel has argued that some ends are constitutive of our selves — we are not an 'unencumbered self' standing at a critical distance from our ends (e.g. Sandel, 1982, 55-9, 161-5), whilst MacIntyre suggests that we decide how to live our lives from within given social roles (e.g. MacIntyre, 1981, 204-5). Whilst both of these theses are controversial, I would seek to avoid their most controversial implications. My argument here is not that society plays a determining role in shaping our projects, or that because our selves are partly constituted by some ends, any particular end is immune to revision. Rather, my point is that standing back from all our most personal projects and coolly evaluating them, then changing them in one Gestalt-type switch is difficult, if not impossible. Because this is impossible or difficult, our choice between different moralities with different basic intuitions may not be so underdetermined. Occasionally, people may be so struck by a moral theory (for example, in a religious or paranormal experience) that their deep commitments change overnight. I would suggest that the experience of most people would be that to a certain extent we cannot discard or disregard our deep commitments in such a manner. I am not denying of course that over time, the value we attach to certain deep commitments can shift, and the equilibrium with which they cohere shifts also; however, these attachments seem much more fixed over a short time span. There are two possible claims. The first, and strongest, says that it is impossible for people to disregard their constitutive commitments. In this case, we should not ask people to do the impossible. The second, weaker, claim is that it is *difficult* to jettison such commitments. Whilst I do not wish to argue that we can never reasonably expect people to do the difficult, I do want to suggest that something being difficult is a consideration bearing on how reasonable it is to expect something of somebody.[40]

---

[40]   It might be the case that this 'standing back from our ends' would be possible yet difficult for some, and impossible for others. Some communitarians would of course argue that it is logically impossible for anyone.

Ground Projects As a Basis for Rejecting Some Moral Claims

If the first point is that we have deep considered commitments which are difficult to shift, the second is that the shift may not be desirable, and that instead we can reject certain moral theories because they conflict with, or do not give sufficient weight to, our personal projects. Two proponents of this view are Bernard Williams and Samuel Scheffler.

Williams, in chapter one of *Moral Luck*, is concerned with the idea that 'an individual person has a set of desires, concerns or as I shall often call them, projects which help to constitute a 'character'' (Williams, 1981, 5), and that these projects have implications for impartial and utilitarian moralities. Williams criticises utilitarianism, and even Kantianism, because if a conflict arises between impartial moralities and that 'nexus of ground projects' which give a person's life meaning,

> impartial morality, if the conflict really does arise, must be required to win; and that cannot necessarily be a reasonable demand on the agent. There can come a point at which it is quite unreasonable for a man to give up, in the name of the impartial good ordering of the world of moral agents, something which is a condition of his having any interest in being around in that world at all (Williams, 1981, 15).

Thus, on Williams' account, we can reject the demands of moralities when they conflict with our most deeply held projects. Not all of what I would term deep commitments need be as important as the ones which Williams feels are crucial to us living with any kind of purpose. The argument, I believe, could be extended so that less crucial deep commitments would count incrementally in deciding which moral theory to adopt. Thus, if there were a choice of moralities, we would be better off with the one which requires us to violate our current deep commitments the least.

Scheffler makes similar points in his attack on utilitarianism. A morality may be more or less demanding on individuals, partly because 'neither the cost of satisfying its requirements, nor the extent to which those requirements are confining, need be the same for everyone' (Scheffler, 1992, 99). In advocating an argument that morality should be humane or moderate, rather than excessively 'stringent', Scheffler says that supporters of the moderate view 'believe accordingly, that moral norms should be capable of being integrated in a coherent and attractive way into the life of the individual agent. And they regard this requirement as imposing a significant constraint on the content of morality' (Scheffler, 1992, 101). It is thus a reasonable development to see some kind of coherence with, and allowance for, an individual's deep attachments as properly influencing her initial *choice* of morality. This would justify her holding one morality rather than others which may have the same impersonal justification but do not allow for her deep commitments.

This is an issue about personal well-being or happiness and consequently about our motivation to be moral. A morality that does not acknowledge our particular deep commitments or ground projects will be seen as excessively demanding. This means that we will be less happy in our moral — and psychic — life, and incidentally we may be less likely to follow what this morality demands of us. However, as Scheffler notes, this does not mean that our personal projects should 'trump' the demands of morality. Instead, a balance between the two, so that selfish projects are regulated by morality, is required. Bradley wrote that 'A man is moral because he likes being moral; and he likes it, partly because he has been brought up to the habit of liking it, and partly because he finds it gives him what he wants, while its opposite does not' (Bradley, 1962, 62–3, footnote 1).

This quotation hints at the (to my mind plausible) idea that regulation is a desirable function of morality. It seems that a component of justification on this understanding of morality is the happiness or well-being that would result from the correct choice of regulatory framework. Bradley's quotation is also useful in prompting two important criticisms of this view of morality. These are first, that on the view that morality is partly rooted in happiness or well-being, some reduction of the moral to the non-moral is taking place; and second, that this methodology will tend to sanctify an individual's 'moral habit'. Both of these criticisms, I believe, are misplaced.

The first point questions the role of non-moral considerations of personal well-being in the process. However, because morality has on this view a regulatory function (amongst others), there is a constant tension between selfish interests and morality, rather than the latter merely being the expression of the former. Morality will not be reduced to self-interest, although the argument maintains that psychic happiness and overall well-being ought to be a consideration in moral motivation and justification. I recognise this is a controversial position. Proponents of what Scheffler terms 'demanding' moral views will hold that my well-being and happiness are irrelevant (perhaps except to the extent that it is a concern that might prevent me from acting morally). However, we are still at the level of metaethical justification rather than particular ethical judgements, and it is not clear how morality can be justified in purely moral terms; consistency, for example, is not a moral term. Here, as throughout the reflective equilibrium process, both moral and wider non-moral considerations are appealed to. If our choice of moral system can only be justified by its morality, then circularity appears to beckon. If we want to avoid the circle, a consideration of the well-being of ourselves and our 'significant others' would be a good candidate to be included — though I cannot discuss these wider questions here.

I believe that the second objection of moral conservatism can be swiftly dealt with. The deep commitments employed are to be considered ones; the reflective equilibrium process is meant to weed out those commitments that are irrationally held. Nor are deep commitments being used at the first stage of the process to decide between justified and unjustified moralities, partly because they are inherently subjective. Instead, their role is that of a tie-breaker. Our intuitions, as highlighted by Williams and Scheffler, feel depth of commitment should be reflected in the process. However, this role can accommodate the fact that we sometimes have irrational commitments.

The primary examples of these kinds of deep commitments for my purposes are strongly held and considered moral judgements. I have shown in the previous section how these act as 'provisional fixed points' in the process of reflective equilibrium. If, in the case of any particular one of these judgements, we are still committed to it when the stage is reached of choosing between justified moralities, then I want to suggest that this commitment should influence our choice. The point here is that from the impersonal standpoint of reflective equilibrium the set of considered moral judgements should fulfil the same role in the process, whatever the specific content of the judgements. However, the *content* of each individual's set of considered moral judgements will be different, and coherence with each individual's set can be used as a mechanism for deciding between moralities which share the same impersonal level of justification. This logic could be extended to non-moral considered judgements and projects that also form important constituents of our character. These strong commitments that form part of our identity are important in turn because of their relation to our well-being, psychic happiness, and — for want of a better expression — human flourishing. Judging those moralities which survive reflective equilibrium by the lights of these deep commitments effectively constitutes a second stage of justification. Beyond the stage of *impersonal* justification is the possibility, if necessary, of *personal* or subjective justification.

Thus, in this section I have argued that the way to show that theory choice is not underdetermined is to point to important personal commitments as a personal or subjective set of reasons for choosing, or choosing to stick with, a morality. Strongly held considered moral judgements constitute one such set of important commitments. This account will also aid the coherence relativist in explaining prominent features of our moral life, as I will argue in the next chapter. In support of this contention, we can utilise the arguments of theorists who believe that (1) it is difficult or impossible to dismiss our deep commitments and (2) that such considerations ought to inform our morality.

Conclusion — Coherence Relativism?

This chapter, through its analysis of reflective equilibrium, has been concerned to trace the possibility of a distinctive relativist account of reflective equilibrium. This account argues that at least one plausible interpretation of reflective equilibrium is relativistic, in the *a priori* sense that it sets out criteria for justification — standards of coherence and consistency — which can be met by several possible moral systems. To distinguish this approach, it can be termed 'coherence relativism'.

In examining considered moral judgements and their role in equilibrium, I have suggested that relativism can most profitably adopt a set of relatively low constraints on what counts as a considered moral judgement, so as not to import a substantial idea of impartiality into the notion of what makes a 'considered moral judgement' *considered*. Coherence relativism sits happily with the idea of considered moral judgements as provisional fixed points because this provides a way to answer the charge of indeterminacy in theory choice. I have tackled three key problems for this approach. First, I argued against Nielsen's idea that reflective equilibrium cannot be relativistic. Second, I have contended that coherence relativism can claim a plausible account of objectivity for itself and for the particular outcomes of equilibria — answering the demand in chapter two that moral judgements must carry force or authority. Third, I also argued in chapter two that it is problematic for an account of moral justification to provide no or little guidance in a hypothetical or real choice situation between moral theories. As coherence relativism allows for several justified moralities, a powerful potential objection to relativism is that it leaves our choice radically underdetermined. I have sketched out in this chapter how using considered moral judgements and deep commitments in a tie-breaker role can answer this criticism.

The other accounts of relativism examined in chapter two do not provide any such answer.[41]

Thus, in this chapter I have discussed two of the issues in our moral life with which a satisfactory relativism must deal. The remaining three elements of our moral experience which potentially pose problems for relativist accounts — of (1) dealing satisfactorily with moral disagreement, of (2) setting out an account of moral criticism and (3) giving us a response to moral horror — are the subject matter of the next chapter. It is my argument there that coherence relativism satisfies these demands, and in addition provides an important part of a compelling argument for toleration.

---

[41] Though this is not to say that alternative answers are not available, nor that the approach I outline here cannot be used in defence of Wong's or Harman's accounts.

Chapter 5

Coherence Relativism and Its Implications

Introduction

The previous chapter outlined a model of relativism couched within the framework of reflective equilibrium. This chapter continues to examine the way in which this coherence relativism might be thought to explain important features of our moral life. In chapter two, I indicated five features of our moral life which serve effectively as tests of a relativist approach. Having examined two of them in chapter four, chapter five addresses the remaining three: (a) how relativists explain moral disagreement, (b) the account the relativist gives of the capacity for moral criticism across moral frameworks, and (c) whether relativism requires us to tolerate the abhorrent. I will argue here that coherence relativism can provide satisfactory responses on these three issues.

I believe that (a) is relatively straightforward, and can be dealt with here. I argued in chapter two that contemporary relativist accounts could understand moral disagreement as being 'pragmatic' in nature — an idea proposed by Wong (1986). Coherence relativism, it seems to me, is not significantly different in its response to moral disagreement. If X and Y hold different moral positions on the same question, whilst neither position might be uniquely true or justified, and so not logically incompatible, they nevertheless conflict as recommendations for action. Both answers to the moral question could not be implemented simultaneously; they are in conflict and contradict each other.

Laying moral disagreement to one side, this chapter addresses the remaining two tests (b) and (c). Outlining a relativist response to moral criticism (b) will involve a discussion of what it is for a view to be universal. I will suggest that we can separate two elements of universality, and that each of these elements can provide the basis for a different kind of moral criticism. Explaining the senses of moral criticism available to the relativist is the task of section one. My response in section two to (c) — the charge that relativism leaves us helpless in the face of abhorrent moralities — has two parts. The first part looks at the ways in which coherence relativism can rule out prominent examples of abhorrent moralities, i.e. consider them un(der)justified. The second discusses a general defence of a relativist argument for tolerance. I interpret (c) as an issue partly about what moralities the relativist ought to tolerate and why — about whether relativism requires us to tolerate the intolerable. This allows me to discuss a common objection against relativism. For many philosophers, any link between relativism and tolerance has been seen as dubious, if not absurd.[1] Later in this chapter I propose precisely such a link, by arguing that relativism can form part of a 'liberal' argument for toleration.

Universality and Moral Criticism

In this section I want to answer a general worry about the possibility of relativist inter-morality criticism which underpins concerns about criticism of other justified moralities and our response to moral horror. That is, how we can criticise someone when we cannot apparently justify our morality to them. We have seen in chapter three that for universalists, moral criticism is understood as resting on principles that are, well, universal. However, the relativist allows that some different moralities will be equally justified — there will be limits to the universality of relativist reasoning. If moral criticism must be universal in character, then how can the relativist criticise? Shouldn't relativists be left biting their tongues instead? Answering this question will involve looking closely at the universal character of moral criticism. The position I will eventually defend maintains that what I will term *evaluative criticism* is always available to the relativist. Criticism which fulfils a stronger role by providing compelling reasons for change (*compelling criticism*) is possible in the case of those who possess unjustified moralities, determined on the 'objective' criteria that coherence relativism stipulates. Thus, my answer relies on a split between the two categories of morality defined by the stan-

[1]   Notably Bernard Williams, as I will discuss below.

dards of coherence relativism, those that are equally justified, and those that are not. Mirroring this is a split between two kinds of moral universality. I will begin this discussion by drawing a distinction between the universal *application* and *justification* of morality.

Universal Application and Universal Justification

My relativist response to the charge that relativists cannot allow for moral criticism begins by arguing that universality has two aspects — application and justification. To *apply* a morality is to use it as a standard of judgement across the actions of ourselves and others. For a morality to be *justified* is for ourselves and others to have compelling reasons to accept it. The idea of universality in these two respects is the thought that a morality can be justified or applied to everyone. My purpose here is to split these two aspects and to ask the question, 'Can principles yielded using relativist premises be universal in *application*, though not universally *justified*?' Answering this question will leave us with a much clearer picture of the kind of moral criticism available to the relativist.

The terms in use here require further explanation. For someone to believe their morality has universal justification is for them to believe that the justification they have for their morality constitutes a justification for everyone (or perhaps for all rational people).[2] On such an account, what counts as a good reason for me to do X must be one for everyone else as well.[3] To the extent that someone believes that their good reason for doing X can be overruled in other people's moral systems, their morality is non-universal with regard to justification. The scope of application of a morality, by contrast, concerns the sphere of people, or perhaps of life, for which it is to be taken as a valid criterion of moral action. The scope of application says nothing in itself about whether the application of a morality to someone can be justified to them. A claim of universal application amounts to the claim that 'other

---

[2]   People who hold this position are endorsing what Gaus has described as a 'strongly externalist' view of justification. Such a view, which says that what counts as a justification for me, must count as a justification for others, is incompatible with relativism (Gaus, 1996, 35). In its most extreme form, this disregards any epistemic authority people might be thought to have over their own sets of reasons, so that something could by justified with regard to me, without my assent being gained.

[3]   I think this position can be qualified in various ways. For example, the morality might only be justified to 'reasonable' or 'rational' people — terms that could be interpreted in different ways. The morality might be 'justifiable', implying that hypothetically, it *could* be justified to everyone. See also the use of counterfactuals by Larmore below.

people ought to do X' — or, that we can judge others' actions right or wrong according to the extent to which they do X. As an example, suppose that a Christian who believes that we should repay injury with kindness meets a Confucian who believes that we should only repay kindness with kindness.[4] Suppose that both hold their position to be the moral one on the grounds that they should follow the teachings in one case of Jesus, in the other of Confucius. In this situation both have grounds to apply their morality to judge the actions and beliefs of the other. However, I take this case to be one where justification which the other would find compelling will be hard to come by — 'because Jesus teaches this' will not prove a good reason for the Confucian to change his view, and vice versa. This is an example of where, quite properly, application of a morality outstrips the successful justification of that morality. I want to maintain, like David Wong, that 'a moral principle can have universal scope; that is, it can apply to all moral agents' but 'it may not be *universally justifiable* to all agents' (Wong, 1986, 189). A relativist must accept that she will not be able to convince others to believe X for reasons A, B, C, etc. because not everything that would be considered a valid reason for the relativist would be considered a valid reason by others.

Charles Larmore, while maintaining that he is not offering a 'sort of ethnocentric relativism' (Larmore, 1996, 59), also proposes a similar solution to what he terms the 'crisis of the enlightenment'. This solution is that 'we reject the idea of universal justifiability . . . while keeping that of a universal content' (Larmore, 1996, 57). Drawing on Wong and Larmore, my suggestion is that the bounds of application can outstrip the bounds of justification. This idea can be seen in the limits that universalist moral theorists place upon the possibilities of justification. For example, we cannot justify ourselves to animals, nor is it counted a problem for moral theories that they cannot be justified to pure psychopaths. Limits of the rational or reasonable circumscribe the outer bounds of the universalist's scope of justification. The limits of the community of reasons shared by the relativist and others similarly circumscribe the relativist's scope for justification.

To say that principles can have universal application without universal justification is to argue that in such a situation, relativists could at least say, 'from where I'm standing, that is plain wrong' or 'you should not do that'. Metaethical relativism provides no reason not to *judge* other people's moralities by our own standard. However, in cases where our morality was being

---

[4]   Confucius, The Analects, Book XIV, 34.

applied beyond the scope within which it could be justified, the relativist would have to accept that this application could not impugn the reasons people had for holding conflicting moral beliefs. Such relativism can supply judgement, but judgement without a justification compelling to others. If a relativist believes X because of reasons A, B, C, then she would be able to apply her morality, but not justify the application, to people for whom A, B, C were not at all good reasons. As such, relativism always provides the possibility of an evaluation of another morality from the standpoint of our own.

One way in which it might be thought the relativist could go further than this is through the use of counterfactual justifications. It would be true in the counterfactual case that *if* the non-believer did believe A, B, C, *then* they would have a good reason to believe X. Counterfactual justifications can appear to underlie the application of 'universally valid' principles to those who nevertheless do not accept them. For example, Larmore, talking of his basic principles which are avowedly 'correct' and 'valid' (Larmore, 1996, 145), says,

> How then should we understand the way these principles are addressed to those who do not share that commitment? The proper answer would seem to be that they should be justifiable to those people as well, though with the justification premised on the (counterfactual) supposition that they do prize most the norms of rational dialogue and equal respect (Larmore, 1996, 142).

Such justification seems vacuous. Certainly it does not advance the argument for view X with regard to those people who do not accept it. It might serve as a psychological justification to other believers for the imposition of that view on non-believers. Alternatively, it could be a way of appealing to the idea that the non-believers in fact did find A, B, C persuasive. On either account, it is a tool of persuasion rather than strict justification. If the relativist can go further, it is not through counterfactual justification.

Two Kinds of Moral Criticism

The above account of moral criticism, whilst allowing the relativist the possibility of moral criticism, will not always go far enough in satisfying our intuitions about the criticism we make in our moral lives. A critic of relativism will argue that in some cases it will just not be enough to say 'that's wrong according to my moral scheme', nor is that the force we want our heaviest condemnation to carry. Therefore I want to look in this section at cases in which the relativist can try to go further and invoke a distinction, introduced by Harman, between evaluative criticism and criticism that offers a compelling reason for another to change their view.[5] I will term this latter kind compelling criticism. The criticism that I discussed above is the former; though it could perhaps be expressed very strongly ('your action offends everything I believe in'), the force would be purely comparative or evaluative. The application of one's morality beyond the justification of that morality can simply be shrugged off. Compelling criticism, on the other hand, says something about the reason why one holds a certain view and offers a reason for another to change her view. Compelling criticism can be given where the application of our morality *can* be justified. It supports an evaluation of a moral position by providing good reasons to believe that the justification for that position is flawed. The relativist will be able to offer compelling criticism in the case of an inadequately justified morality. In such a case, where the morality is being criticised because of inconsistency or incoherence, a relativist can offer compelling ways in which the other morality is wrong. For example, its conclusion might not be supported by the premises, or it might invoke factual claims which are not justified on the model of factual inference held. In such a case, the relativist can not only condemn, but also condemn for reasons which are compelling to the other person.[6]

To summarise this, the coherence relativist can always provide reasons for her criticisms of other moralities. These might well stem from her 'deep commitments', for example. However, where we are criticising an equally justified morality, those we criticise can shrug off the reasons behind the application of our morality. In other cases where the morality we criticise is not justi-

---

[5]   However, I do not want to suggest that Harman would place the line between the two exactly where I will. In *Moral Relativism and Moral Objectivity*, the use of the distinction is based on Harman's account of quasi-absolutist terminology, and the distinction between objectivity and OBJECTIVITY which he draws. I do believe that his meaning, interpreted outside quasi-absolutist terminology, is broadly similar to the distinction I am drawing here. Despite his position in the original book that all moralities are equally justified, a clarificatory comment in Harman, 1998, indicates that he can give a sense to less justified moralities, based on the idea of a moral framework 'taken to be a system of corrected values, made coherent with each other and the facts' (Harman, 1998, 208).

[6]   In the next part of this chapter I will show how this kind of criticism could work.

fied, we will be able to find compelling criticism to support our assessment.[7]

In chapter two, I briefly discussed agent- and appraiser- relativism. I suggested that there might be a sense in which both agent- and appraiser- relativism are available to the relativist, and here I want to pursue this idea. I have argued above that relativists can judge other people according to the relativists' values. This sounds like what Lyons and subsequent objectors termed 'appraiser relativism' (Lyons, 1976). 'It says, in effect, that a moral judgement is valid if, and only if, it accords with the norms of the appraisers social group' (Lyons, 1976, 109). Disregarding the concept of 'social group', I am saying that one set of moral criticisms are those based on the appraiser's standards. However, the kind of criticism I want to allow for is also agent-relative, in that if it does not take into account the content of the agent's moral framework then it will not provide compelling reasons for change. Such criticism will only succeed against a backdrop of a common account of reasons — an 'objective' shared meta-framework. One form such criticism could take is criticism of inconsistency within the agent's moral framework. This approximates Lyons' 'agent-relativism', that 'an act is right if, and only if, it accords with the norms of the agent's group' (Lyons, 1976, 109). Again disregarding the group-speak, I am saying that an act can be judged wrong if it does not cohere with the agent's norms (moral framework). The coherence relativist must argue that the reflective equilibrium framework provides the most objective set of good reasons, so that moralities rendered unjustified by that model can be criticised in an 'agent' way — a way in which the criticism will be found compelling by the agent in question. In summary, my position is that the application of our morality to someone without giving reasons for the application that they can accept is 'appraiser' relativism. This will always be a possible form of criticism for the relativist. In cases in which the application can be backed up by shared good reasons it will take a more compelling 'agent' form, challenging the reasons another holds for their view and providing a reason to change that view. Coherence relativism argues that standards of coherency and consis-

---

[7]   In a similar vein, Charles Taylor has argued that we should aim for grounds which our opponents 'cannot but accept' (Taylor,1996, 209). One such ground, for Taylor, is our opponents 'own anomalies'.

tency provide a substantial basis for shared reasons in such a case.[8]

Of course, there are other models of the criticism people can offer between frameworks. Alasdair Macintyre has offered one of the most prominent of these accounts. MacIntyre has argued that despite the fact that we can conceive of radically different traditions of thought, each with their own standards of rational justification, there remains the possibility of strongly objective judgements about their worth. In briefly examining the grounds on which objective criticism can be offered in MacIntyre's scheme, I will point out similarities and differences with that of the coherence relativist. MacIntyre writes,

> It is first of all untrue . . . that traditions, understood as each possessing its own account of and practices of rational justification, therefore cannot defeat or be defeated by other traditions. It is in respect of their adequacy or inadequacy in their responses to epistemological crises that traditions are vindicated or fail to be vindicated (MacIntyre, 1988, 366).

Such an epistemological crisis is a situation where a tradition meets an internal incoherence or a new fact in need of explanation, and the explanatory power of the tradition cannot overcome it. In the terms of my argument, MacIntyre is saying that the response to an epistemological crisis can constitute a universal 'good reason' to either accept or reject the claims of a tradition. He recognises that for long periods of time, such traditions can stand in an equilibrium of incommensurability (MacIntyre, 1988, 366). However, there always remains the possibility of universal rational rejection or acceptance. A coherence relativist, it seems to me, can acknowledge that the ability to deal with internal problems is of objective importance – which says nothing more than it is commonly a bad thing to have huge holes in a theory and no way to plug them. Indeed, the coherence relativist's criteria of justification may be very close to this. We can construe an epistemological crisis as an instance of incoherence and inconsistency, and I have contended that these are two bedrocks of relativist moral criticism. To this extent, the coherence relativist may be saying something similar to MacIntyre.

However, there is also a significant problem with MacIntyre's analysis. MacIntyre specifies that for a tradition to be in a real epistemological crisis it must be 'recognizable as such by its own

---

[8]   Gerald Dworkin discusses inconsistency as a flaw in moral views in Dworkin (1975), 125–8.

standards of rational justification' (MacIntyre, 1988, 364).[9] The *authority* for determining the presence and resolution of an epistemological crisis lies with the members of the tradition who are struck by the crisis. The only compelling judgement of whether there is a discrepancy, and how this discrepancy must be resolved, must come from within the tradition. However, if each tradition comes with its own conception of rationality, then each tradition may have a different interpretation of what it is to resolve an epistemological crisis. It seems we can only examine these interpretations from within our own tradition. However, this position does not provide the kind of vantage point from which we are able to provide a compelling judgement of another tradition which is in crisis (or not) — we do not have the authority to judge. MacIntyre can mitigate this point with the answer that common elements of the idea of rational enquiry will emerge (MacIntyre, 1988, 359). Thus, we *can* always have common standards on which to judge. I have suggested that we can indeed identify some contingently common, maximally interpersonal standards. However, I am less sure than MacIntyre that these will suffice to determine by themselves whether ourselves or others are in epistemological crisis and if so, what the way out is. Even if 'patterns will appear' (MacIntyre, 1988, 359) in traditions of rational enquiry, each tradition might have a different interpretation of what these patterns of rational enquiry require. The difference between the kind of relativism I have been outlining here and MacIntyre's approach thus lies in the coherence relativist claim that compelling reasoning must be come from within the framework of those we criticise. MacIntyre's acknowledgement of the tradition-relativity of being in crisis and judging others to be in crisis is, to my mind, undermined by his desire to posit some common standards.

Having discussed MacIntyre's proposal, we are now in a position to summarise the work of the chapter so far. I have argued that relativists can criticise other moralities without inconsistency. In her criticism of Harman, Sarah Stroud identifies a 'middle position' between the view that 'there is a single maximally correct moral framework' and that of Harman that '*all* moral frameworks are maximally correct'. This middle position is that 'some moral frameworks are maximally correct, while others are

---

not' (Stroud, 1998, 190).[10] This is the ground where coherence relativism stands, and because it occupies this position it offers two possibilities for moral criticism: (a) the moral condemnation of other perspectives, which is always available and (b) criticism which provides compelling reasons to change for those we criticise. (b) is desirable to back up the moral condemnation of (a), but it will not always be easy to come by. Of course, for this account to be intuitively plausible, it remains to be shown that the class of moralities which we can criticise compellingly contains those moralities, such as Nazism, which we would want to place 'beyond the pale' — an exercise that I will undertake next. Nevertheless, this section has argued that moral criticism is always available for the relativist. Section two will further this analysis by asking, in the case of abhorrent moralities, whether these two kinds of criticism will suffice.

Abhorrent Moralities, Relativism and Toleration

Part 1: Relativism and Abhorrent Moralities
The most serious problem with this methodology as outlined above is one that seems, as I indicated earlier, to afflict most relativist proposals. That is, it will let into the realm of the 'justified' some moralities which we find abhorrent. The task of this section is to examine the relationship between relativism and moral horror. In so doing, I will show how relativist criticism of moralities can work, and discuss how much tolerance can be supported by the relativist account. The problem for relativism is that we are — quite rightly — resistant to extending the notions of justification (or tolerance, as I will go on to discuss) to moralities which sanction extreme human suffering. Nazism is often taken as the paradigm case of a morality that lies 'beyond the pale'. Part one of this section, then, aims to assess whether such horrific moralities are justified on my relativist account, and then discusses the consequences of my answer to this question. Part two of this section discusses the linked question of the relationship between relativism and tolerance. Another way of raising the same 'abhorrent moralities' objection is to argue that for relativists 'anything goes'. What does relativism say about tolerating other moralities, and what kinds of limits does it draw?

---

[10]   Of course, if Harman's account allows for some moralities being less well justified than others, then we can properly identify him with the middle position also.

It is my overall contention in part one that prominent examples of abhorrent moralities will fall outside the realm of justified moralities. In my argument below, I draw upon several examples of racist and fascist discourse to support my claim that they will fail the standards required of a justified morality, and to illustrate *how* such moralities will fail the standards. However, this is not to claim that *every* morality we find distasteful will fail the standard of interpersonal justification on the coherence relativist account. Thus, I will also consider the objection that a number of abhorrent moralities could pass the tests required of a justified morality in my schema and the resultant question of what would follow if some did. On these issues, I argue that accepting we cannot crack the justificatory system of an abhorrent moral view does not mean we should refrain either from criticising it or from coercing those who believe it. However, it ought to give us pause for thought before we do so.

The brand of relativism I have defended offers two potentially 'objective' criteria for justification (in the sense discussed in chapter four), and thus two factors which can always ground compelling criticism. The first is consistency with facts and within a belief system. The second is coherence, i.e. the mutual support of various elements of a person's moral framework. Advocating reflective equilibrium as an account of moral justification, the relativist can also draw on the importance of *reflection* on considered moral judgements. My account allows for several ways in which a moral system can be un- or under-justified in terms of a lack of consistency and coherence. It is my contention that these features allow the coherence relativist to rule out many repulsive moralities.

In this section I will illustrate this claim with reference to the following ways in which repulsive moral systems can be under-justified.

(i)   Inconsistency with the facts, where these, or the norms which determine them — e.g. ideas of scientific discovery and evidence — are accepted by the system.

(ii)   Internal inconsistency between different components of the framework.

(iii)   Latent inconsistency, where a framework is held by someone who, whilst she expresses support for that framework, also has a 'submerged' or unnoticed commitment to something at odds with it.

(iv)   The absence of rational reflection, when instead ideas appeal to and are endorsed immediately by the emotions alone. This can constitute the violation of the weak criteria for considered judgement that I outlined in chapter four.

These areas can be interlinked and overlap, as my brief analysis below will show.

I do not want to conduct here in-depth, systematic analyses of the meaning, core features and typology of racism, fascism or indeed any prejudice that I use to illustrate my contention below. Whilst such an analysis would strengthen my argument, it would also lengthen it considerably. Similarly, whilst I talk about some forms of abhorrent morality here, I do not, and cannot discuss them all. The continuum of acceptable-to-abhorrent moralities will vary for each person (though I believe cases such as fascism are held, and ought to be held, in common). Also, whilst I believe that sexism, for example, shares some features with racism, arguing that the same objection applies in both cases runs the risk of over-simplifying the relationship. Conversely, a separate analysis of all the moralities that I considered abhorrent, or that I considered that the reader would think beyond the pale, would needlessly over-complicate this section. Instead, my response below serves to indicate the kinds of ways in which the justifications for repulsive moral frameworks can be undermined.

(i) Inconsistency with facts and the norms that ought to determine them

Theories of racism can rely on scientific evidence of racial superiority to support discrimination, suppression or elimination. Many of the factual claims made in support of racist beliefs are simply false. For example, the neo-fascist West European Federation claimed in its 'racist catechism' of 1963 that 'racial hierarchy is an irrefutable and natural fact; the Aryan race is hierarchically superior to other races' (quoted in Griffin, 1996, 327). Racial science is evident also in the justification of the apartheid policy in South Africa (Dubow, 1995). For example, in support of a policy of segregation and the power of white South Africans, the psychologist M. L. Fick concluded that 'the available objective data point to a marked inferiority on the part of the native in comparison with Europeans' (Fick, 1929, 56). Proof that contemporary racial science is still an important contributor to racism is found in texts such as the journal Mankind Quarterly, or in *The Bell Curve*. Murray and Hernstein, the authors of *The Bell Curve*, maintain that raising IQ would cut crime, and that the difference found between the intelligence of whites and blacks is largely due to genetic differences between the races (Bell in Delgado and Stefancic, 1997, 534–7). A debate continues as to the extent to which the authors' presuppositions, prejudices and stereotypes determine their analysis, as well as being determined by them.

What is wrong with scientific racism is a failure to adopt agreed scientific standards in the research, for example in these three ways. First, it can be biased — for example, research into race under the Third Reich began from an assumption of Aryan superiority. Second, it can rely on out of date data — e.g. Jensen's 1969 reiteration of the argument that blacks are less intelligent than whites relied on data produced by William Galston a century before (Rosen and Lane in Delgado and Stefancic, 1997, 529). Third, it might draw conclusions about causation from instances of mere correlation, by failing to allow for environmental factors. For example, in *The Bell Curve*, Murray and Hernstein show a statistical *correlation* between IQ and social problems, but 'they repeatedly describe low IQ as a 'factor in,' 'a significant determinant', and a 'strong precursor' of various social maladies' (Judis, in Delgado and Stefancic, 1997, 531).[11]

Often, the bias itself can cause errors in reasoning or in the use of data. Of course, it can be claimed that there is no 'neutral' science, such claims often being accompanied by a demand for reflexivity and a greater sensitivity to the underlying assumptions of research. Even on this account, the bias I am talking about is constituted precisely by the failure to question the assumptions and motivations of the research. These errors constitute ways in which scientific racism fails to justify, or to form part of a justificatory circle with, racist belief and policy. Indeed, mistaking correlation for causation is not limited to 'scientists'. It can also be found in beliefs linking race, unemployment and laziness, or race and the decline of ancient civilisations.

Away from the racial-scientific realm, other factual inaccuracies occur in historical/empirical claims. These include the arguments behind Holocaust denial,[12] and the claim made by the Nazis in the 1930s that Germany was 'under attack by Jews' who had infiltrated German business and Government. This was used as a justification for a defensive war to eliminate them. For example:

[11] This book has attracted a large critical response. I quote an example of it here, 'the Bell Curve, with its claims and supposed documentation that race and class differences are largely caused by genetic factors and are therefore essentially immutable, contains no new arguments and presents no compelling data to support its anachronistic social Darwinism' (Gould, New Yorker, Nov. 28 1994, 139).

[12] Although I think a distinction can be made between those who argue the Holocaust never happened and those who argue it was not the result of a systematic policy of genocide, neither version is defensible.

> The history of Jewry is the history of the decline, not of the Jews, but of the people who offered Jews hospitality and rights of residence. Right from the start Jewry used the most ruthless ploys to attack him [a Nazi Author]. Or it operated so cleverly disguised within the German state apparatus that the man in the street could scarcely detect when and how the Jew was at work (Anon, quoted in Griffin ed. 1996, 145).[13]

The claim of a conspiracy of people in power and/or Jews against 'Aryan man' is still a common feature of neo-nazi discourse.[14]

(ii) Internal inconsistency (contradiction between beliefs)

The first section above, concerning different kinds of inconsistencies with agreed facts or agreed ways of determining the facts[15], is actually a subsection of a broader category of inconsistencies between beliefs (I take facts, entering belief-systems via perceptions, to form the basis of some reasons and beliefs). Under this heading I want to discuss, quite apart from the factual basis of the beliefs, inconsistencies between the beliefs themselves. For example, Allport argues in *The Nature of Prejudice* that stereotypes often contain contradictory statements, but have the capacity to absorb opposites so that one can be applied to a situation where the other is not applicable. Allport recounts the following conversation in his research;

> Mr A: I say the Jews are too much alone; they stick together and are clannish.
>
> Mr B: But look; in our community there are Cohen and Morris on the community chest, several Jews in the Rotary club and Chamber of Commerce. Many support our community projects.
>
> Mr A: That's just what I was saying, they're always pushing and elbowing their way into Christian groups (Allport, 1979, 195).

Allport picks out other instances of contradiction — e.g. the assertion that black people are aggressive and pushy, but also too laid back. I want to consider this in more detail later as part of a discussion of Goldberg's critique, which I will outline shortly.

---

[13] Notice that the Jews' influence could 'scarcely be detected', pointing to a lack of evidence in support of this claim.

[14] For example it surfaces as a justification for race war in *The Turner Diaries*, (Pierce, 1978).

[15] The Irving case exposed the extent to which, as far as Irving and similar revisionists are concerned, the Holocaust was not an 'agreed fact'. The debate must then move to the evidence or methodology utilised in generating the 'fact'.

(iii) Latent inconsistency

Apart from inconsistency within racist stereotyping and ideology, another inconsistency can lie latent between someone's professed beliefs and their intuitions. Could someone be a Christian who followed the teachings laid down in the Bible whilst simultaneously holding with Goebbels that Christ was a Nazi because 'life is an act of sacrifice for our neighbour and my neighbour *is he who has the same blood*' (Goebbels in Griffin ed. 1996, 120, my italics)?[16] How can someone hold simultaneously two such conflicting beliefs? Either one belief or the other must lie dormant (in some sense) before the contradiction is exposed. Similarly, could someone profess sincere compassion for the disabled, yet concur with the Nazi line that 'no pity is to be shown to those who occupy the lower categories of the inferior groups — cripples, epileptics, the blind . . . . (Von Saloman, quoted in Griffin ed. 1996, 119). In these cases we have a potential inconsistency and the moral framework is certainly not coherent. A person could rescue their position either by arguing that the two positions could sit alongside each other, or by jettisoning one of them. Nevertheless, the situation still constitutes a challenge to them to reflect on their belief system and the way they describe it.

(iv) Anti-rationalism

Whilst fascists and racists can and do concoct appropriate scientific, philosophical and factual claims as required, much of the appeal of such ideologies lie in their anti-rational nature, as Griffin notes (Griffin, 1996, 5-6). This anti-rational nature has, it seems to me, two components. First, the message is generally delivered charismatically, an appeal to the emotions rather than the intellect. In the oratory of racism, non-sequiturs, dubious connections and as we have seen, dubious factual claims matter little provided they are delivered correctly. For example, an Italian Fascist Magazine in the 1930s argued that:

> the mysticism of Fascism is the proof of its triumph. Reasoning does not communicate, emotion does. Reasoning convinces, it does not attract. Blood is stronger that syllogisms. Science claims to explain away miracles, but in the eyes of the crowd the miracle remains; it seduces and creates converts (Anon, quoted in Griffin 1996, 55).

---

[16] Of course, a contradiction only exists here if a Christian believes Jesus' commandment to 'love one's neighbour as oneself' extends beyond their own ethnic group. This is clearly the intention found in the doctrines of Catholic and Protestant churches; the fact that it is not always adhered to by individual church members — e.g. in Rwanda — merely points out the prevalence of inconsistency in individuals' moral systems.

Second and correspondingly, the reason for people adopting a racist or fascist standpoint can be fear or an appeal to threatened self-interest. There is a correlation between times or areas of economic depression and the adoption of racist beliefs, where immigrants or 'others' become an apparent immediate threat to prosperity and security. Manipulation of the emotions, especially pride and fear, is fascism's stock-in-trade. My contention here is that the appeal of fascism often lies in circumstances — the emotion of the 'patriotic' moment, rhetoric, fear — which fall foul of even weak constraints on considered moral judgements. These circumstances are not those in which we produce considered moral judgements. Whilst I do not want to argue that there is no role for the emotions or 'passions' in an account of morality and moral motivation,[17] an appeal to them which aims to bypasses rational judgement on the 'spur of the moment' (and which then catches up by rationalising the stance taken) must be seen as problematic. I argued in the chapter concerning reflective equilibrium that moral judgements made in certain circumstances are liable to error. The circumstances in which fascism 'seduces and creates converts', it seems to me, fall into this category. I also argued there that manipulated judgements, while perhaps being 'considered' in that rationalisations have been constructed for them, are likely to be uncovered by reflection. In this connection, I would add that an external critique of a person's justification can be a stimulus for this kind of reflection.

Problems

I have shown that coherence relativism can maintain that at least some abhorrent moralities are unjustified, in the kinds of ways I have indicated above. Here I want to consider two further points: (1) the extent of this coverage: are all abhorrent moralities doomed to fail the standard of justification? and (2) what bearing does the justified or unjustified nature of these moralities have on the criticisms we can make of them (and the action we are permitted take in response)?

(1) Will all abhorrent moralities fail to reach the standard of justification?

Goldberg, in *Racist Culture* (1994), argues that not all racisms are illogical or irrational, in two senses. First, they satisfy the common

---

[17] Indeed, my account places 'deep commitments' at the heart of moral motivation, and some (though by no means all) of these commitments could be emotional attachments.

criteria for rational systems of belief. Second, they are instrumentally rational in marrying means and ends. Goldberg stresses that for a system to be termed internally inconsistent, strict criteria have to be applied. In the case of the research cited by Allport, we are left not knowing whether the statements were made on similar occasions or over a period of time, with the person's view changing. If this had been the case, if the views were not held with regard to circumstances and persons that were relevantly similar, then there would be no inconsistency. Furthermore, some of the other contradictory statements Allport cites can be rendered consistent, so even were they pronounced at the same time about the same subject, the way in which they cohered could be explained (Goldberg, 1994, 130–3). Goldberg also argues that not all racist positions need include scientific evidence to support them, and stereotypes can be employed with degrees of generalisation to reduce the inaccuracy in applying them.

However, in turn, I think there are considerations limiting the application of Goldberg's criticisms. Whilst the logic of a racist might not be worked out well enough to satisfy strict inconsistency, that does not mean that when teased out it would not be inconsistent. Nor indeed that the position is not *incoherent*, in that the different aspects do not back each other up. For example, studies of racist attitudes toward Blacks in America during the 1950s found that they were seen as both scruffy and concerned about their appearance, laid back and aggressive (Allport, 1979, 196–8); these statements might perhaps be rendered consistent, but would still seem incoherent. That is, they would not be in strict logical contradiction, but they would seem to pull in different directions.[18]

Whilst Goldberg might be right that racist views reflect an appropriate marriage of ends and means, this does not count in their favour on either my own (nor a universalist) account of what is wrong with them. Furthermore, it seems to me that claims about the broad-based anti-rationalism of such ideologies have considerable basis in fact.[19] Goldberg fails to consider this as a feature of racism that has a bearing upon its rationality. In the end,

---

[18] They could be rendered consistent by explaining that blacks are laid back with regard to some things, and pushy with regard to others, for example. But for these two views to cohere, a story has to be told connecting the two, a story which has in turn to cohere with other elements of the racist world-view. Thus, coherence might be more difficult to satisfy in the face of sustained examination.

[19] One need only examine the amount of rhetoric and mythology produced by the Third Reich or Mussolini's Italian fascists while in power to see this in operation. Latter day fascists and racists too, operate by an

racism has to believe that some races or ethnic groups are superior to others. There has been no conclusive, valid proof to support this claim from science or philosophy. Fear and threatened pride unsupported by reflection, being exactly the kind of things that are likely to influence our 'considered moral judgements' unreasonably, are inadmissible as justification. The result is that such beliefs will always lack compelling justification, and so can always be condemned as wrong with powerful supporting reasoning.

However, this is not to say that there has never been, or never will be, an abhorrent morality with reasoning behind it we cannot fathom or refute by standards that the holders of that morality must accept. One cannot give any *a priori* argument which can prove that each and every morality we find repugnant can be refuted in this way. In some cases, there may be no compelling reasoning available to support our condemnation of such moralities. This, I want to go on to say here, prevents us from neither condemning nor coercing, but it should cause us to pause for reflection upon our own moral framework.

(2) Abhorrent moralities: criticism and restraint

I argued in section one that the coherence relativist can offer two kinds of criticism. Evaluative criticism of other moralities will always be available. In addition, in the case of unjustified moralities, a compelling critique of the justification for the abhorrent moral stance can be provided to back up the evaluative criticism. This means, for example, that when we confront the Nazi and he asks for reasons to support our rejection of his morality, we can give ones that he finds compelling. Coherence relativism, as a view about the nature of justification, says nothing by itself about the kind of responsibilities we have towards other moralities, justified or otherwise. Thus, it might be dangerous to speculate on exactly how abhorrent moralities should be treated. I do not believe that the answer I give here is *entailed* by preceding discussions of the nature of coherence relativism. However, I do want to venture some suggestions in this area, which seem to flow naturally from the way in which the problem is set out here.

As argued in section two of this chapter, the application of our morality can extend beyond the justification which others must

appeal to abstract ideas of glory and heroic spirit, combined with a calculated manipulation of fears of powerlessness and displacement. (An overview of the rhetoric of the KKK, Aryan Nations, and other hate groups can be found at www.hatewatch.co.uk. See also Solovyov, Klepikava, 1995).

accept. We can criticise without being able to justify our morality compellingly. So, even if an abhorrent morality is justified, in that we can find no flaws or errors beyond the fact that it disgusts us, we need not refrain from criticising it. Such a morality, despite its justification, might also fall outside the bounds of toleration. If we find a morality abhorrent and can criticise it strongly from within our moral scheme then nothing in the relativist programme prevents us from converting our criticism into action by coercing people who sign up to such a morality. Coercion might be justified, for example, by threats to civil peace or the violation of the established rights of other citizens.

However, relativism in justification perhaps justifies caution in how we treat other justified moralities. It is arguably appropriate that if we find a view offensive, but cannot find ways in which it is confused or contradictory, we ought not just to dismiss such a view out of hand. For one thing, to do so might limit the possibility of social criticism. The next step should be to examine our own views, to see whether *they* consist of mere prejudice. If we remain convinced that a view is both dangerous (taking into account wider considerations of social utility) and wrong, then we can still criticise it and coerce those who hold it,[20] though not necessarily on a basis that those who hold it would find convincing.

It might be objected that this strategy requires us to doubt ourselves too much, to consider our own morality and reflect upon whether we are wrong before standing up for what we believe. The account I am outlining, however, is not a novel answer to questions of what to do when we meet conflicting moralities. I did not intend to produce a Millian account of what to do with offensive moralities, but the account sketched above does share several features with his. It can be buttressed by Mill's passionate defence of the reasons for refraining from intolerance. Offence alone is not a sufficient ground for coercion. Freedom of opinion brings us to a livelier realisation of the truth, whether that is contained in our own views or those of our opponents, or to some measure in both (Mill, 1991, 59). I am not proposing, nor am I claiming Mill's support for, the idea that when someone presents us a moral view which deeply offends our most basic values, we should immediately be thrown into confusion as to what to do. But if we cannot find any factual evidence against their claim or flaws in their reasoning, if they are living their lives by it (i.e. it makes a broad kind

---

[20] This is not meant to imply that a view must be dangerous and wrong before we can criticise it; we can criticise it in any case, but it seems to me that the clearest prima facie case for coercion is where a view is dangerous, in that it incites hate, lawlessness, rights violations etc.

of sense) then we should reflect upon our own morality and engage in debate before automatically assuming they were wrong and we are necessarily right.

This idea sounds better applied to humanity's past than our humanitarian present. We can all agree that the sooner the slave owners considered the arguments against slavery, or the sooner arguments for sexual equality were listened to and conceded, the better. And we can all see the absurdity of the Pope's imprisonment of Galileo for his scientific position (which was not officially acknowledged as correct until 1992). 'We have progressed since then', a counter-argument might proceed, 'now we should not be asked to consider views that are obviously abhorrent and false'. I remain sceptical about the force of such a claim. Its tendency is to insulate us from the reality that we can and do make moral mistakes. If 'we' have indeed progressed, reflexivity and a willingness to see the others' side are surely two features of that progress.

Part 2: Relativism and Tolerance

The first part of this section applied my model of relativist moral criticism to the moral horror objection, discussing the criticism that on the relativist account, such moralities are equally justified and that no criticism can be offered. Another way of casting the same objection is to argue that the relativist might be required to *tolerate* such moralities. I want to approach a response to this claim through an analysis of the limits of toleration for a coherence relativist account. To complete my answer to the question 'what is the relativists' response to abhorrent moralities?' we must ask about the nature of the premises and conclusions of an argument linking toleration and relativism. Indeed, the question of the limits of toleration for the relativist is intimately linked with the kind of moral criticism relativists can offer, for to tolerate a view we must first think that it is wrong. Without an account of a relativist argument for tolerance, we will be unable to answer the question of whether relativism requires us to tolerate the intolerable. However, the question of the link between relativism and tolerance is both an important and controversial question in its own right. It will also provide an important link into part two, which looks at the relevance of relativism for arguments about neutrality. Nevertheless, partly because toleration is important in completing my account of the relativist response to moral horror, and partly because my analysis in chapters six and seven concentrates on neutrality in terms of state policy, I discuss this issue here rather than later. Therefore, the final part of this chapter discusses what a relativist argument for tolerance might look like.

Exactly what can relativism contribute to a justification of toler-ance? I intend to approach this question through an argument presented by David Wong. He contends that relativism forms a premise in one argument for toleration. Here, it should be said, I am taking a relatively uncontroversial definition of toleration, which I understand as being refraining from persecuting some-one despite having both motive and opportunity.[21] I conceive of toleration as a response to diversity on the part of individuals or groups, including (but not exclusively) the state. For the state, a concern about toleration is linked to the demand for neutrality, as I discuss in chapters six and seven. I will argue that coherence rel-ativism can contribute to a distinctive liberal justification of toler-ation, and discuss some possible objections to my position. This will involve setting out the precise premises and conclusions of such an argument and meeting a number of common objections. In particular, I want to discuss at some length the objection that ethics or morality is in some sense independent of questions about the nature of moral meaning and justification. The concern here is that metaethical analyses of issues such as relativist accounts of moral justification do not impact on normative ethical questions. An analysis of this question also allows me to locate the role of relativism in my argument for toleration.

David Wong's Argument: Relativism and the Justification Principle

As I have mentioned, Williams dismisses the possibility of relativ-ism grounding tolerance as 'absurd' (Williams 1973, 34). For crit-ics such as Williams the argument they are criticising proceeds thus:[22]

(a) Neither side can prove his case

Therefore

(b) Neither has a right to impose his own views.

---

[21] This definition is given, for example, by Susan Mendus (Mendus, 1988, 3–5).

[22] Geoffrey Harrison, in his analysis of the argument from relativism to tol-erance, argues that it confuses two positions we can take on morality. Relativism is a view of morality — the view of what Harrison terms an 'observer'. By contrast, toleration belongs to the concrete realm of moral judgements. Thus the argument proceeds by deriving 'a participant's conclusions' from 'an observer's premises' (Harrison, 1976, 132–3) — a move he thinks is illegitimate. This split between observer and partici-pant, or metaethics and ethics, is something I will examine shortly.

As Wong points out, Williams is right when he criticises such an interpretation; and he is also right that a number of people, amongst them 'notorious' anthropologists such as Herskovits, appear to hold just such a view.[23] However, a better interpretation can be given of arguments that proceed from relativism to tolerance. Wong writes

> The relativist arguments for tolerance that nonphilosophers give are typically vague and incomplete. They are subject to multiple and conflicting interpretations . . . Harrison and Williams neglect the possibility that the relativist arguments of nonphilosophers also can be interpreted as arguments from moral relativism and one or more ethical premises to tolerance (Wong, 1986, 180).

Wong interprets such arguments as containing a 'suppressed ethical premise'. If we set out this premise, they would run more like this

(a) Neither side can prove his case

(b) It is wrong to impose one's views on another person unless one can justify them to him or her

Therefore

(c) Neither has a right to impose his own views.

This premise (b) is an ethical premise, supplied, if it is to be supplied at all, by the agent's own moral viewpoint. Wong believes that Kantianism and Millian rule-utilitarianism both contain formulations of this idea, which he calls the justification principle, that 'one should not interfere with the ends of others unless one can justify the interference to be acceptable to them' (Wong, 1986, 181).[24] Wong takes some version of this principle to be held by many liberals, and it is this principle combined with metaethical relativism that yields tolerance. This combination allows that a view about the nature of ethics might be relevant to the individual in deciding how to react to other ethical systems.

---

[23] Brian Barry is another thinker who has criticised this kind of argument. He writes 'a remarkably hardy fallacy is the idea that moral relativism can be invoked as a basis for religious and other forms of toleration' (Barry, 2000, 133).

[24] Whether either approach buys into the justification principle is not something I want to go into detail about here. I discuss later how widespread some version of the justification principle might be. I *am* concerned, in chapters six and seven, to show how contemporary liberal accounts adopt this kind of principle.

Coherence Relativism and the Justification Principle

I want to suggest that the argument Wong makes can be utilised pretty directly by the account of coherence relativism which I have given. Whilst I have criticised Wong's account of relativism because of the universalistic limits it set on the sphere of adequate or justified moral systems, I believe Wong's account of the argument for toleration is accurate, and can be used independent of his larger relativist schema. In the form I want to advance here, his argument might be written thus:

(a)   There are a number of equally justified moralities

(b)   It is wrong to take action to impose our views on others unless ours are better justified.

Therefore

(c)   It is wrong to take action to impose our morality on others who possess an equally justified morality.

The above formulation assumes something about the nature of being 'better justified'. I take this notion to consist in an appeal to intersubjective superiority in the relevant factors. For the coherence relativist, for example, these factors would be coherence and consistency. Premise (a), fully explained, would have to say something about the nature of justification to explain how multiple justified moralities could result. As I argued in chapter four, coherence relativism holds that some moralities may share the same amount of justification on an account of justification as coherence and consistency. In such a situation, from an overview of the moralities of others and ourselves, we could have no reason for saying that our morality was superior.

The argument for toleration I have outlined is supported by a relativist premise (a) about the nature of justification, and what I would hesitantly call a liberal moral premise (b), which determines what ought to be done about the moralities justified or unjustified by the relativist metaethical view.[25] The justification principle, i.e. the liberal moral premise, is common to the work of modern liberals such as Rawls and Larmore, for whom it forms an explicit part of their arguments for state neutrality.[26] As I argued

[25]   This is not to say that the moral premise concerning justification I supply here is the *only* moral premise that could be held in conjunction with the relativist premise (a).

[26]   Rawls, for example, insists that a 'public and shared basis of justification' would be required 'to mark the difference between comprehensive beliefs as such and true comprehensive beliefs'. It is unreasonable, on Rawls' account, to 'insist . . . on what they take to be true but others do

earlier, this liberal premise need not be held hesitantly by a relativist, or as a purely subjective or powerless thought. It can be used to judge action, and attain (backed by appropriate justification) objective force. The metaethical premise is supplied by many forms of relativism, including the coherence relativism that I advocate here. The moral premise (b) is crucial to the argument. Whilst relativism informs us that the nature of justification is such that there can be several equally justified moralities, it says nothing about how we should treat them. However, this should not be taken to mean that the relativist metaethical premise does no work in the argument. Consider if (a) were replaced with

(a1) There is a single true morality — my own.

Then combined with the justification principle, no duty to tolerate need be yielded.[27] Whilst premise (b) is an injunction to tolerate all moralities of set [X], premise (a) defines the content of set [X]. In any given situation, deciding whether to tolerate another morality or not is a conclusion reached from both these premises.

There is no logical reason why relativism must be allied to the justification principle. Different principles or different accounts of the justification principle will set the boundaries of tolerance circumscribed by such an argument differently. For example, the moral premise might be one dictating no link between justification and toleration, and instead indicating that we should allow other people freedom for their moralities only to the extent their morality matches our own. Such an account, if it referred to other justificatory factors other than those allowed by coherence relativism (e.g. to explain why one morality was uniquely correct), would not constitute an argument from relativism to intolerance.

Possible Objections

The above sketch of the relationship between relativism and toleration is open to a number of objections, some of which I shall address below. David Wong answers many in an instructive discussion following his proposal linking the two ideas(Wong, 1986, 184–90). These include explaining why a relativist might hold a Kantian justification principle, and a specific response to Harrison's arguments against the link (see footnote 22 in this chapter).

---

not' (Rawls, 1993, 61). I discuss Rawls' position in more detail in chapters six and seven.

[27] Of course various modifications to the argument, including additional premises, could still yield this conclusion. For example, one precept of the sole true ethical view could be tolerance of those moralities which were wrong.

Here I want to concentrate on three important objections. (1) One might challenge the assumption underlying this argument, that metaethical conclusions can form premises in normative arguments. As a substantial issue in moral philosophy in its own right, I want to examine this issue at some length here. As well as explaining the sense in which questions of the nature of morality can impact on questions of how we should act morally, an examination of this debate also allows a clearer picture of the role of metaethical and ethical premises in the argument. (2) We can question the scope of the argument; how many people really hold something like the justification principle? Does this argument have relevance beyond liberalism? (3) One can ask about the status of the injunction to tolerate, and the limits to this principle of toleration.

(1) Ethics and metaethics

It is often thought that the study of ethics proceeds on two levels; on the first level, *normative ethics*, we ask what it is that we ought to do. On the second level, *metaethics*, we ask how we should understand moral claims and how we ought to decide what it is that we ought to do. The argument for tolerance that I just considered includes, I have argued, a premise about the nature of justification — what I take to be a metaethical claim — and results in the decidedly normative claim that we should tolerate others. I suggested, following Wong, that a moral premise had to be added to the argument to make sense of it. However, the exact role of the metaethical premise in such an argument is hard to characterise accurately. Discussing this issue here clarifies how relativism contributes to a defence of toleration and thus contributes to my defence of relativism against the charge that it leaves us helpless in the face of abhorrent moralities.

Before examining this question, it is necessary to define more precisely the terms involved in this debate. Metaethics, as I use it here, is comprised of questions concerning the purpose and nature of ethics. It concerns the basis upon which we can evaluate different moral theories and what truth or justification consist in with regard to ethical questions. I want to use the term metaethics in a wider sense than that in which it has sometimes been employed. Originally, metaethics was associated with 'an analysis of the language and logic employed in the moral discourse' (Finnis, 1983, 27). Such a meaning became attached to the term during what Harman calls 'the period of linguistic philosophy . . . when many English-speaking philosophers toyed with the idea that philosophy might be nothing but the analysis of language'

(Harman, 1977, vii). Thus, the metaethical analyses of Hare, Foot, Stevenson, Ayer and others focused on questions of the meaning of moral terms.[28] Subsequently, the content of metaethics changed as philosophers argued that metaethics was concerned with the nature of moral justification, the nature of the link between morality and reason, and the account we give of moral reasons (Finnis, 1983, 28). For example the metaethical component, for Harman, of 'philosophical ethics' lies in a 'properly philosophical account of the meaning and justification of moral judgements' (Harman, 1977, vii). I want to take metaethics in its second broader sense, in which questions of justification and reasoning, as well as meaning, are the explicit focuses.[29] Questions of the nature of moral justification are questions about the nature of ethics. By contrast, normative ethics is associated with 'the study of our substantive moral conceptions' (Rawls, 1972, 52), and thus, with deciding what we ought to do.

Argument has continued over whether the two realms of the ethical and metaethical are largely independent of each other. Certainly, the conclusion that concepts of truth and justification are relative to individuals' moral systems seems far removed from the concrete solving of moral problems such as abortion or tolerance. A good example of this is Rawls' argument for the independence of normative ethics. In 'The Independence of Moral Theory' Rawls suggests that 'a central part of moral philosophy is what I have called the comparative study of moral conceptions, which is, in large part, independent' (Rawls, 1999a, 301). In the paper, Rawls discusses the claim that moral theory is independent in particular from moral epistemology and a theory of meaning, areas which are often regarded as 'methodologically prior to it' (Rawls, 1999a, 302).[30] His later liberalism is 'political' in part

---

[28] For example, Hare refers to metaethics as 'the logical study of the language of morals' (Hare, 1972, iii).

[29] This does not commit me to a full account of the meaning of moral terms, and the fact that my argument focuses on the 'justification' component does not imply that I deem discussions of meanings unimportant. One cannot discuss the nature of moral justification without discussing the meaning of moral justification. Conversely, discussing the meanings of the terms 'moral' and 'justification', without discussing what renders a moral judgement justified, does not take us very far.

[30] Indeed, Rawls indicates that in some sense, normative ethics might be prior to metaethics. He believes that doing normative ethics will eventually make disagreements in metaethics more tractable: 'if we can find an accurate account of our moral conceptions, then questions of meaning and justification may prove much easier to answer. Indeed some of them may no longer be real questions at all' (Rawls, 1972, 50).

because it wants to utilise concepts of public reason and reason-ableness to bypass questions of the nature of truth.

There are two particular ways in which normative ethics can be seen to involve questions of metaethical truth and justification. We can see this in Rawls' use of reflective equilibrium — a concept central to the exposition of coherence relativism. Here, following Griffin, I will argue against the idea that the 'comparative study of moral conceptions' (Rawls, 1999a, 301) can be completed without straying into metaethics (Griffin, 1996, 145). The first point, iden-tified by Griffin, is the idea that reflective equilibrium cannot be fully explicated without giving answers to questions about *how* it justifies. He denies the possibility of a 'test powerful enough to rank competing normative views, while ignoring questions about objectivity, truth, and knowledge' (Griffin, 1996, 144). Our confi-dence in, and the power of, any coherence test requires us to answer important metaethical questions first.

The second point reinforces this view. Wide reflective equilib-rium draws upon a wide area of justification, comprising various moral and non-moral ideas. Some components of a coherent wide equilibrium are to be found in other non-moral areas of philoso-phy, such as ideas of personal identity; others include prudential interests which must be taken into account. It is impossible to achieve a wide reflective equilibrium without considering ques-tions of what counts as a good reason to hold a moral position, and without giving an account of elements such as objectivity. A coherent theory that can give no answer to the question, 'that con-clusion is fine for you, but why should I accept your reasons for it?' is surely problematic. Any sufficiently deep questioning of a coherent moral position would involve asking for metaethical reasons, reasons which concern the nature of the justification and truth being offered, at some point in the regress.

I have suggested that ethics and metaethics cannot be con-ceived of as being entirely independent.[31] Hence, there is no bar-rier to relativism providing a metaethical component of an ethical argument for toleration. Metaethical relativism will not, by itself, entail a particular moral outcome. Nevertheless, a commitment to relativism can influence the conclusion by requiring us not to act in a way inconsistent with that belief. Metaethical relativism, or any of the competing views about the nature of moral justifica-tion, will operate at a deep level in any moral theory in wide

[31] My argument here has been directed against Griffin's interpretation of Rawls, rather than necessarily Rawls himself. Rawls comments that he does not care 'for independence too strictly understood' (Rawls, 1999a, 302).

reflective equilibrium, and can be used as a reason to support action. Consider the following case, of B asking A to justify his position.

A: 'We ought to tolerate that morality.'

B: 'Why?'

A: 'I believe that intolerance is only justified by the fact that my morality is superior to someone else's. And in this case it isn't.'

B: 'Their morality is as good as ours? By what standard?'

A: 'I believe that moralities are justified only to the extent that they are consistent and coherent.'

At a certain level in the argument, the reasons for a normative ethical position become metaethical ones. Any metaethical position determines what reasons are available to a moral view at this level of the debate. It does not determine a unique conclusion, but does determine the range of compatible and incompatible metaethical reasons. In the case of metaethical relativism, the inclusion of a premise saying that there is no single justified morality would render untenable any appeal in the same argument to the idea that there *is* a single justified morality. The determination of a range of reasons might lead in practice (though I will not take this suggestion up here) to the determination of a range of conclusions.

(2) The justification principle

So far, I have clarified the role that the metaethical premise can play in the argument. However, potential problems also cluster around the ethical premise. An objector might well argue that if the justification principle is a liberal one, this justification of toleration is only for liberals. For those who do not hold something like the justification principle, the above argument is irrelevant. This criticism, I believe, has some force. Wong's argument is intended to show that there is an argument for toleration, involving relativism, made by relativists within liberal societies. My adoption of the argument, resting on a particular specification of a relativist idea of justification, shares the limits of Wong's. It is worth pointing out, however, that these limits may not be as severe as they appear. I noted above that Wong also finds an argument for the justification principle in the works of Mill. Wong argues that the justification principle is a way of protecting what Mill would conceive of as a fundamental component of well-being, individual autonomy. 'When an individual's freedom is restricted in such a way that it cannot be justified to him or her, the kind of growth that Mill thought essential to well-being is frustrated. It is reasonable to lay down the justification principle to protect the general welfare' (Wong, 1986, 184).

Wong's exegesis of Mill is controversial, to say the least. Nevertheless his basic point that a justification principle is *one possible* way to protect people's freedom is, I think, a fair one. Moreover, we can interpret justification as being close to an idea of informed consent. Informed consent can only be gained by offering a justification for the proposal at issue, which is then assented to. The preference of liberals for informed consent is an endorsement of the idea that reasons should be offered and accepted as a legitimation of a proposal. Thus, the justification principle might be thought of intrinsically valuable as a requirement for informed consent, or as being instrumentally valuable as a way to promote autonomy or the common good. This second thought might appeal to those who find it an appropriate response to diversity for the political realm, if not always governing the private.

The justification principle can find purchase wherever people are committed to giving reasons for actions or positions — though this should not be taken to mean that, by virtue of feeling the need to give justifications, people would be committed to the same *version* of the justification principle. The problem arises of exactly how we specify the justification principle; whether we are required to justify intolerance to people *as they are*, or people *were they rational or reasonable*. Different comprehensive moralities, different varieties of liberalism even, will have different views on this. Consequently, the amount of toleration required by the combination of the justification principle and relativism will vary with the interpretation of the principle. Furthermore, as I noted above, if someone believes himself or herself in possession of the sole moral truth, the justification principle will not yield toleration (unless the sole moral truth itself implies toleration). All this serves to clarify what we can expect from the justification principle. It is not a panacea, and operates most easily as *part* of a *liberal* argument for toleration.

(3) The limits of toleration

My central concern here is with two strands of criticism of relativism. On the one hand, the charge is that relativism cannot justify toleration, and on the other, relativism stands accused of requiring us to tolerate the morally repugnant. So far, I have looked in more detail at the content of and relationship between the two *premises* in an argument linking relativism and tolerance. Here I want to examine the *conclusion* and highlight its limits, in order to show that relativism does not prompt unlimited toleration. The conclusion of the argument I have examined is not that we should *always* tolerate, nor that toleration can *never* be overridden for other moral or even prudential reasons. If it did, it would be supplying what it could not justify. As well as the variable content of the justification principle, the exact weight given to the injunction to tolerate vis-à-vis other moral judgements would differ between moral systems. It is quite possible that a conflict could arise between the principle of toleration and other duties or principles that might be considered more important by the agent. In such a situation, toleration need not win, and I suspect that this matches our intuitions. The existence of such ethical conflicts, and the overturning of toleration for the sake of other values is consonant with at least some liberal views of toleration. For liberals other ethical demands place limits on the principle of toleration — one such common limit is that we need not tolerate the intolerant.[32]

There is another way in which my proposal limits the sphere of views to be tolerated; that is, the argument above only requires toleration of equally justified moralities. I have assumed here that the major reason for intolerance is the surety and superiority of one view vis-à-vis others. The argument only addresses this particular reason for intolerance; it supports the obligation to tolerate those moralities that are equally justified. Because of its limited scope, its silence on other moralities does not imply that there are no possible reasons for tolerating moralities that are not equally justified. There may be considerations — another moral injunction within one's moral framework, or prudential considerations, or charity in a situation of incommensurability — which mitigate in favour of tolerance of moralities that do not share the same amount and kind of justification. It is also possible that the duty to tolerate at least those equally justified moralities will on occasion be weighted against other values and will 'lose'. This, as I indicated above, is not a problem for the argument, but rather a qualification of its force. Furthermore, qualifying the conclusion like this makes the argument more attractive rather than less, for this surely matches our experience. A requirement to put toleration first every time is counter-intuitive. Thus, in this part of my response to the 'abhorrent moralities' charge, I have outlined an argument linking coherence relativism and toleration. I have

---

[32]   Of course, we might still be willing to tolerate some people who espouse intolerant views, for example if they did not have the power to translate them into practice.

been careful to note, however, that relativist tolerance need not be boundless.

Conclusion

This chapter has examined coherence relativism and its relation to our moral experience. Having examined some of the demands of our moral experience in chapter four, the purpose of this chapter has been to discuss two further important elements of our moral experience. The first was that relativism must allow us to engage in moral criticism. The second, linked to this, was that relativism had to give us a response to abhorrent moralities. The second of these areas also demanded that I examine whether relativism prompted tolerance, and if so, how much tolerance. We are now in a position to respond to these questions. Two kinds of moral criticism are open to the coherence relativist. The relativist always has the possibility of condemning (evaluative criticism), and will be able to back that up with compelling reasons (compelling criticism) whenever they encounter an unjustified morality. In response to the second point, I have argued that prominent examples of abhorrent moralities are unjustified on a coherence relativist scheme. But what about those abhorrent moralities that are justified? Relativism can form part of a distinctive justification of tolerance. However, this tolerance is not boundless and the argument should be viewed in the context of a wider moral scheme, of which tolerance is only a part.

Having argued that relativism can serve as part of arguments for toleration, I now move on to the second part of the book. I will argue there that it forms part of liberal arguments for neutrality. This is the work of chapters six and seven. Of these, chapter six will provide an overview of neutrality and a discussion of political liberalism's arguments for neutrality. Chapter seven will set out my argument for the relevance of relativism.

Part 2

Chapter 6

Liberal Neutrality

Introduction

The second part of this work shifts the focus away from questions of metaethics and ethics to ones of political theory. In the previous chapter, I argued that relativism could contribute to a distinctive liberal defence of toleration. This part examines the relevance of relativism for contemporary liberal defences of state *neutrality*. In my initial survey of liberal ideas of state neutrality, I will postpone questions about the relevance of relativism until chapter seven. This chapter analyses the idea of liberal neutrality between differing conceptions of the good. I shall begin by considering the nature of liberal neutrality, and setting out the terms that I use in my analysis. I then move on to examine liberal defences of neutrality. I will argue here that such defences can be divided into two types, neutral and non-neutral. Neutral justifications of neutrality are those providing a justification which all could accept without disregarding their own cultures or ways of life. Non-neutral justifications are based on controversial ethical premises, which may limit their appeal.[1] I take Mill's justification of state neutrality as an example of a non-neutral justification. On the other hand, theorists such as John Rawls and Charles Larmore have attempted to provide neutral justifications of neutrality.

The central contention of this chapter is that these defences are all problematic, though some more than others. In particular I want to contend that they fail to deliver a *neutral* justification of neutrality, and that whilst denying the presence of controversial

---

[1] By controversial, I mean that they are contingently viewed as such by people. On this definition, whenever a justification is not controversial, it is neutral.

metaethical foundations, all in fact have controversial and confused metaethical positions at their base. The focus of my analysis is on the metaethical foundations of these approaches and the character of the *neutral justification* of neutrality they offer. All the defences of neutrality examined here are rich and complex, and to consider them in their entirety lies beyond my scope. I will concentrate here on these metaethical issues, the discussion of which provides the crucial first stage of my argument (concluded in chapter seven) that relativism can provide a plausible set of metaethical foundations for political liberal arguments.

The Idea of Neutrality Between Conceptions of the Good

I am concerned in this chapter with the idea of neutrality as a lack of bias applied to the arena of state policy. Work on neutrality by thinkers such as Raz (1986), Arneson (1990), Kymlicka (1989b, 1990 199–207), Rawls (1993), Waldron (1989) and Dworkin (1985) draws distinctions between kinds of neutrality. I want to invoke a distinction, common to most of these analyses, between neutrality of *outcome*[2] and neutrality of *aim* or justification.[3] According to the former, a state policy is neutral if it has the same impact on all people or conceptions of the good. This neutrality of effect contrasts with what has been termed neutrality of justification or aim. According to this latter idea of neutrality, a state policy is neutral if it does not draw its justification or purpose from any particular controversial conception of the good. It is entirely possible that a policy neutral in aim — not intended to further a particular idea of the good — nevertheless impacts differentially on different ideas of the good. For example, suppose that a democratic government institutes a rule that bladed weapons should be banned for reasons of public safety. Though not justified by reference to a particular conception of the good, nevertheless it will disproportionately affect the ways of life of martial artists and followers of some religious traditions — for example, druidism. Like all the liberal neutralists and their critics whom I cited above, my primary concern here is with neutrality of aim.

[2]   We can distinguish between various meanings of 'outcome' here. For example, equal outcome can refer to an equal effect on the welfare of those affected, or equal success, in the sense that the proposal works equally well in respect of those affected.

[3]   A further distinction between ideas of neutrality of *justification* and *aim* could be introduced. However, for my purposes I assume that the aim of a project ought to constitute a large portion of its justification. I should also make clear that I will not discuss here neutrality of *procedure*, which requires that the process determining state policy should be agreed-upon by all.

The focus for neutrality, as it is used by most egalitarian liberals, is the conceptions of the good held by citizens. A conception of the good is a set of commitments that a person values — what Waldron refers to as their 'tastes, aims, and ideas' (Waldron, 1989, 76). It can be thought of in terms of preferences, as in Dworkin's case of 'the television-watching, beer-drinking citizen who is fond of saying 'This is the life' (Dworkin, 1985, 191). However, the language of commitments should, I believe, be preferred for doing less injustice to people — religious or secular — for whom preference might not capture the strength of their feeling about their way of life. It should be noted that Rawls prefers the term 'comprehensive doctrine' to describe such a more or less consistent and persistent set of beliefs and ideas about the world, and I use the terms more or less interchangeably here.[4]

Neutral and Non-Neutral Justifications of Neutrality

Having explained what the kind of neutrality I am concerned with here involves, I want to invoke a distinction, most recently used by Colin Bird, between different *justifications* for neutrality (taken as the position that the state policy should not rest on a particular controversial conception of the good). Some possible justifications, says Bird, are themselves *non-neutral*. That is, they justify neutrality of procedure on grounds that are controversial, or perhaps potentially controversial. Bird suggests we should strive for a *neutral* justification of neutrality; a neutral justification being one 'which displays a certain kind of neutrality toward individuals' controversial conceptions of the good; just as the neutral state must not rank or favor particular moral ideals, a neutral justification must not involve such controversial moral ideals' (Bird, 1996, 63).

Non-neutral justifications rely on a conception of the good that some dispute. Their justificatory force is limited to those who accept or can accept the controversial conception. However, many recent defences of liberal neutrality have claimed to provide *neutral* justifications. In this chapter I will discuss defences by Rawls, Larmore, and Bird. Other thinkers who aim to provide such a neutral justification include Dworkin (1985), Arneson (1990), Feinberg (1973), and Ackerman (1980, 1989). Later in this chapter I discuss these justifications to see if they attain a suffi-

[4] Rawls lays down quite a strict idea of what constitutes a fully or partially comprehensive doctrine (Rawls, 1993, 13). I see this as one liberal theorist's working out of the idea of a conception of the good. Whilst it might differ from other liberals' interpretations in various ways, I do not believe this difference is important to the central thrust of this chapter.

cient degree of neutrality.[5] First, as an exemplar of a non-neutral justification of neutrality, I will briefly set out Mill's argument for a kind of neutrality.

J.S. Mill's Non-Neutral Justification of Neutrality

As an example of what a non-neutral justification looks like, we need look no further than J.S. Mill's *On Liberty*. There Mill argues that state and public toleration of different ways of life should be based on the supremely important good of individuality. Mill writes,

> free development of individuality is one of the leading essentials of well-being ... it is not only a co-ordinate element with all that is designated by the terms civilisation, instruction, education, culture, but is itself a necessary part and condition of all those things (Mill, 1991, 63).

Individuality, for Mill, has 'intrinsic worth', and this explains why society should allow the freest possible expression of different ways of living. Like almost any interpretation of a thinker, this view of Mill is controversial. Mill does think there is a case for the government to have a role in 'giving advice and promulgating information' (Mill, 1891, 603). However, 'laisser faire should be the general practice: every departure from it, unless justified by some great good, is a certain evil' (Mill, 1891, 609).[6]

For those who do not share Mill's commitment to the value of individuality, his assumptions of the possibility and desirability of autonomy make the proposal problematic. Such critics include those who endorse what Larmore has termed the 'romantic' critique of individualism (Larmore, 1996, 129). Communitarians such as MacIntyre and Sandel will find much to argue with, asserting instead the primacy of social roles in character and belief formation, and of a society based on a 'politics of a common good' (Kymlicka, 1990, 216).[7]

Charles Larmore's Neutralist Proposal

By contrast with Mill's approach, many contemporary liberals — Rawls and Larmore for example — aim to provide a justification

---

[5]   I assume here that as well as being entirely neutral or non-neutral, we can distinguish *degrees* of neutrality.

[6]   Support for my interpretation of Mill comes, for example, from Joseph Raz who characterises Mill's harm principle as a defence of toleration by the state (Raz, 1994, 158).

[7]   Whilst I do not think communitarians would endorse Mill's characterisation of individuality as necessarily primary and intrinsically valuable, this is not to say that they could not advocate policies which mirrored those of Mill.

of neutrality which is itself neutral between conceptions of the good life. In *Patterns of Moral Complexity* and *The Morals of Modernity*, Larmore offers a powerful argument for building the state on neutral principles. 'Neutral principles' writes Larmore, 'are ones we can justify without assuming the validity of those views of the good on which people reasonably disagree' (Larmore, 1996, 126). Furthermore, Larmore is concerned to offer a neutral justification of this ideal, in the sense that

> we must look to a core morality that is, as much as possible, common ground. It may be too hopeful to expect that this moral basis will escape every element of controversy. But it must certainly be neutral enough to accommodate people who value belonging and custom (Larmore, 1996, 133).

In this section, I intend to present, and then criticise, Larmore's justification for neutrality. I argue that it is problematic, primarily because it is itself predicated on a contentious view of the good. It thereby fails the criterion for a 'neutral' justification in exactly the way that Larmore says it should fulfil it.

Rational Dialogue and Equal Respect

Larmore's justification of liberal neutrality relies on two moral 'norms' which he believes command wide assent and thus do not violate the requirements of a neutral justification; it is, in that sense, a 'minimal' justification. The norm of rational dialogue says that if people face disagreement on a particular issues, they

> should respond by retreating to neutral ground, to the beliefs they still share, in order either to (a) resolve the disagreement . . . by means of arguments that proceed from this common ground, or (b) bypass the disagreement and seek a solution of the problem on the basis simply of this common ground (Larmore, 1996, 135).

For example, consider a hypothetical debate concerning pornography. Two people can disagree about whether pornography ought to be prohibited, but still agree on some common reasoning. For example, they might agree that individuals had rights to self-expression, or that one duty of the state was to protect people from pernicious material. This common ground could constitute the kind of idiom within which one person could justify her position in terms the other could understand (indeed, Larmore thinks justification necessarily involves common ground (Larmore, 1996, 135)), or constitute the basis for a compromise solution weighing these two considerations.

As Larmore says, 'If the people still wish to solve the given problem, and if they are committed to solving it through rational discussion, then they have no choice but to find the solution on the basis of beliefs they both share' (Larmore, 1996, 135). The above norm only tells us what to do if we are committed to finding reasonable agreement. What we need is a reason to adopt this commitment. For Larmore, this reason is the norm of equal respect for persons. This is expressed by the Kantian formula of treating people never as means, but rather as ends in themselves. Larmore writes:

> What is prohibited by the norm of equal respect is resting compliance only on force. For the distinctive feature of persons is that they are beings capable of thinking and acting on the basis of reasons. If we try to bring about conformity to a political principles simply by threat, we will be treating people solely as means, as objects of coercion (Larmore, 1996, 137).

Coercion is a clear case of treating people as means. Thus, Larmore is able to draw unequivocal support for equal respect from the Kantian position. However, he does not intend it to be the *only* source of justification for equal respect. Indeed, his proposal claims to be neutral precisely because communitarian critics of Kantianism can also assent to it.

Before setting out my criticisms of this position, two further elements must be added to complete my account of Larmore's argument. First, Larmore maintains that the people involved have to be interested in forming a political community; otherwise, their first response to diversity could be 'disband, or to switch their allegiance elsewhere' (Larmore, 1996, 143). Second, Larmore's position presupposes that citizens reflecting on questions of political organisation are required to put the norms of equal respect and rational dialogue above their other commitments; these two ideas take priority. Part of the reason why these ideas take priority is that Larmore also insists the two norms are valid and correct, not simply taken as such (Larmore, 1996, 146). I think this contention is significant, and will return to it below.

I believe that the status and content of these two norms are sufficiently controversial for reasonable people not to agree on them, and certainly not on the priority they are given. 'Reasonable people' says Larmore, 'are those who think and converse in good faith and apply, as best they can, the general capacities of reason that belong to every domain of enquiry' (Larmore, 1996, 169). The first question to be asked is whether the retreat to neutral ground really does constitute a 'norm' of rational dialogue for reasonable people. One way to approach this might be to ask whether Larmore's reasonable disagreements do in fact possess a significant amount of neutral ground. It is not always easy to divine in arguments exactly what is common to two opposing positions;

this is because often what varies in positions is the weighting attached to different values. I want to discuss and criticise two potential aspects of the idea of 'neutral ground'.

One aspect concerns the substance of the disagreement. Larmore might argue that positions share the same views on some meaningful, substantive propositions — as in the pornography case above. In response, my first claim might be put like this: in many persistent, reasonable disagreements, there is in fact very little neutral ground to retreat *to*, and that is exactly why these disagreements are reasonable and persistent. Thus, we can interpret the above case of pornography legislation as a situation where, whilst both positions share the same considerations, the different *weightings* produce the different views. For there to be substantive neutral ground, what is required is agreement in weighting or ranking of considerations; otherwise, the neutral ground is illusory. In chapter three, I discussed this issue with regard to contingent universalism, but noted that universalists need not be committed to equal weighting, merely a certain common set of principles. The problem for Larmore is more pressing, since substantive neutral ground is more demanding than an unranked list of common moral values. For that neutral ground to be substantive, it has to consist not only of agreement that some issues are relevant, but also agreement on the weighting attached to those issues. If weightings are not considered important then what we count as neutral ground will actually disguise a fundamental aspect of the disagreement. Such a foundation would not be an adequate one on which to reach agreement. Conversely, we will be unlikely to find a disagreement characterised by general agreement on issues and their weighting, because in such a case we would not expect a persistent disagreement. [8]

Furthermore, the idea that 'facts' would constitute common ground has limited applicability for disagreements where the 'facts' themselves are the subject of the dispute. For example, different sides of the abortion debate will regard the idea that an embryo constitutes a person after a certain time as either a true fact, or seriously mistaken. [9] Opposing sides would also weigh the

---

[8]   These comments foreshadow what I say in chapter seven, where I discuss how we understand this kind of disagreement.

[9]   As I noted in chapter four, for the relativist there might easily be disagreements about 'the facts', because of the possibility of these apparent truths being generated by different frameworks of norms; for example, by empirical scientific methodologies or metaphysical claims about the world. What is needed is at least a shared set of norms upon which to decide what constitutes a fact.

rights of the potential mother and the rights of any potential child differently. It is far from clear, however, that disagreements between different people will also involve areas of agreement. Otherwise, there might be no persistent disagreement to begin with. For Larmore's idea of neutral ground to constitute a 'norm' there has to be a number of cases where there is meaningful common ground, but not so much that in fact the disagreement is minor, or has been already resolved.

Larmore may instead be thinking of a deeper (and initially more promising) kind of neutral ground. Both parties in a dispute might share a common idea of what counted as a reason — perhaps in the sense of the second account of objectivity I gave in chapter four — and what kinds of reasons should be produced in any given case. This might work especially well in abstract reasoning about the basis of political association. From this core of reasons, a solution could be produced which *incidentally* reflected either, both or neither of the positions, yet could be justified by the common and correct sorts of reasons and considerations. If both parties consent to the reasoning process, then whatever the resulting agreement, it would be justified by that consent. It would be, in this way, a kind of procedural justice.

The problem for such an interpretation concerns the question of whether reasons that were common to two different positions could determine a single correct outcome. If they sufficed to determine such a solution then the disagreement would not exist, unless both sides had a different understanding of the reasons that were or were not applicable to this particular situation. This second interpretation of the idea of neutral ground turns out to be vulnerable to similar objections to the first. If both sides share common reasons and a commitment to a neutral procedure, then where does the disagreement come from? Alternatively, if there is scope for people to understand these common reasons differently or weight them differently, then the neutral ground is illusory. People can misapply a common conception of a reason, resulting in disagreement, but then this disagreement is amenable to resolution, at least in principle. As I will go on to examine in chapter seven, it is not at all clear that this kind of mistaken disagreement is the kind which Larmore needs for his argument to go through. If this idea of 'common reasons' were the common ground to which Larmore is referring, it is difficult to see how it could provide an outcome, yet not speak on issues upon which Larmore wants to remain silent. For example, he wants to say nothing about the source of people's reasons (Larmore, 1996, 139), nor does he argue that public standards of reasoning should be higher than those endorsed in private life.

Another problem with Larmore's account arises from his claim that we *ought* to retreat to neutral grounds. There might be two components to this; the first that it is prudentially correct, the second that it is the most fair or reasonable approach.[10] The 'prudential ought' fails to provide a reason and also fails to give an adequate interpretation of the moral element in Larmore's argument. The first thing to note about the claim that it is in our best prudential interests to retreat to neutral ground, is that the calculation would depend on the interests to be weighed. The prudential interest in co-operation (or less likely a desire for co-operation for its own sake) has to outweigh that of holding out for my point of view. People have to be prepared to value agreement, even when it does not endorse their position, more than the stubborn endorsement of their position. In the real world, it would appear that this norm seldom dominates the thinking of parties in political disagreement. In negotiation, maintaining one's position without compromise or concession on what are seen as crucial questions is a common strategy; for example, the situations in Northern Ireland or the Middle East. It is simply not the case, in public or private life, that agreement should be at any cost; and it is equally the case that maintaining one's position and refusing to compromise can produce significant concessions in any resulting settlement. Strategic considerations could plausibly outweigh a prudential 'ought' claim by Larmore.

This leaves the second alternative, that the retreat to neutral ground is justified on the basis that it is the fair response to disagreement. That the norm of rational dialogue is thought to be legitimate or fair is made clear by its backing from the explicitly moral idea of equal respect. According people respect means not using coercive state power without justification. This idea provides a strong reason to seek their assent. In fact, if we are aiming to provide justification then this *must* involve engaging with the views of others to produce an argument to which we can expect people to assent.[11] With intolerance or repression apparently

---

[10] Larmore, as I will discuss shortly, sees his two norms as moral judgements which 'trump' other considerations of value. If this is assumed, then they will constitute a 'best interest' to co-operate. I will go on below to explain why such an assumption is problematic.

[11] There is some small room left here for repression. For a justification of coercive state action need not work — the people who it affects may not find it compelling. I mentioned in chapter five that Larmore thinks a counterfactual justification 'were these people reasonable, then they

ruled out, neutrality is our only option. However, we must also seek people's assent to the idea of a retreat to neutral ground. If we fail to convince people of the authority of neutral ground, then we will fail to respect them when using coercive state power in accordance with the result of any neutral deliberation. Successful justifications must appeal to neutral ground. But we must have secured people's prior assent to the idea of neutral ground in order for our conclusions to bind.

A final question concerns the status of these two norms. Much of my discussion might seem to be rendered academic by Larmore's supposition that 'citizens are required to rank the norms of rational dialogue and equal respect above their other commitments' (Larmore, 1996, 141). Given that Larmore says, 'the constitutive ideals of the good life belong to our very sense of what is valuable, to the basis of our choices' (Larmore, 1996, 139), what kind of status do these norms have to 'trump' the very source of value? They are, Larmore asserts, 'true' and 'correct'. For Larmore, our moral perspectives remain as correct as before; his project, like Rawls' (as I will examine shortly) claims not to have sceptical implications (Larmore, 1996, 171–2). Larmore accepts that his proposals are limited in scope primarily to those who accept the two norms, and the status they are allotted. He writes 'with those who reject the norm of equal respect or rank their conception of the good life above it, we will usually be unable to converge on any political principles that are as justifiable to them as to ourselves' (Larmore, 1996, 142).

My argument above has been intended to show that the idea that we should always seek neutral ground in disagreement is problematic. There may be little neutral ground to seek, or our view may be in fact sufficiently important to us for us not to want to stand back from it in order to reach agreement. Furthermore, I have contended that we can only justify coercing people on the basis of neutral grounds to those people who *accept* the idea of neutral grounds. If, as I have argued, people can reasonably reject the importance and validity of neutral grounds, the population of people who value the norm of equal respect or rational dialogue might be smaller than we think. Larmore's proposal appeals to a limited constituency. Either we are 'all liberals now', in that we think we should resolve disagreement by reference to neutral procedure, and should respect other people too much to coerce

---

would find the justification compelling' might suffice. As I noted there, I think such an argument is unsatisfactory.

them without gaining their consent, or we are not. If not, then Larmore's proposal does very little to speak to us.[12]

This might be thought to indicate a challenge to the internal coherence of my argument. After all, in chapter five I argued that there are similar limits to the appeal of the justification principle. Isn't the coherence relativist principle left open to exactly the objection I press against Larmore's argument here? In response, three things should be noted about the position of Larmore and the coherence relativist. First, whilst the coherence relativist can attempt to justify the norm of equal respect to others, she recognises serious potential limitations: Larmore appears much less concerned with the limitations to his proposal. Second, the coherence relativist is in no way claiming that her account constitutes a neutral justification for toleration. Larmore, by contrast, is presenting his account of a neutral justification for neutrality. Third, Larmore's formulation of a justification principle based on equal respect is only one interpretation of this idea. As I indicated in chapter five, I think commitment to some version of the justification principle, perhaps for different reasons to the ones Larmore gives, is more widespread.

The limits of the community who would accept the primacy of equal respect and rational dialogue illustrates how controversial that primacy is. I have argued, then, that Larmore's proposal is controversial, and confused in its account of the neutral ground from which justifications can be given. Larmore's theory possesses additional shortcomings that I will discuss in chapter seven. Notably, what is missing from my discussion here is an account of the reasonable disagreement to which Larmore's proposal is a response. I want to save my account of this aspect of Larmore's theory for later, since this takes us into murkier realms than norms of respect or dialogue. Larmore separates his account of political liberalism from his account of reasonable disagreement. I follow his lead for now, though I will argue that the two are ultimately connected. Of course, Larmore is not the only political liberal to provide an account of how we arrive at a neutral justification of neutrality. Perhaps the most prominent account has been provided by John Rawls. I turn now to Rawls' defence of liberal neutrality.

---

[12] It must be said that Larmore perhaps does not intend his theory to be entirely neutral. He takes the main focus for neutrality of justification to be the debate between individualist and romantic communitarian ideas (Larmore, 1996, 127–32).

Rawls' Priority of Right[13]

Rawls terms his neutralist proposal 'the priority of right over the good' (e.g. Rawls, 1993, 173) because he feels the term neutrality to be potentially misleading. His proposal in *Political Liberalism* is nevertheless straightforwardly neutralist. The political conception 'seeks common ground — neutral ground — given the fact of pluralism' (Rawls, 1993, 192). The priority of right is defined in terms of the neutralist idea that the state 'is not to be designed to favor any particular comprehensive doctrine' (Rawls, 1993, 194). It relies on an ostensibly neutral justification which aims to avoid philosophical disagreement.

To understand Rawls' argument, it is necessary to examine the context in which the demand for neutrality, and his justification for it, arises. For Rawls, this is a condition of 'reasonable pluralism'. He writes,

> The diversity of reasonable comprehensive religious, philosophical and moral doctrines found in democratic societies is not a mere historical condition that may soon pass away; it is a permanent feature of the public culture of democracy ... a diversity of conflicting and irreconcilable — and what's more, reasonable — comprehensive doctrines will come about and persist (Rawls, 1993, 36).

He argues that oppressive state action is the wrong answer to this diversity. Instead, we should look to the support of reasonable people, who want to live in a 'fair system of co-operation'. Such reasonable people are willing to accept that different conceptions of the good are reasonable, and that it would thus be unreasonable to use the power of the state to insist on their own beliefs.[14] This diversity of reasonable beliefs arises from what Rawls calls the 'burdens of judgement', which I discuss in more detail later. These include elements such as differences in the evaluation of conflicting evidence and weighting, and the existence of a number of conflicting normative considerations which

---

[13] I will not discuss here the international dimension to Rawls' approach that he sets out in *The Law of Peoples*. As Rawls regards the Law of Peoples as the extension of his liberal conception of political justice (Rawls, 1999b, 3–4,) it might be expected that much of what I say here is applicable. Nevertheless, there are (to my mind at least) significant disjunctures. Notably, *The Law of Peoples* is not concerned with state neutrality and its justification but rather with tolerance and a much more limited moral-political conception of justice at an inter-state level.

[14] The notion of reasonableness is a complex one. In chapter seven I distinguish between an epistemic and moral component to the idea. Here, following Rawls, I rely on an intuitive idea to carry me through the sketching of his argument. Detailed discussions of reasonableness are undertaken by Caney (1995) and Wenar (1995).

are difficult to assess (Rawls, 1993, 56–7). Crucial here is a test of reasonableness. This allows Rawls to set aside questions about the truth of particular doctrines. Everyone will of course believe that their beliefs are true; but it may not be reasonable to act on those beliefs. He argues

> reasonable persons see the burdens of judgement set limits on what can be reasonably justified to others, and so they endorse some form of liberty of conscience and freedom of thought. It is unreasonable of us to use political power, should we possess it, or share it with others, to repress comprehensive views that are not unreasonable (Rawls, 1993, 61).

Reasonableness, says Rawls, requires neutrality. Rawls terms his approach political liberalism, because it aims to be purely political; it is restricted to the public or political realm. Within that realm, rather than have a divisive debate about the truth and falsehood of conflicting ideas of the good, Rawls aims to employ substitute notions which command widespread consent without getting embroiled in controversial philosophical questions.

Notably, debates about what Rawls terms 'constitutional essentials' and 'basic justice' are conducted on the basis of public reason (Rawls, 1999b, 133). This is a core of common reasoning for the public political realm that comes about when people agree on a conception of justice. Public reason is much like Larmore's neutral ground. Because everyone should talk the language of public reason when they engage in political debate, proposals can be publicly justified in terms of this common reasoning. For Rawls, this expresses an 'idea of political legitimacy' by holding that 'our exercise of political power is proper only when we sincerely believe that the reasons we would offer for our political actions . . . are sufficient, and we also reasonably think that other citizens might also reasonably accept those reasons' (Rawls, 1999b, 137). Rawls introduces public reason partly in an effort to replace 'the whole truth' with 'reasons that might be shared by all', because insistence on truth is 'incompatible with democratic citizenship' (Rawls, 1999b, 138).[15] This is one important kind of neutrality which Rawls' proposal aims for. As we shall see here and in chapter seven, this kind of public reason may be hard to come by.

---

[15] Of course, this is only a sketch of some of the key features of public reason. As Rawls indicates, public reason will require different things from holders of different positions in the state. Furthermore, there can be a family of political liberalisms, each with a slightly different conception of public reason. Rawls discusses these aspects in more detail in Rawls, 1999b, 132–80.

Rawls' approach aims to legitimise liberal principles by founding them on people's consent. In particular, Rawls refers to the consent of reasonable people as an 'overlapping consensus'. Rawls' emphasis on the paramount importance of consent generates several problems for his theory. Some of these I will indicate here; others must await a fuller explanation of the role of reasonable disagreement in his theory, which I provide in chapter seven. As Rawls is perhaps the most prominent modern liberal egalitarian theorist, his account has already attracted a large amount of scholarship, much of it critical. My purpose here is to bring out two particular respects in which Rawls' apparent stance is objectionable. These are concerned with the burdens of judgement and the Rawlsian conception of objectivity. In addition, these are problems of a particular kind; they both involve Rawls in questions of metaethics.

The Burdens of Judgement and Scepticism

According to Rawls, all reasonable persons assent to the burdens of judgement. They explain why, for Rawls, reasonable people should be tolerant people who institute a neutral state. The consequence of us not being able to justify our view to the general public is that we should not impose it on them. The burdens of judgement tell us why we are not to expect agreement on many contentious political and philosophical questions. Those explicitly listed by Rawls are:-

(a) The evidence bearing on a case is conflicting and complex, and thus hard to assess.

(b) Considerations of weighting can cause disagreement even if the evidence is agreed upon.

(c) All our concepts are vague and subject to hard cases. Indeterminacy means we must rely on judgement and interpretation.

(d) People's different 'life experiences' shape the way in which they weigh moral and political values.

(e) Different normative considerations of different force on both sides of an issue can produce difficulty in making an overall assessment.

(f) No system of social institutions can incorporate the full range of moral and political values.[16]

---

[16]   Summarised from Rawls, 1993, 56–7.

These features, says Rawls, make disagreement reasonable, and reasonably expected. They have the status of what Rawls calls a 'general fact' (Rawls, 1993, 36). I want to suggest, following Scheffler (1994) and Wenar (1995), that the burdens of judgement have, *contra* Rawls, definite sceptical implications, which will make people unlikely to assent to them if they hold certain reasonable world views. In fact, I will raise three problems with Rawls' use of the burdens of judgement.

(a) The burdens of judgement as an obstacle to overlapping consensus

The first problem is that they jeopardise the possibility of an over-lapping consensus — i.e. widespread support amongst reasonable people — for Rawls' political doctrine. Wenar argues

> religious doctrines typically deny that the burdens of judgement obtain. This, on reflection, should not be surprising. The burdens of judgement are meant to explain (among other pluralisms) why some people believe in one faith, while others believe in other faiths, and still others are agnostics and atheists. The explanation essentially says that questions about religion . . . are hard to think through even under the best of conditions, and that people answer these questions differently because of particular life experiences (Wenar, 1995, 44).

Referring especially to burdens (a)- (d), this is in sharp contrast to the way much religious doctrine presents itself as 'universally accessible to clear minds and open hearts' (Wenar, 1995, 44).[17] Wenar concludes, after citing the example of Catholic doctrine, that there is an incompatibility here between the burdens of judgement and religious claims to know easily and with absolute certitude. The burdens of judgement provide an account of the sources of pluralism which conflict with the account offered by much religious doctrine. Thus religious people might be in the position of endorsing justice as fairness as a political conception, but of 'characteristically' rejecting the grounds — the burdens of judgement — on which it partly stands (Wenar, 1995, 44–5). Thus, at the same time as strengthening the justification for his political liberalism, the burdens of judgement damage the inclusivity of the overlapping consensus. I think this argument can be extended in two further ways, as points (b) and (c) below.

---

[17] This is not to claim that all theological positions think that truth is revealed uniquely in their religion. Some theologians will allow the explanation of diversity posited by the burdens of judgement.

(b) The burdens of judgement and the conditions of scepticism

The first issue above discussed *incompatibility* between political liberalism and some comprehensive doctrines. The second concerns one important reason for this incompatibility — scepticism. Despite Rawls' avowals to the contrary, the burdens of judgement have sceptical implications. Rawls talks about scepticism as 'a philosophical analysis of the conditions of knowledge . . . after examining our ordinary ways of enquiry, they come to the conclusion that we cannot know those objects because one or more of the conditions of knowledge can never be satisfied' (Rawls, 1993, 63). Operating on this account, he denies that the burdens of judgement are sceptical in effect. He writes:

> Political liberalism does not question that many political and moral judgements of certain specified kinds are correct and it views many of them as reasonable. Nor does it question the possible truth of affirmations of faith. Above all, it does not argue that we should be hesitant and uncertain, much less sceptical, about our own beliefs (Rawls, 1993, 63).

We must be clear about the nature of Rawls' claim. 'Hesitancy' and 'uncertainty', it might be contended, are psychological rather than philosophical terms; they are attitudes with which we can hold beliefs. The justified and truthful nature of these beliefs, if they are to be termed correct, is a separate issue on this account. Rawls' scepticism is defined in terms of the latter, but I do not believe they can be so sharply divided.[18] Let us consider an example. I believe X to be the case. Furthermore, I believe it without hesitancy or uncertainty. However, I also endorse Rawls' account of 'the many hazards involved in the correct (and conscientious) exercise of our powers of reason and judgement' (Rawls, 1993, 56). If I accept that this is a hard case, should my judgement become less *justified*, because I become more aware of the possibility of error, or should my judgement merely become less *certain*? If certainty is linked to the confidence I have in the justification for my belief, then the two cannot be separated. The first problem I want to raise with Rawls' rejection of sceptical consequences for the burdens of judgement, then, is that the latter are exactly the kind of considerations we appeal to in order to cast doubt on another's position. This is perhaps because a claim of justification is often based on the idea that mine is the only possible explana-

---

[18] Rawls is operating on what appears to me a specific and rather dense (i.e. closely packed) definition of scepticism. A. J. Ayer, for example, treats philosophical scepticism and certainty as linked issues. Scepticism attacks certainty for 'without a basis of certainty all our claims to knowledge must be suspect' (Ayer, 1971, 41).

tion, or an explanation that is much more probable to be correct — the 'best explanation'.[19] If I were arguing against someone who believed that God was the only explanation of creation of the world, I might point to the existence of other explanations, offered by science. I would probe hard cases (e.g. the existence of evil) and I would examine whether background or upbringing, rather than any claim to objective reasons, were the motivators behind a view that might be thought to lack supporting evidence. I would do all this in the expectation that I could cast doubt upon the reasons she had for holding her belief. Similarly, she could invoke scientific hard cases, the incomplete explanatory power of scientific explanations, or my failure to open my mind to possibility of the truth in an attempt to make me doubt my stance. Surely, it is questionable whether a belief could be held with the same confidence if we took the burdens of judgement into account. Perhaps such a questioning is not feasible. It is hard to compare the 'presence' and 'absence' of the burdens precisely because the burdens of judgement are taken into account as reasons for being less certain in making some judgements anyway. They already affect the degree of probability attached to our judgements.[20]

The problem is complicated by the relation between reasonable people holding opposing beliefs, and other people *justifiably* (in some sense) holding opposing beliefs, which is discussed below and in chapter seven. At the very least, Rawls' view needs an account explaining how the burdens of judgement can leave my view that my position is best justified by the evidence intact — and will not even affect the certainty with which I hold it — whilst acknowledging that other people can reasonably come to the conclusion that a different explanation is the best justified. For now, I just want to note that Rawls' lack of an account of justification and certainty is a significant *lacuna* in his argument; in chapter seven I will discuss the way in which relativism can provide a resolution of this problem.

_____

[19] The issue of the relationship between scepticism and claims of justification is one I will discuss in greater detail in chapter seven, particularly in my discussion of Barry.

[20] Do the burdens of judgement provide an expectation of reasonable disagreement without indicating that my confidence in my belief is unreasonable? Perhaps I can still believe that my belief offers the best explanation, but without the same degree of certainty as before. Again, this may have damaging consequences for reaching a consensus between the advocates of different conceptions of the good.

(c) Scepticism prompted by reasonable divergence in belief

The above account began by considering whether the burdens of judgement in themselves are sceptical in content — i.e., if they are 'reasonable doubt'-provoking when held by someone in conjunction with beliefs. It ended in the muddier ground of whether the *possibility* of other reasonable people holding opposing beliefs is a reason for holding beliefs with less certainty. A slightly different question is whether acknowledging the *presence* of other reasonable conflicting views can cast reasonable doubt on my own. This case can usefully be examined with regard to a courtroom situation. The defence in a courtroom situation aims to establish reasonable doubt — to leave the jury with the view that there is reasonable doubt over whether the crime has been committed. The testimony of experts is one way such reasonable doubt can be established, for example if there is a disagreement between pathologists as to the conclusions to be drawn from forensic evidence. Whilst each expert can be certain of his or her own view, the overall impression left on the jury might well be that the evidence is inconclusive. Will not the presence of other people, as reasonable as ourselves, with conflicting views, lead us to the idea that the evidence is not conclusive? This is presumably the idea behind the need for unanimous verdicts. If the evidence does not convince some 'reasonable' people, then there is reasonable doubt. If we take an overview of a problem on which reasonable people differ, the presence of divergent views will lead us to think that the evidence is inconclusive and there is doubt as to the correct solution.[21]

To sum up my position, I have argued for three claims. (1) The burdens of judgement conflict with claims of universal certainty made by religious doctrines. (2) The burdens of judgements are sceptical (in a broad sense)[22] in effect because some of them —

---

[21] Interestingly, Raz discusses the courtroom case to provide support for Rawls (Raz, 1994, 104). He maintains that a court might find me guilty beyond reasonable doubt despite my innocence, and their judgement should not impinge on my assessment that I am innocent. We might want to characterise such cases as ones which I will discuss in the next chapter as 'mistaken' disagreements. For if I am innocent, the jury must have made a mistake in their reasoning or their assessment of the evidence. On the other hand, if I had motive and opportunity, DNA and fingerprinting evidence pointed to me, the murder weapon was found in my house along with my blood-stained clothes, then it seems to me that the jury's lack of doubt ought to trouble my assessment of my innocence.

[22] As I have already noted, Rawls seems to provide a particularly limited definition of scepticism. I use scepticism here to represent the more general idea that our standards of proof should be subject to doubt. The bur-

particularly (a), (b), (c) and (d) — encourage us to consider the possibility of other better explanations. (3) The consequences of the burdens of judgement, that different reasonable people will believe different answers to the same question, ought (if the analogy with the courtroom is correct) to provide us with a reason to be less certain. These problems mean that Rawls' attempt to avoid controversy at the level of the foundation of his theory fails. The burdens of judgement encourage scepticism, despite Rawls' protestations to the contrary, and such scepticism will be damaging to Rawls' attempt to provide a legitimising consensus behind his proposal. This consensus will be undermined precisely because the burdens of judgement, as I have indicated, are themselves controversial. I now want to turn to another area where the emphasis on consensus is problematic. This is Rawls' account of objectivity. Again, we may have a conflict here with the claims made by reasonable conceptions of the good.

The Political Account of Objectivity

When Rawls sets out his account of public reason and reasonableness, he also discusses the nature of the objectivity he claims for this account i.e. the standard of objectivity for the political realm. Rawls wants such a standard to 'establish a public framework of thought sufficient for the concept of judgement to apply and for conclusions to be reached on the basis of evidence and reasons after discussion and due reflection' (Rawls, 1993, 110). Rawls notes: 'Kantian constructivism holds that moral objectivity is to be understood in terms of a suitably constructed social point of view that all can accept. Apart from the procedure of constructing the principles of justice, there are no moral facts' (Rawls, 1980, 519). As with Rawls' explanation of disagreement, most reasonable comprehensive doctrines already possess a view of the sources of normative authority. Rawls' view of the public realm is expected to garner their support in an overlapping consensus. Otherwise, there will be a continual tension between the standards by which people judge the basis of important political claims, and the standards by which they judge the rest of their lives.

Whilst it should be stressed that Rawls intends for this conception of objectivity to govern only the political realm, Rawls does want the account to assign reasons to reasonable people. They

dens of judgement certainly seem to bear in leading us to expect that our standards of proof need not be the only reasonable ones, and that they need not determine a uniquely correct answer.

'are to act from these reasons, whether moved by them or not; and so these assigned reasons may override the reasons agents have, or think they have, from their own point of view' (Rawls, 1993, 111). As Wenar points out, again this will conflict with some comprehensive doctrines, as

> comprehensive views, as we know them and expect them to remain, are settled in their explanations of the origins of normative force . . . if a person, to be a reasonable citizen of a just consensus must believe that constructivism provides the real reasons for just action, then there are now no such reasonable people. None, that is, save adherents of a comprehensive Kantian constructivism (Wenar, 1995, 55).

It might be objected that Rawls' political constructivism need not go as far as either of the other two views of objectivity that he discusses, the Kantian and the rational intuitionist. For example, whilst Rawls says rational intuitionism might go so far as to say that 'a reasonable judgement is true, or probably true . . . of an independent order of values', political constructivism need 'neither assert nor deny that. For its aims . . . the concept of the reasonable suffices' (Rawls, 1993, 113). However, at least in the private realm, rational intuitionists would not believe that *mere reasonableness* is sufficient. Rawls' description of the political realm is continuous with rational intuitionism, but only in the sense of a 'highest common factor'. The rational intuitionist will want more than Rawls' account provides. Asking the intuitionist to use Rawls' account for the public realm, and his own for the private, would lead to two problems highlighted by Wenar. He writes, 'this sort of public reason would inevitably result in hypocrisy (where people publicly endorse policies which they would privately reject) or cheating, (where people bend their public reasoning toward the conclusions they are really convinced of)' (Wenar, 1995, 57). If people endorsed constructivism as a compromise, a common ground between their own and other views, the result would be public reason as a *modus vivendi* rather than an overlapping consensus.

However, this area indicates another, deeper problem with his proposal. Rawls appears to believe that his theory is neutral with regard to metaethical disputes because it leaves the 'concept of a true moral judgement to comprehensive doctrines' (Rawls, 1993, 116). Even if Rawls' account uses the word reasonableness rather than truth, this does not suffice to show that his account of reasonableness is not freed from suppositions Rawls makes about the nature of justification. Indeed, Rawls' account of the status of the political judgements and their power as guides to action does not remain neutral with regard to its account of the sources of justification. Of course, being distinct from other accounts of objectivity does not render his proposal non-neutral. Instead, the way in which his political account *conflicts* with more thoroughgoing accounts of objectivity leads me to this conclusion. It is political in the sense that it applies to the political realm, but in fact it makes substantial claims on a wider sphere. In Rawls' own words, it establishes an 'order of reasons' upon which any individual can be found mistaken, and makes 'a distinction . . . between reasoning and judgement, however sincere and seemingly correct, and what is true or reasonable' (Rawls, 1993, 112) which will be applied outside of political questions. Rawls' account of objectivity is thus more than merely political or minimal. It is in conflict with other accounts of objectivity, and hence controversial.

A similar situation arises with regard to Rawls' idea of 'commonsense reasoning'. Rawls' public reason is intended to operate on the basis of 'guidelines and rules . . . specified by reference to forms of reasoning and argument available to citizens generally, and so in terms of common sense, and the procedures and conclusions of science when not controversial' (Rawls, 1993, 162). At the very least, this stands in need of an account of what constitutes 'common sense' — as Gaus points out, people have different ideas of what constitutes common sense (Gaus, 1996, 132-6). If we allow that different reasonable people have different reasonable standards of judgement, the burdens of judgement imply that we could not impose a single set on people without being unreasonable. Therefore, people have to hold the same commonsense norms. Here a similar problem arises to that with the political account of objectivity above. Individuals' accounts of which modes of reasoning are and are not commonsense will differ. Even if we take the 'highest common factor' of their accounts of commonsense reasoning, we will produce an account which is incomplete. That is, it will not include all that individuals want from an account of commonsense reasoning; they are left endorsing one standard for the public and another standard for the private.

The central question here is whether Rawls' disavowal of the use of 'true' and 'false' as being unnecessary to a *political* theory is sufficient to make Rawls' theory and its justification neutral. Criticism that it does not has come, for example, from Joseph Raz. [23] Raz holds that we cannot assert something without asserting it to be *true*. He terms the position that a theory can be recommended

---

[23] Estlund is another theorist who identifies problems of truth and justification in Rawls' work (Estlund, 1998).

as reasonable without being true a strategy of 'epistemic abstinence' (Raz, 1990). Rawls' claim to allow everyone to realise the
fact of reasonable pluralism without scepticism might rely on
what Raz describes as 'the dubious epistemological claim that
there can be reasons for belief and action which are quite reasonably not recognised as such by people generally, but which are
valid nonetheless' (Raz, 1990, 45).[24] Raz is surely right to pin
Rawls down here, because maintaining your account is true, and
maintaining it is objectively justified, both amount to advocacy of
the account. If Rawls provides an account of justification which is
controversial in itself, then the fact that he ducks questions about
the truth of his account does not suffice to make his proposal 'neutral'. I want to pick up this theme later by indicating how Rawls'
account leaves room for a relativist theory of moral justification. I
do not, at this stage, want to argue that Rawls' account ought to
have a relativist foundation. Such a controversial claim requires
more support than I give it here. Chapter seven offers a fuller
account of Rawls' argument, and does ultimately reach that conclusion. My purpose here is merely to draw out the complexity of
Rawls' stance on questions of justification.

I have already discussed the role of the burdens of judgement in
justifying neutrality. I argued that their presence implies, despite
Rawls' protestations to the contrary, a substantive idea of 'reasonable doubt' in his theory. This draws him into questions of scepticism and justification.[25] Thus, I have now considered two areas in
which Rawls' theory is both internally problematic and
embroiled in debates in metaethics. In the first case, questions
concern the link between reasonable pluralism, certainty and
scepticism. In the second, these concern the nature of objectivity.
Because Rawls wants to provide an account of why we should
expect reasonable disagreement, and how we can claim objectivity for reasoning in the public realm, Rawls cannot avoid
metaethical issues.

Both Larmore's and Rawls' accounts have indicated the difficulty in advocating liberal neutrality without foundations. Chap-

---

[24] However, a *relativist* might be able to assert something as true, however,
whilst denying it was the only possible valid position on a particular
question; and would also be able to assert that reasons are valid, but not
for everyone. Indeed, such a claim is definitional of the kind of relativism I have been defending in this book.

[25] I am not alone in reaching this conclusion. Peter Jones for example, has
argued that the priority of the 'right' over the 'good' in Rawls' work only
works if 'my beliefs were not securely grounded enough to warrant their
continued assertion in opposition to the principles of justice.' (Jones,
1989, 61).

ter seven will look in more detail at the difficulties of such a project.

Conclusion

This chapter has examined attempts to provide a fully neutral justification of neutrality. I have argued that these attempts fail. Where common moral premises are appealed to, these are less common and unproblematic than might be supposed. Furthermore, any account has to say something about the status which it accords its basic norms, and the authority which they wield. To do otherwise leaves either a substantial gap in the theory or leaves it vulnerable to a 'what's that theory got to do with me?' objection. Larmore and Rawls need to establish the basis of neutrality as authoritative. Whilst Larmore is vague as to why his norms of equal respect and rational dialogue should be considered as paramount, Rawls attempts to provide a widely acceptable account of objectivity, upon which the political principle of neutrality can stand as objectively justified. This claim of authority for neutrality, I want to suggest here, cannot be achieved without a metaethical justification. This is what the failure, especially of Rawls' justification of neutrality, demonstrates.

Despite their rejection of controversial moral and philosophical questions, both Rawls and Larmore start with controversial bases for their justification of neutrality. This is an idea I want to examine further in chapter seven, where I look in more detail at the nature of reasonable disagreement and the role it plays in Rawls' and Larmore's arguments. In particular, I will suggest that the argument from the burdens of judgements, via reasonableness, to toleration, ultimately makes the best sense only if we accept a wider metaethical theory in which to situate its claim. The accounts I have examined here can perhaps claim to be *more neutral* justifications of neutrality, but not entirely so. Indeed, this chapter raises the question of whether an entirely neutral justification is possible. Perhaps the best we can ask for, as Gaus suggests, is a 'justificatory liberalism' which is explicitly non-neutral, though robust in the sense that it can be embraced by a wide variety of theories (Gaus, 1996, 6). Exactly what justificatory liberalism might look like, and whether relativism can make a significant contribution to the development of a justificatory liberalism, is the subject of my next chapter.

Chapter 7

Reasonable Disagreement and Relativism

Introduction

In the previous chapter, I argued that the foundations of Rawls' neutralist proposal were unclear and potentially controversial, and that Larmore's argument for liberal neutrality was not itself neutral. This chapter takes on these issues in more depth by looking at the contentions on which political liberal arguments rest. It argues that political liberalism stands in need of clear foundations, and that relativism can provide the appropriate set of foundations. In so doing, it looks at the possibilities for what, following Gaus, I want to term a *justificatory* rather than *political* liberalism; i.e. political liberalism plus an account of justification and reasonable disagreement. It aims to answer this question: given that political liberalism, as argued above, needs an account of moral justification, why should liberals accept relativism as such an account of moral justification?

In chapter five, I argued that there is a consistent relativist proposal which provides an intuitively satisfying account of moral criticism and can combine with a 'liberal' moral premise to provide an appropriately liberal answer to the question of toleration. As I briefly indicated there, neutrality is a related, though distinct, idea. In particular, while we can talk of toleration on the part of individuals or groups, neutrality in its most common form is concerned with the state.[1] Nevertheless, it might be thought that just as relativism contributes a part of a liberal defence of toleration, it can straightforwardly take the same role in a liberal defence of neutrality. However, the argument we must make to ground such a claim is significantly different, for three important reasons. First, as we have seen in chapter six, the political liberal approach aims to be neutral in its justification of neutrality, which is founded on the legitimising power of consensus. Any argument about relativism and neutrality must take into account and address this distinctive aspect of the approach. Second, an argument demonstrating how relativism can form part of an argument for toleration is not as ambitious as one that claims relativism *ought* to *underpin* liberal defences of neutrality. Because of this greater level of ambition, the claim requires correspondingly greater examination and justification. Third and relatedly, this examination and justification takes place against the background of much greater opposition. As I indicated in chapter five, a link between relativism and toleration has often been assumed, or at least considered. The claim that relativism can form part of a reason to tolerate, though contentious, is less so than the claim that relativism has a place at the heart of contemporary liberalism. Given that relativism has been thought to undermine liberal commitments, liberals may well be resistant to any claim that relativism is *compatible* with, let alone should form the *foundation* of, political liberalism.

My discussion will begin with a more detailed account of the nature of reasonable disagreement. I will contend that political liberalism, to succeed, must embody a relativist account of reasonable disagreement; that is, an account which allows for there to be no single justified morality. To illustrate the points I make, I set out Larmore's analysis of this phenomenon, in addition to re-examining Rawls. I then move on to analyse the arguments of Brian Barry, who aims to give a sceptical interpretation of reasonable disagreement in order to yield neutrality between conceptions of the good. My aim is to show that relativism is the ghost at these banquets, providing a plausible set of foundations for a justificatory liberalism. In analysing this idea, I also argue that liberalism makes a distinction between those reasonable beliefs with sufficient credibility and justificatory force (and command respect because of this), and those without. Such a proposal as to what marks off the reasonable, in at least one of its senses, maps

---

[1]   Horton and Nicholson, for example, note that a defence of toleration at the political level can take the form of a principle of neutrality (Horton and Nicholson, 1992, 4).

onto the line drawn by relativism between justified and unjustified moralities. In chapter six, I identified a problem concerning the sense in which 'certainty' can remain in a world characterised by reasonable disagreement, and this problem also recurs in Barry's work. In this chapter I argue that relativism can also provide a plausible account of this certainty. Thus, it can help resolve the problem of scepticism that Rawls encounters. These considerations help establish the claim that a relativist metaethics can make a positive contribution to a defence of political liberalism.

I then speculate on the costs and consequences for political liberalism of adopting such a set of foundations. I will discuss various possibilities for legitimating a liberal neutralist regime founded on controversial relativist ideas of justification. I conclude that liberals should accept that there are many framework-relative justifications for liberal principles. Liberal principles could thus be converged on for many different reasons. However, in conjunction with this approach, the relativist liberal should simultaneously advocate one particular relativist set of reasons in public debate with the aim of securing rational assent.

Reasonable Disagreement and Liberalism

In the last chapter, we saw that an idea of reasonable disagreement was a crucial feature in the arguments of Rawls and Larmore. I want to begin this chapter by looking in more detail at what reasonable disagreement involves and the role it plays in political liberal arguments. Political liberalism, as I have already noted, is in part a response to the degree of diversity of conceptions of the good. In order to command a justifying and legitimising consensus, the justification of liberal principles offered must be capable of commanding widespread assent, i.e. be uncontroversial. It is often claimed as an advantage of political liberalism that it has found a minimal, straightforward foundation that nevertheless has considerable intuitive power. This foundation is the phenomenon of reasonable disagreement.

This section makes two related claims about the idea of reasonable disagreement: (1), that liberals such as Larmore and Rawls need to provide an expanded notion of reasonable disagreement, rather than simply relying 'neutrally' on the mere presence of the phenomenon; and (2), that such an expanded notion of reasonable disagreement must be a relativist one. In taking on the first task I will concentrate on Larmore's characterisation and support my contention with reference to Rawls as well. The second task is taken up by subsequent sections on Brian Barry's analysis of reasonable disagreement and on the features of relativism that make it suitable to underpin political liberal arguments.

What is reasonable disagreement? Larmore talks of disagreement between people who 'think and converse in good faith and apply, as best they can, the general capacities of reason that belong to every domain of enquiry' (Larmore, 1996, 168). For Larmore, reasonable disagreement is a 'phenomenon' in which such people disagree about fundamental questions of value. Similarly, we have seen already that what Rawls, perhaps misleadingly, terms the 'fact of reasonable pluralism' (Rawls, 1993, 63) is a *fact*. We can observe disagreement all around us. But when should we accept that people disagreeing constitutes reasonable disagreement?

I want to begin an examination of this question by looking at how we classify the mistakes made by reasonable people. The mistakes I am cosncerned with in this section are those made in the application of Larmore's 'general capacities of reason'. I take such mistakes to be the misapplication of, or failure to implement, these generally held standards. I want to argue that it makes a difference to the plausibility of liberal arguments whether or not we stipulate that for disagreement to be reasonable, the views which are in conflict must be mistake-free. Alternatively, we could conceive of reasonable disagreement as disagreement between people who are generally reasonable, even though one or both the conflicting views in question violate generally held standards of reasoning. We might want to argue that when generally reasonable people make mistakes with regard to the particular issue on which disagreement has arisen, then their views are to be counted as unreasonable. Thus, it might be the case that disagreement between other reasonable people and myself on a particular question was unreasonable, in the sense that with regard to that topic everyone who disagreed with me was simply mistaken in their application of generally held standards of reasoning. Another possibility is that they could be reasoning in 'bad faith' in this instance.[2]

On this view, the fact that the two people who are disagreeing are both reasonable does not suffice to render the *disagreement* rea-

---

[2] For reasons I will explain below, this does not mean that reasonable reasoners have to be perfect reasoners. For reasonable disagreement to form a plank in an argument for neutrality, it is not the case that there must be no mistakes on questions where there are reasonable disagreements. Instead, what is required is that instances of reasonable disagreement cannot all or mostly be reduced to 'unreasonable' mistakes by one side or the other.

sonable. Whether we ought to call a disagreement in which one party affirms something in violation of generally held standards of reasoning an 'unreasonable disagreement', or a 'mistaken reasonable disagreement', is, I believe, largely a terminological issue. We could equally well distinguish between unreasonable and reasonable disagreement, or between mistaken reasonable disagreement and truly reasonable disagreement. Instead, the reason why the issue of mistakes in relation to reasonable disagreement is significant is because of the role that reasonable disagreement plays in liberal theory. I set out the liberal argument for neutrality below, indicating exactly what difference the issue of mistakes makes to the strength of the argument. I argue that only reasonable disagreement not resulting wholly from mistakes can provide a straightforward foundation for this position; mistaken or unreasonable disagreement cannot.

The Link Between Reasonable Disagreement and Neutrality

Political liberals argue that accepting the fact of reasonable disagreement leads to neutrality.[3] I think the argument can be sketched in the following form.

(a) In a situation of reasonable disagreement, we cannot successfully justify our conception of the good to others.

(b) Our respect for other people requires that we do not generally impose where we cannot reasonably justify.

(c) Therefore, we should remain neutral with regard to conceptions of the good, and not seek to impose a particular one.[4]

Of course, the emphasis placed on different parts of this argument, and the meaning of key terms in this argument, vary between thinkers. I hope that (a), (b), and (c) capture the basic spirit of political liberal arguments.

Before looking at this argument, I want to note two apparent advantages it possesses by virtue of incorporating reasonable disagreement. First, the standard for *reasonableness* or *justification* is good deal lower than *truth*, so political liberals need not engage in the messy business of establishing whether or not a particular

---

[3] For the claim that it 'leads to' neutrality, see Rawls, 1993, 59. For Larmore, political liberalism is the 'response' to disagreement about the good (Larmore, 1996, 132–3).

[4] (b) and (c) could be said to form the *moral* component of reasonableness. As I go on to examine, (a) expresses the *epistemic* component.

conception of the good is true. The epistemic component of reasonableness instead lies only in accordance with generally held standards of reasoning. As we have seen, Larmore refers only to 'the general capacities of reason' (Larmore, 1996, 168). The avoidance of questions of truth is indicative of the way in which political liberalism aims to avoid controversy, or 'extend toleration to philosophy' (Rawls, 1993, 10). If political liberalism can avoid these kinds of questions, consensus will be much easier to arrive at. Second, it relies on the intuitive power of the undeniable presence of disagreement. Reasonable disagreement has the status, says Rawls, of a 'general fact'. Similarly, Larmore notes that 'we do not need an explanation to recognise the phenomenon' (Larmore, 1996, 171). Reasonable disagreement and the inability to justify the use of coercion to others are important components of the justification of neutrality. This argument makes reasonable disagreement fundamental to the justification of neutrality, and thus increases the chance that people who recognise the presence of this reasonable disagreement will adopt a posture of respect for others. Larmore endorses a variant of this argument and bases his whole position on the idea of reasonable disagreement. For him, it is the force which animates the liberal demand for neutrality. Reasonable disagreement prompts the 'norm' of a retreat to neutral ground (provided we want to continue the conversation), and only then does the norm of equal respect surface to supplement it.[5]

The focus of this section is on the consequences of allowing disagreement to be characterised as reasonable even when it results from mistakes. An example may help to clarify what I mean. Take the case of a Nazi who believes in good faith that scientific evidence justifies the inferiority of other non-Aryan races. He affirms generally held standards of reasoning, including those governing the scientific domain. However, he has misapplied them with respect to his belief by mistaking a correlation between poverty and race for proof that non-Aryans are stupid. This, of course, is only an example. Gaus recounts many possible examples of such logical fallacies in our everyday reasoning (Gaus, 1996, 54-59). If this is a situation of *un*reasonable disagreement, if the Nazi's error is made relative to a standard of generally held reason, then we can in principle successfully point out to her the error of her ways. Only insincerity or further errors on her part will prevent her

---

[5]   This brief summary relies on my examination of Larmore's defence of neutrality as a whole in chapter six.

from seeing that we are correct.[6] Larmore should especially appreciate this argument as he draws on a distinction between proof and justification — proof only constitutes justification when it appeals to common ground.[7] If we accept that such a mistake renders a view unreasonable, then no requirement to remain neutral is generated by the argument. Only in cases where reasonable disagreement is untainted by mistakes is neutrality yielded. Therefore, liberals who wish to propose this argument as a solution to situations of reasonable disagreement cannot think that the phenomenon or fact of persistent reasonable disagreement is wholly due to mistaken reasoning.

A second consideration points in this direction. If part of reasonableness is adherence to shared standards of reasoning, and mistakes involve the *mis*application of such standards, then there is a conceptual barrier to mistaken reasonable disagreement. The two notions, on these definitions, are incompatible. This might be thought to indicate a problem with the definitions of reasonableness or mistakenness rather than an incompatibility between the ideas. However, there is a serious problem in allowing mistaken disagreement to count as reasonable disagreement. Namely, if a failure to meet common standards of reasoning does not make a view unreasonable, then what does? If mistakes are reasonable, then what, if anything, is unreasonable?

The idea that the correct application of reason by different persons produces reasonable diversity and reasonable disagreement requires, then, that we accept that reasonable disagreement is not the result of a mistake by one of the parties. This view can sound implausible however. It might be objected that reasonable people can and do make mistakes which do not impugn their reasonableness. For example on a complicated mathematical question, or one of quantum mechanics, it is perhaps inappropriate that people should be judged unreasonable for their failure to arrive at the correct answer. Furthermore, these general standards of reasoning, which I am arguing are important to the idea of epistemic reasonableness, need not themselves always provide a conclusive standard but instead an occasionally vague and incomplete one. Both of these points can be acknowledged without undermining the basic argument. Reasonableness in the application of general standards of reasoning should not by itself be expected to lead to correct answers in very specialised areas. What reasonableness

---

[6] It is no accident, as I will go on to discuss, that the description of this situation looks a lot like the distinction between evaluative and compelling criticism introduced in chapter five.

[7] I discuss Larmore's proposal in more detail later.

may instead require in such a case is an honest admission of insufficient knowledge or understanding of the problem. Reasonableness can be thought of as a disposition or application of a procedure rather than a body of knowledge. Furthermore, it can be admitted that in dealing with knotty analytical or logical problems, the idea of general standards of reason might not determine by itself a uniquely correct answer (this, after all, is what liberals might believe about conceptions of the good). This is partly because the content of reasonableness is hard to pin down and subject to hard cases. Rather than perfect application of general canons of reasoning, epistemic reasonableness requires imperfect but sincere and self-aware application — a willingness to admit error (such as the errors of rationality described by Gaus) and correct it. We can admit that reasonable people will make some errors in cases of reasonable disagreement without making mistakes the sole cause of reasonable disagreement.

Thus, I have argued that *mistaken* reasonable disagreement cannot serve the role required of it by the liberal argument. Reasonable disagreement that rests on mistakes is in principle amenable to rational resolution. In cases of mistakes, we can plainly justify the correct view over the incorrect one. Thus, no neutrality is required in such cases. Were we to preserve the duty to be neutral and instead hold that neutrality was required even when disagreement was unreasonable, too much neutrality might be required. Allowing mistakes would weaken the case for neutrality by introducing a countervailing intuition, that in cases where someone is plainly wrong, correction (or perhaps toleration) rather than a stance of neutrality is what would be required.

If liberals are not to affirm that reasonable disagreement is characterised by mistakes relative to commonly held reasoning, then the proposal stands even further in need of an explanation of its nature. For the idea that reasonable disagreement does not boil down to some people simply misapplying common concepts *entails* the claim that the sincere application of commonly held modes of reasoning does not suffice to distinguish between multiple possibly correct answers. No single answer is uniquely reasonable. Liberalism stands particularly in need of justifying this interpretation of the situation to those who believe their position is uniquely and compellingly justified by the available evidence, such as some Creationists, who believe that the earth and the Bible are compelling evidence of God's existence. Suppose your position holds itself to be true and uniquely endorsed as such by commonly held standards of reasoning. You would be justified in asking a liberal how you could assert this but also understand reasonable disagreement not as people making mistakes in their reasoning, but as holding an alternative view, the truth or falsehood of which is independent of its reasonableness. In other words, there is a tension in asserting that your truth is available to all those who affirm sincerely common justificatory standards, and simultaneously holding that the application of commonly held modes of reasoning need not determine a uniquely correct answer.[8] The liberal has to show how and why the reasonable does not equal the true, or even what we have a good reason to believe, against people who would argue that all reasonable people ought to accept their position.

Thus, I wish to draw the preliminary conclusion that the problem for political liberalism has two parts. The first is that liberalism claims to offer a neutral justification of neutrality, in which reasonable disagreement is a fact that almost no-one would dispute. This appearance is inaccurate, for the liberal has a particular characterisation of reasonable disagreement that makes controversial claims. The second, which follows from this, is that the commitment to the liberal account of reasonable disagreement faces a problem in motivating a consensus behind it. This is because, as I have just indicated, plenty of people will hold a view of disagreement with implications that are incompatible with the liberal account.

However, my view is not simply that in the abstract, liberals need to specify the nature of disagreement in this kind of way, despite the problems attached. It is also that political liberals *do* characterise reasonable disagreement in what I will show to be a 'proto-relativist' way. Rawls' account embodies confused though potentially relativist assertions about the nature of justification, whilst the account Larmore offers is more straightforward. I suggested at the end of the last chapter that Rawls' account necessarily brought him into metaethical territory. I now want to recap his argument, looking in more depth at the ways in which it might be thought relativist. I will then move on to examine Larmore's account.

Rawls and Relativism

An analysis of Rawls' argument for neutrality clearly demonstrates that relativism lies at the foundation of his proposal. One reason for reasonable people to be tolerant of reasonable conceptions of the good, and to institute a neutral state, is Rawls' denial

---

[8]   As I will discuss shortly, Brian Barry identifies this as a central dilemma facing advocates of liberal neutrality on the basis of reasonable disagreement. (Barry, 1995a, 168–9).

that a single morality can be uniquely publicly justified.[9] A claim that our beliefs are true, says Rawls, is a claim 'that all could equally make' but which 'could not be made good by anyone to citizens generally' (Rawls, 1993, 61). I want to suggest here that Rawls' account of disagreement in the political realm only works against the backdrop of a wider theory of moral justification on which what counts as a good reason for me need not be a compelling reason for others. The fact of reasonable pluralism, where others are reasonable but nevertheless *quite wrong* by standards I know to be correct, need not motivate toleration. Rawls' account does not work without the idea that other competing reasonable doctrines are reasonable, where part of the connotation of 'reasonable' is 'justified'. That is, 'since there are many reasonable doctrines, the idea of the reasonable does not require us, or others, to believe any specific reasonable doctrine' (Rawls, 1993, 60). Such a claim might seem at first sight to be very close to the kind of relativism that I have been advocating elsewhere, which holds as its central claim that there is no single justified morality ('specific reasonable doctrine').

However, Rawls' argument for neutrality is only meant to apply in the public or political realm. Rawls, it might be said, is *for* suspending judgement on issues where coercion is at issue, but does not deny that there might be a single justified moral view. Certainly remarks such as 'we recognize that our own doctrine has, and can have for people generally, no special claims on them beyond their own view of its merits' (Rawls, 1993, 60), which might be taken as advocating a kind of relativism, occur in the context of a discussion of the use and abuse of state power. Rawls might simply be saying that for purposes of coercive implementation, we cannot compellingly show others that ours is the uniquely correct moral framework, and this should bring us up short in wanting to be intolerant. Thus formulated, his argument looks like a version of the justification principle I discussed in chapter five, rather than any more grandiose relativist claim about morality as a whole. He is merely claiming that coercion requires justification.

However, I argued there that for the justification principle to yield tolerance, it had to be married to a premise dictating the circumstances under which we would be unable to justify our beliefs to others. Rawls' account hints at, without unambiguously spelling out, such a premise. It certainly stands in need of an explana-

---

[9]   Furthermore, given his account of the way in which public reason is objective, it can be said that for Rawls there is no single objectively or universally justified morality (Rawls, 1993, 110–3).

tion of how and why we lack the ability to justify our comprehensive moral view, and hence cannot coerce others on the basis of it. I want to maintain here that this ambiguity about the relationship between the 'reasonable', the 'true' and the 'justified' leaves room for relativism.[10] More strongly, we can say that Rawls recognises framework-relative barriers to justification, at least in the public realm, and this idea is characteristic of relativism.

Larmore, Contextualism and Relativism

Having looked at the possibility of finding proto-relativism in Rawls' account, I want to turn now to Larmore's account. In chapter two of *Morals of Modernity*, Larmore offers a distinctive account of the nature and purpose of moral justification. This account argues that justification is tradition-bound, but only invoked in cases when we have sufficient reason in our belief system to doubt one of our beliefs. 'We can regard our moral convictions as necessarily rooted not in reason as such, but rather in one or several traditions of moral thought and practice that are historically contingent . . . and that we can elaborate or even change in part, but never completely leave behind' (Larmore, 1996, 56). Thus for Larmore, the 'ultimate source of authority' for our moral beliefs, is our 'form of life' (Larmore, 1996, 57). Larmore claims he is not advocating an 'ethnocentric relativism' because his theory of the nature of justification allows for undoubted principles of universal range (and perhaps the possibility of universally justified principles).[11]

Critics of my argument might argue that Larmore's theory of justification is separable from his proposal for a neutral minimal moral core. However, I include a sketch of his proposal here because it clearly underlies the particular way in which Larmore disavows that his account is sceptical. For example, Larmore writes:

---

[10] However, there is an alternative route that Rawls can take here. It might not be the case that there *is no* uniquely justified morality, just that we *cannot* know which morality is correct. Such an answer does not involve a relativist metaethical commitment. It does however, involve a heavily sceptical one, and I want to suggest that relativism constitutes a more desirable commitment than such a thoroughgoing scepticism, particularly given Rawls' desire to leave certainty intact.

[11] In particular, for Larmore it is the case that 'not belief itself, but change of belief, forms the proper object of justification' (Larmore, 1996, 60). This apparent difference with coherence relativism is something I will examine later.

> we examine the worth of an existing belief always in the light of other things we already believe, if only because we could not otherwise establish the positive grounds for doubt that alone make it necessary to seek the justification of that belief. As a result where we have no positive grounds for doubt, we should regard our view as true, however much it may be the subject of reasonable disagreement.

or again;

> When our own background beliefs thus clash with those of someone else, this is not (as I observed in Chapter two) a sufficient reason for us to suspend allegiance to these beliefs and re-examine them. To call them into doubt we need some positive reason to think they may be false, one that we must be able to recognise as such by our own lights; for that, after all, is the standpoint from which we judge (Larmore, 1996, 172).

Both of these passages reveal the reliance of Larmore's political proposal on the theory of justification he sets our earlier in the book. This theory of justification is something I will examine in detail shortly. At this point, it is worth recalling that Larmore maintains he does not require an explanation of reasonable disagreement 'to recognise the phenomenon'(Larmore, 1996, 171). Whilst it is true that Larmore does not provide an account of how reasonable disagreement comes about, I would argue it is not correct to say that his account rests merely on a recognition of the phenomenon, with the implication that this recognition is somehow neutral, uncontroversial, or unphilosophical. A particular account of moral justification is integral to his understanding of what reasonable disagreement is, and his justification of neutrality would be incomplete without such an account.[12] He contends that the reasonable and the true or justified are separate; but he is also concerned to provide a particular account of the nature of justification.

I do not want to maintain that Larmore advocates exactly a form of relativism, but his position at least advocates things that many universalists would want to deny. For example, it denies that what is a good reason or successful justification for me must also constitute a good reason or successful justification for you. Larmore makes it very clear that the only good reasons for us are ones we can recognise by our own lights. Reasonable disagree-

---

[12]   This is not to say that Larmore must produce the exact model of justification that he does as part of his justification for liberal neutrality. However, it would have to be replaced with something that considered the same question, of how reasonable disagreement is to be characterised and provide a similar answer which ruled out mistakes as the main cause of reasonable disagreement. I will argue in this chapter that a relativist proposal could fulfil this role.

ment involves presenting 'our opponents with the reasons for our views and explaining in a detailed way what errors prevent their agreeing with us' but ' they may be able to do the same with regard to us' (Larmore, 1996, 172). Larmore maintains a distinction (interestingly introduced in his justification of liberal neutrality rather than chapter two of the book) between *proof* and *justification*. He writes 'whereas a proof consists simply in the logical relations among a set of propositions, a justification is a proof directed at those who disagree with us . . . It can fulfil this pragmatic role only by appealing to what they already believe, thus to what is common ground between us' (Larmore, 1996, 135).[13] Thus, something can constitute proof for me of a fact, whilst the absence of common ground means it can find no justificatory foothold in the beliefs of others. We have epistemic authority over what counts as a successful occasion for doubt, and justifications must appeal to what is common between our frameworks. Larmore paints a picture of humanity 'fundamentally divided' along 'divergent structures of purposes, significances, and activities' (Larmore, 1996, 172–3) and accepts that our justifications can only appeal to such divided sets of background beliefs.

In summary, Larmore has a substantive commitment to a certain conception of reasonable disagreement according to which the justification for what I believe to be true can quite easily fail to prompt doubt in your framework. Because good reasons are framework-relative, Larmore's approach shares features of coherence relativism. Of course, there is a way in which Larmore's approach might be rendered compatible with strongly universal reasons and values. The only way for Larmore to assert that good reasons are common is to assert that only a reason which is powerful and capable of creating doubt for *everyone* is a good reason. But Larmore also says that we can have good reason to believe as true more than what we can attain reasonable agreement upon. If such reasons were 'good for everyone', then they would be included in the category of generally accepted reasons. If Larmore believes that the only good reason is a universally compelling one, then reasonable agreement would 'contain' all the good reasons, and no other reasons would be significant. Precisely because Larmore states that the reasonable does not suffice to determine justification within an individual's framework, there must be good reasons for me, on Larmore's view, which are not good reasons for others.

---

[13] Larmore is not unique in drawing this distinction, e.g. Rawls, 1972, 580–1.

There is one key problem with Larmore's contextualist model of justification. An important element that distinguishes it from the kind of relativism I am advocating is Larmore's position that justification is only an issue in the presence of doubt — that justification is only required when we have within our system 'positive grounds for doubt that alone make it necessary to seek the justification of that belief' (Larmore, 1996, 173). This is what enables him to claim his position has no sceptical implications, so that 'we should regard our view as true however much it may be the object of reasonable disagreement' (Larmore, 1996, 173). Unsurprisingly, this is where I think the problem lies. Larmore fundamentally underestimates the amount of justification that this will leave us doing. Justifications, understood as the reasoning that supports our conclusions, are not something we only consider when they are called into question by others, at least partly because justification does not require an actual challenge. We constantly consider the 'proof' (reasoning) for our judgements whenever we come across a situation which requires a judgement, for it is the reasoning which allows us to weigh potential responses and choose one for good reasons.[14] Furthermore, the strength of the reasoning behind our judgements is relevant to deciding the question of whether there are positive grounds for doubt or not. The question of whether the positive grounds for doubt compel us to justify our system itself requires a *prior* assessment of the strength of our justification to determine whether there are any grounds for doubt at all. Thus, I am unconvinced by Larmore's position that justification can only occasioned by 'positive grounds for doubt' within our framework. Justification ought to be, and is, a more widespread exercise than Larmore thinks.

This section has examined the idea of reasonable disagreement, expanding on my characterisation of it in the work of Rawls by introducing the account of the phenomenon advanced by Charles Larmore. I have argued that it is not the bare phenomenon of reasonable disagreement that motivates the 'neutral' justification for political liberal neutrality. Instead, liberals must assert at least that reasonable disagreement is not due wholly to mistakes in the application of shared standards. I have looked at the way in which this idea is expressed in the thought of Rawls and Larmore,

---

[14]   It might be responded that this is because of doubt as to the right course of action. But if this is a case of doubt, then we are always in doubt. However, we can rehearse the reasons we have for performing an action without entertaining 'positive grounds for doubt', and I would maintain that we regularly do this. We can consider without being hesitant or doubtful.

and argued that we can find relativist claims in the foundations of both of their approaches.

Liberalism, Scepticism and Relativism

Having examined the role of relativism in arguments for liberal neutrality, it is worth turning now to scepticism, because the latter is sometimes seen as both a problem and an alternative foundation for liberalism.[15] It is a *problem* for liberalism because the position of political liberals is contradictory on this issue. Thus, as we have seen, Rawls' argument holds that (a) no-one's proposal in uniquely justified, but that (b) this should not dent our confidence that our proposal is uniquely justified. In this form, his position is mystifying. Larmore similarly offers a defence of certainty despite elements which pull him in the opposite direction. Only his particular account of when justification is necessary allows Larmore to avoid scepticism, and I have argued that this account is flawed.

However, scepticism about the possibility of justification could perhaps serve as an *alternative* to the relativity of justification. I have argued in this chapter that reasonable disagreement contains elements of relativism. Nevertheless, it could be objected that pushing political liberals into the relativist camp is problematic because there are viable alternatives to relativism as a metaethical foundation. One of the most prominent of these alternatives is found in Brian Barry's interpretation of political liberalism. A form of scepticism constitutes Barry's *solution* to the problems of political liberalism. He argues for a forthright ethic of scepticism to underpin the liberal commitment to reasonable disagreement. I want to examine his argument here to determine whether it really offers an alternative to a relativist understanding of reasonable disagreement.

Brian Barry, Reasonable Rejectability and Scepticism

By contrast to Larmore, Brian Barry is one liberal neutralist who believes that the phenomenon of reasonable disagreement requires explanation, and does not often get it (Barry, 1995b, 329). It needs explanation because reasonable disagreement forms a core justification of liberal neutrality, by supporting a liberal response to cultural diversity for reasons beyond those of mere

---

[15] Of course, some thinkers have argued that neither scepticism nor relativism should be invoked in support of liberalism (e.g. Waldron, 1989, 73). My position here will be only that relativism must be invoked as part of 'political liberalism', properly understood.

mutual advantage (Barry, 1995a, 164). Barry holds that one fundamental feature of reasonable disagreement stands especially in need of elaboration: 'the proposition that there is no conception of the good that cannot reasonably be rejected' (Barry, 1995b, 329). This expectation that others can reasonably reject opposing views is, as I have argued, incompatible with reasonable disagreement being solely due to mistakes. It is also a key claim about the nature of reasonable disagreement which underwrites liberal arguments for neutrality. Thus Barry, looking at possible ways of interpreting what happens when reasonable people disagree, holds that 'the only one that seems to me adequate is to deny that there is any conception of the good that nobody could reasonably reject' (Barry, 1995a, 169). In holding this, Barry might appear quite close to what Gaus terms a 'relativism of reasons'.[16] Certainly, his claim entails a denial of the view that what counts as a good reason for me must count as one for everyone else as well. There is no set of reasons in support of a conception of the good that cannot be overturned or defeated in someone's framework. However, Barry argues in *Justice as Impartiality* that the best argument for liberal neutrality needs 'moderate' scepticism in order to justify this understanding of reasonable disagreement.

> How then are we to establish that there is no conception of the good that nobody could reasonably reject? The answer that I wish to defend is that no conception of the good can justifiably be held with a degree of certainty that warrants its imposition on those who reject it (Barry, 1995a, 169).

Barry thus links the case for justified rejection of conceptions of the good to justified *doubt* about all conceptions of the good. This move lies at the heart of Barry's argument and is, I will go on to show, intensely problematic. I want to examine Barry's adoption of what he calls moderate scepticism in two stages. First, I will examine the content of Barry's scepticism and the relationship between that and his claim that no conception of the good stands immune to reasonable rejection. Second, I will examine the argument Barry gives in support of his sceptical conclusion. I believe that both these components possess problems. I conclude my assessment by arguing that Barry's position is far from the most satisfactory elaboration of reasonable disagreement, and that relativism, as I will go on to propose in this chapter, is substantially less problematic.

---

[16]   Gaus gives a simple characterisation of a relativism of reasons thus: 'Given Alf's perspective . . . it is possible that he has no reason to believe Beta, while given our system of beliefs, we do' (Gaus, 1996, 39).

Barry's Argument from Scepticism

For Barry, scepticism refers to doubt that I have knowledge rather than the denial of the possibility of knowledge. Thus, his scepticism suggests that 'certainty is ill-founded' rather than 'belief is ill-founded' (Barry, 1995a, 169). He proposes that we should remain certain enough for ourselves to live our lives by a conception of the good, but not certain enough to impose our beliefs on others. In terms of my brief discussion of Rawls and scepticism in the previous chapter, he is using scepticism as an attack on confidence rather than knowledge. What remains ambiguous, however, is the link between the two. Exactly what is the difference between knowing, and knowing for certain? And doesn't the undermining of confidence in a conclusion involve raising doubts about the justification for that conclusion?

Barry sees scepticism as the response to a dilemma — 'why should I not impose my views when I am confident they cannot be reasonably rejected?' Barry's apparent answer makes two claims:

(1) A *sceptical* claim: 'no conception of the good can justifiably be held with a degree of certainty that warrants its imposition on those who reject it.'

(2) A *reasonable rejectability* claim: 'there is no conception of the good that nobody could reasonably reject', i.e. all conceptions of the good can be reasonably rejected (Barry, 1995a, 169).

If I am correct about the apparent structure of Barry's argument, the first of these — the sceptical claim — is meant to provide a reason for us to accept the second, reasonable rejectability, claim. As it stands this argument is problematic, for reasons I will now go on to demonstrate.

To illustrate the way in which Barry constantly allies reasonable rejection and certainty, let us look in more detail at the way his argument runs. The liberal neutralist wants to describe a situation in which people are certain of their own view in a plurality of views, but do not want to impose their view on other people. The problem Barry identifies is what to say to people who believe that their conception of the good 'is one that nobody can reasonably reject' (Barry, 1995a, 182). He writes 'I question whether certainty from the inside about some view can coherently be combined with the line that it is reasonable for others to reject that same view' (Barry, 1995a, 179). For Barry, the way to render this situation coherent is for people to have only limited certainty in their beliefs. Thus, 'I should recognize the inherent uncertainty of these beliefs. While having enough confidence in them to live by them, therefore, I should at the same time recognize that others can reasonably reject them' (Barry, 1995a, 178).

So, Barry thinks that an affirmation of moderate scepticism is the correct response to the political liberal's problem. But what makes people have less certainty in their beliefs if their beliefs still possess the same amount of justification?[17] For example, let us suppose that I am certain that X is the case. What makes me certain of this is a set of reasons that, as far as I am concerned, justify my belief. Now, either my reasons are good ones, in which case I am justifiably certain, or else they are bad ones, in which case my certainty that X is the case is ill-founded or unjustified. What can weaken my certainty that X is the case? Perhaps some deep-seated insecurity or self-doubt comes to the surface. But what *ought* to weaken my certainty? Surely only a change in how justified my beliefs are. Justification and justified certainty have to be linked. I think Barry recognises this: he wants to weaken our certainty by a definite amount — to the point at which we no longer feel certain of our righteousness in imposition of our conception of the good. As I will examine shortly, Barry attempts to do this by providing reasons which weaken our justified certainty to the required degree.

If justified certainty in a view is what is at issue, then Barry's argument relies on a premise about justification rather than certainty. He is saying to the non-liberal 'you should not be absolutely certain that your beliefs are correct' — but why? If we replace the concept of certainty in these situations with the other thing Barry's account already commits him to denying, the possibility of one single uniquely reasonable conception of the good, then the force of what he is saying becomes clear. I cannot believe that my belief is uniquely justified whilst simultaneously holding that people can reasonably reject it. If unique justification is required for Barry's justified certainty, then of course he is correct in what he is saying. Our certainty should be undermined by other people plausibly rejecting our view and holding a different one. However, he is mistaking the effect — 'I do not hold this view with absolute certainty' for the cause — 'my view is not uniquely justified'.

Either *justifiable* surety is reliant on no one else being able to *reasonably* reject your point of view, in which case the certainty claim collapses into the reasonable rejection claim, or placing the stress

---

[17] Of course, people might have a well-justified belief which they are uncertain about (perhaps through constant pressure or ridicule from others); but that is different from maintaining that people ought to or should be less certain of a well-justified belief.

on certainty rather than *justified* certainty means that Barry is positing the bald fact that we can never be certain enough to impose.
In this second case, whether our view can be reasonably rejected,
or the amount of justification it possesses, is irrelevant. Even if it
could not be reasonably rejected, we would not be confident
enough to impose it. Either certainty is what is important, so there
is no need for the idea of *reasonable* rejection, or else (and this is
what I strongly suspect) the real work is done by the claim about
the constant possibility of justifiable rejection, of which a decline
in justifiable confidence is merely an epiphenomenon.[18] On this
account, Barry's argument rides on the back of a relativist account
of justification, or at least requires an account of justification on
which I can be justified in living my life by a principle but cannot
justify that principle to others in a way they are committed to
accepting. Something like this must underpin his claims about
certainty.[19]

In summary, Barry is wrong in thinking that scepticism about
justified certainty lies at the base of an elaboration of reasonable
disagreement. Instead Barry's scepticism, as the erosion of justified certainty is a *consequence,* either philosophically or psychologically bound up with the possibility of reasonable rejection.
Barry's assertion that 'scepticism supplies the premise that is
needed to get from the desire for agreement on reasonable terms
to the conclusion that no conception of justice should be built into
the constitution or principles of justice' (Barry, 1995a, 172) is
undermined by his reliance on the reasonable rejection principle,
as will be shown when I look at his argument for scepticism.[20]

---

[18] As I go on to note, in his argument for scepticism Barry constantly
invokes both reasonable rejectability and justified certainty.

[19] On an alternative relativist account, certainty itself could in a sense be
relativised. To be certain in a world where no conception of the good is
immune from reasonable rejection is to be certain that something is justified by my standards even though I realize other people's frameworks
might commit them to rejecting it, and that there is no uniquely reasonable answer. This argument, that a kind of certainty could remain in a
world where we recognise the impossibility of successfully justifying
our belief to everyone, is what seems to me the appropriate relativist
answer to the problem of scepticism, and is a subject I will examine later
in the chapter.

[20] It should be noted that Barry's account, I believe, commits him to the
same sorts of criticism of Rawls and Larmore's anti-sceptical stances that
I made above and in the previous chapter. For example, in *Justice as
Impartiality,* he argues that Larmore requires a tacit scepticism for his
argument to work (Barry, 1995a, 173–7).

Barry's Argument For Scepticism

Separate problems arise in the argument Barry offers for his scepticism. These problems are significant, because if scepticism is the foundation of his argument for political liberalism, then we must perforce look at his argument for scepticism in order to assess the overall force of Barry's proposal. Only then can we see whether scepticism really constitutes a viable alternative to relativism. There are two strands to Barry's argument for scepticism. The first is his primary 'argument from experience', arguing that the history of religious toleration shows a failure to attain rational conviction from other people. The second responds to potential criticisms of his account by arguing that the position of scepticism belongs on a different level to those dogmatisms (conceptions of the good that state they cannot be reasonably rejected) that are being criticised.

Barry's primary argument is, I believe, a weak one. He takes the failure of attempts to impose one conception of the good, such as the 'conflicts between Catholics and Protestants in post-Reformation Europe' (Barry, 1995a, 170) as 'evidence in favour of scepticism'. Barry argues that the failure of 'attempts to enforce religious orthodoxy' (Barry, 1995a, 169) should leave us with a sense that all the differing conceptions of the good can be (and have been) rationally rejected by someone. He writes,

> It is hard not to be impressed by the fact that so many people have devoted so much effort over the centuries to a matter of the greatest moment with so little success in the way of securing rational conviction among those not initially predisposed in favor of their conclusion (Barry, 1995a, 171).

Again, it should be noted that Barry is talking about 'securing rational conviction' rather than feelings of certainty. The evidence he offers, if anything, is evidence of a failure to secure rational agreement, but it is a *testament* to the continued strength of certainty that believers felt. It is a history of people plainly believing that they *are* certain enough to impose on others. The historical record surely illustrates the *resilience* of certainty despite a lack of success in converting others. We can see then that Barry's argument is viciously circular. He is offering evidence of reasonable rejectability of conceptions of the good, in order to show that people should not be certain enough to impose their conception of the good, in order to support the idea that no conception of the good can be reasonably rejected. The introduction of scepticism adds no further support for Barry's position; Barry could omit scepticism and support his argument for reasonable rejectability by simply citing the way that throughout history, people have reasonably rejected conceptions of the good. Then he would simply be claiming (1) there is no conception of the good throughout human history that has been accepted by everybody; (2) therefore, it is unlikely that such a conception of the good exists.

It is entirely unclear what scepticism adds to the argument here; instead, it simply draws on the support of the reasonable rejectability thesis. In any case, a religious person could quite reasonably reject Barry's reading of history; and in particular reject the idea that it constitutes evidence that there is no conception of the good which cannot be *reasonably* rejected. Indeed, many of the examples Barry cites as methods of securing rational conviction throughout history would be rejected as unsatisfactory — penalties, persecution and the like. The claim that rational conviction cannot be achieved through persecution is one that dogmatists, I would guess, are quite willing to concede. This in no way, however, impugns the believer's claim that her view would command rational assent if people really listened, or were not swayed by Satan etc. There are alternative interpretations and explanations of continued disagreement.[21] Like the dogmatists he criticises, Barry's arguments here only provide evidence for scepticism for those initially predisposed in favour of this conclusion, and will not compel such dogmatists to accept his view. Barry says, 'I do wish to assert that whether or not dogmatists are actually convinced by the case for scepticism, they ought to be' (Barry, 1995a, 171). In a similar way, dogmatists will assert that while Barry is unconvinced by dogmatisms, he ought to be; certainly, his argument does not suffice to stop the religious believer from maintaining that her view ought not to be reasonably rejected.

My argument above, as Barry notes of dogmatists, might carry the implication that scepticism is equivalent to dogmatism. This is where his second strand is introduced. It is important for Barry's position that scepticism stands in a different relation to the dogmatisms it criticises, perhaps to show it is more 'reasonable'. The reason for this is,

> the impression that there are two positions — scepticism on one side and dogmatism on the other — is misleading. What we really have is scepticism on one side and a host of conflicting dogmatisms on the other. These dogmatisms cancel one another out, in a manner of speaking ... the sceptic is in the happy position of agreeing with each about 99 per cent of what he maintains, that is to say the inherent lack of certitude in everybody else's beliefs. He disagrees with each only at

---

[21]   In a similar vein to some unsuccessful arguments for relativism I have analysed, evidence of diversity does not prompt the acceptance of scepticism; rather, it is a certain *interpretation* of the evidence.

the point where he maintains that his own beliefs provide the unique exception to what he claims to be the case for everybody else's (Barry, 1995a, 172).

Notice that here the religious believer attributes inherent lack of justified certainty to others, rather than reasonable rejectability. Again, Barry swaps between the two terms as if they were identical.[22] In any case, Barry's argument here is unconvincing at best. To say that the believer's claim of truth constitutes 1% of what she maintains underestimates the crucial importance of claiming something as certain. Without wanting to get into the mathematics of Barry's argument,[23] he is doing an injustice to the believers' position by claiming that the truth or justifiable certainty component of a belief system is quantifiable and of minute significance; I would contend that a claim of certainty can permeate the whole or most of a belief system. Furthermore, we are left unclear as to exactly how dogmatisms 'cancel out', leaving scepticism untouched. Barry maintains that the sceptic agrees with ninety-nine per cent of a believer's position. If the claim of certitude constitutes a portion of someone's belief, and Barry's sceptical component fits neatly in the place of that errant component, then that is on Barry's own argument the *only* difference that prevents sceptics from agreeing with dogmatists. The implications of this argument surely puts Barry's scepticism *more* on a par with all the other dogmatisms, rather than *less*.

I now want to sum up my position vis-à-vis Barry. Barry maintains that 'scepticism supplies the premise' in an argument involving agreement on reasonable terms and arriving at a liberal neutralist conclusion. He argues that his argument suffices to justify this position. He thus writes 'the claim I wish to make is not simply that this premise can do the job; I also maintain that it is the only one that can' (Barry, 1995a, 173). I have argued against this conclusion by holding that Barry's strictly sceptical premise adds nothing to the foundation of reasonable rejectability which he builds upon. If anything, it confuses and weakens his claim, by introducing the notion of being certain enough for ourselves, but not certain enough to impose on others. I think this is potentially a

---

[22] Though the religious believer would assert a reasonable rejectability claim as well.

[23] I believe that Barry's mathematical approach here belongs in the distinguished company of Rousseau's (in)famously difficult assertion that 'take away from these same wills the pluses and minuses that cancel one another, and the general will remains as the sum of the differences' (Rousseau, 1993, 203).

separate reason for neutrality, but not a promising one.[24] Barry ignores one obvious alternative, which is to flesh out the idea of reasonable rejectability that in any case his sceptical premise relies on. Thus, I want to conclude that Barry's proposal fails to provide an alternative to a relativist foundation for political liberalism. Instead, his claim collapses into a claim about justification which is relativist in spirit.

Relativism and Justificatory Liberalism

Previous sections have analysed the idea of reasonable disagreement as a component of liberal arguments for neutrality. I have argued that this phenomenon stands in need of explanation in order to fulfil the role asked of it by liberal theory, and that the explanations provided by Charles Larmore, John Rawls and Brian Barry are incomplete or inadequate in various respects. I have briefly indicated where relativism is similar to or differs from the views of justification advocated by liberal thinkers. In particular, I noted that it shared features with Larmore's approach. In this section, I provide more positive considerations to support the claim that relativism presents a good candidate for the theory of justification underpinning liberal reasonable disagreement. This exercise will involve two elements that draw upon the central requirements for a satisfactory account of reasonable disagreement. First, I want to look at the way relativism explains reasonable disagreement, and argue that this fulfils the liberal requirement. I argue that the line drawn by coherence relativism between justified and underjustified moralities is similar to the standard of reasonableness involved in the idea of reasonable disagreement. Second, I want to suggest a way in which a relativist theory of justification can answer the sceptical dilemma identified by Barry and others.

I noted at the start of this chapter that a political liberalism which rests on relativist foundations constitutes what Gaus terms a *justificatory* liberalism. Such a liberal position recognises that the concept of justification is central to liberalism, and so is committed to providing an account of justification. Gaus maintains 'Because there is no such thing as an uncontentious theory of justification, an adequately articulated liberalism must clarify

---

[24] What would support the position of being certain enough for ourselves, but not for others, if not justification? We might invoke respect for others as a reason for a different standard of certainty for our relations with others. However, for reasons given in chapter six I am unsure about the ability of equal respect to function as a neutral justification of neutrality.

and defend its conception of justified belief — its epistemology'
(Gaus, 1996, 4). In this part of the chapter I will come to conclusions which are very similar to Gaus', though for slightly different
reasons. Like Gaus, I believe that political liberalism (despite its
disavowals) does draw on an account of justification, though as it
stands this account is confused (Gaus, e.g. 1996, 3-5; 1998, 259–60).
Again like Gaus, I believe that political liberalism stands in need
of clear justificatory foundations, and such foundations should
recognise the relativity of justification (Gaus, 1996, e.g. 3-6,
292-295). However, my conclusions are reached for rather different reasons; where Gaus interrogates the concepts of public reason and commonsense reasoning used by political liberalism, I
approach these conclusions through an analysis of the idea of reasonable disagreement. I am unsure about the force of parts of
Gaus' arguments, and the relevance of the proposal that follows
from his conclusion. This proposal forms part of the subject for
discussion in the final section of this chapter, which asks the
question of how a justificatory rather than political liberalism
should be legitimised.

(1) Relativism and Reasonableness In Disagreement

However, first it is necessary to examine how relativism interprets reasonable disagreement. We can begin by noting that reasonable rejectability has a dual nature. Reasonableness is both a
line to be crossed and a concrete package of reasoning methods
and tools common to all. Thus, it allows for two constituencies of
reasonably rejectable views. The first constituency comprises
those views which fail to meet a standard of reasonableness: these
views are definitionally unreasonable. However, at least some
conceptions of the good (those termed by Rawls 'reasonable comprehensive doctrines') will pass the standard of reasonableness.
Political liberalism also holds that none of this reduced set of
views is immune to reasonable rejection. With regard to this second constituency of positions, 'reasonable rejection' must mean
rejecting views for reasons which whilst they are not *general* common elements of reasoning, and hence not part of the conception
of epistemic reasonableness, are not *un*reasonable either.

For me to hold a view justifiably, reasonableness is a necessary
condition. However, considerations of general standards of reasoning are not sufficient to determine which reasonable view I
should hold. My reasons for affirming one reasonable view and
rejecting other such views have to be made on grounds which are
not common to everyone (else they would constitute part of the
conception of reasonableness itself) but which nevertheless do

not violate the requirements of reasonableness. Reasonable rejectability thus entails the core relativist claim that there is no uniquely interpersonally justified conception of the good. That a view is reasonable does not entail that everyone must accept it. Rather, a liberal who affirms reasonable rejectability is committed to the claim that there is no single conception of the good which can be successfully justified to everyone. In other words, there will always be reasonable grounds (grounds which do not violate the requirements of epistemic reasonableness) for someone to reject it. She must also be committed to there being a broad standard of reasonableness, below which conceptions of the good are unreasonable. This element appears close to the claim of an intersubjective standard of justification, identified in chapter four as a component of a relativist approach. Furthermore, this standard allows the rejection of conceptions of the good for reasons that do not fall foul of the idea of epistemic reasonableness. The idea of justifications that meet the standard of reasonableness, but are not part of that standard, overlaps with the relativist idea of a further, more personal level of framework-relative justification.

I want to argue that the particular kind of relativism I discussed earlier, *coherence relativism*, maps on to the epistemic component of reasonableness to draw the same line as that drawn by the liberal standard of epistemic reasonableness.[25] First, I will examine in more detail what liberal 'reasonableness' involves with regard to beliefs, so it can be seen more clearly what this standard shares with relativism. In looking at this, I draw upon the argument which Gerald Gaus puts forward for this conclusion. Gaus outlines a difference between *rational* belief and *reasonable* belief. Rational belief is defined by its adherence to a principle of epistemic rationality (Gaus, 1995, 239).[26] This principle says that for it to be epistemically rational to hold a belief, that belief must be justified by credible evidence (including its coherence with other elements of one's belief system), the evidence must be accepted by the person holding the belief, and there is no belief that the holder finds more credible. On the other hand, reasonable beliefs are those generated by agents through the good faith application of their reasoning powers. Gaus contends that reasonable beliefs can be mistaken (or irrational) — much like my analy-

---

[25] This is not to say that the line is absolutely clear; there can and will be cases in which justification is hard to discern, but this again is something that is shared by this line and that of reasonableness.

[26] Gaus offers a weaker and stronger conception of epistemic rationality. For the sake of brevity and clarity here, I do not discuss these two standards, but take the more demanding one.

sis in the earlier part of this chapter — so that reasonable people can nevertheless hold irrational beliefs in some instances. Political liberals cannot appeal to reasonable but epistemically irrational reasons because, as I illustrated earlier, irrational reasons or mistakes can be conclusively rejected; thus, only those reasonable beliefs which are not epistemically flawed should be considered. Liberalism thus operates on a standard of reasonable beliefs dubbed 'sufficiently credible' to count.

Coherence relativism has a similar standard of sufficient justification. The kinds of things which constitute this maximally interpersonal baseline standard are the same kinds of things that are relevant to deciding whether a belief is 'sufficiently credible'. Appeals to both standards involve appeals to basic tenets of reasoning as being the most common or generally held ones. Coherence relativism, as I noted in my earlier outline, looks for a standard of consistency within propositions of a framework and between propositions and the perceived facts, and coherence in terms of mutual support between those beliefs. Generally held standards of reasoning will want to endorse both of these elements as relevant and important to the credibility or epistemic reasonableness of a belief. The link is especially clear because coherence with the rest of a belief set is relevant to credibility or the rationality of the belief (Gaus, 1995, 244, footnote 25). Coherence and consistency are chosen by coherence relativism as a base standard for justification precisely because they represent generally held elements of reasoning. Whilst the standard of justification offered by relativism doesn't say anything in itself about the need for 'good faith' on the part of reasoners, it clearly makes a set of claims which are held in common with epistemic reasonableness. In fact, we can regard relativism as providing a specification of sufficient epistemic rationality.

Thus, the split between justified and underjustified sets of beliefs made by coherence relativism maps onto the standard of epistemic rationality adopted by political liberalism. In accordance with a focus on good faith application of standards in arriving at such beliefs, it provides the account of 'the reasonable' required by political liberalism. I now turn to the second consideration supporting a relativist foundation, which concerns the liberal response to scepticism.

(2) Relativism and the Sceptical Implications of Reasonable Rejectability

As we have seen, political liberals have held that the 'reasonable rejectability' view of disagreement has no implications for the certainty with which a view is held. I have argued that this account is problematic: the dilemma, as outlined by Barry,[27] is how to believe my view to be certainly correct whilst also believing it to be reasonably rejectable. I want to argue here that coherence relativism offers a ready explanation of how a kind of certainty can be consistent with the reasonable rejection of my view by others. Again, this is made possible by the relativist analysis of the two senses in which a conception of the good can be justifiably rejected. The relativist response starts by questioning *what* we are to be certain of or certain that.

I cannot consistently believe (1) there is no conception of the good that nobody can reasonably reject *and* (2) my conception of the good cannot be reasonably rejected. Proposition (2) is doubtless something we could possibly be certain of, and it is perhaps what some thinkers are talking about in the debate over whether reasonable disagreement undermines certainty. The reasonable rejection position *cannot* be combined with the claim that I am certain that my view is uniquely reasonably justified. Thus, reasonable rejectability ought to undermine certainty in (2). However, in the terms of coherence relativism, reasonable rejection can be combined with the claim (2a) that my view is uniquely justified in my framework, by which we mean it embodies our deepest commitments in a consistent and coherent way better than the available competition. (2a) is something, I think, which a person could be justifiably certain of whilst affirming the reasonable rejectability condition (1).

The implication of this is that rather than leaving us less certain, reasonable rejectability affects what we can be said to be certain *of*. The preliminary conclusions of this analysis are twofold. First, that political liberalism does undermine certainty, at least certainty that our view can be successfully justified to others. This is unavoidable given its commitment to reasonable rejectability. As I have noted above, propositions (1) and (2) are inconsistent. Second, relativism — specifically coherence relativism — yields exactly the specification of certainty allowed by liberalism. Whilst on one level this should not be surprising, given my arguments about the similarity of reasonable rejectability and the central relativist claim, it illustrates the degree of sympathy between relativism and this component of political liberalism.[28]

[27] But which also appears in the work of Nagel, for example (Nagel, 1987)
[28] Another point here is that coherence relativism in addition allows us to remain certain that, by our standards, other moralities are not as good as our own.

Does this analysis solve the dilemma for political liberals by leaving us as certain as we want to be? In a sense, the question is misleading, as it emerges that we can be certain *of* two different things. Both presumably admit of degrees, but there appears no inherent reason to be less confident in uttering (2a) that my view is justified (in the relativist sense) than there is to be to be confident of (2) that my view is justified (uniquely, so that my justification of it to others must be successful). Furthermore, this relativist approach offers a way to reappraise Barry's argument. The truth in Barry's conflation of reasonable rejectability and scepticism lies here. If we admit certainty in (2a), and affirm a premise allowing imposition only where it cannot be reasonably rejected (what I have called 'the justification principle'), then the outcome will be an unwillingness to impose our views, which could be expressed as a lack of certainty or confidence in the proposition 'I am justified in imposing my view on others'. Political liberalism cannot allow us any more certainty without violating reasonable rejectability. This feature of political liberalism derails its attempt to find a legitimising consensus behind liberal principles. The liberal must hold that we cannot be certain of our ability to convince others. Plenty of other comprehensive doctrines will find this claim problematic. Political liberalism is thus controversial, and in conflict with conceptions of the good which claim to be certain of more.

Having surveyed various political liberal positions, and examined the role that relativism might play, I want to draw together the core ideas of this chapter so far. Someone might argue that all that has been shown is that relativism is compatible with liberalism: it has not been shown that relativism is required by political liberalism. My response to this is first that even if I have proved only the weaker compatibility claim, then this ought to have serious consequences for the antipathy many liberals have for relativism. However, I believe I have offered considerable evidence for the stronger conclusion. Earlier in this chapter, I offered accounts and criticisms of other competing explanations for the reasonable rejectability claim (I think that Larmore's, in any case, largely maps onto my own relativist approach). Brian Barry's sceptical approach fails to solve the problem, for it collapses into the reasonable rejectability thesis.

On the positive side, I have argued in the two preceding sections that reasonable rejectability strictly, even tautologically, entails justifiable rejectability. We cannot affirm that a view can be reasonably rejected for reason A which meets the standard of reasonableness without affirming that such a view can be rejected by any framework which contains A.[29] If any view can be reasonably rejected, then the core relativist claim that there need be no single justified morality must be correct. I have noted that the standard of maximally interpersonal justification endorsed by coherence relativism maps onto the standard of accordance with general standards of reason which forms the core of the idea of reasonableness. Lastly, I argued that relativism provides an answer to the question of the sceptical implications of reasonable rejectability. Confusion over whether liberalism can supply a defence of certainty and assert reasonable rejectability can be eased by determining exactly what we are meant to be left certain *of*. Thus, this argument for neutrality rests on foundations which are relativistic in character. Furthermore, I have argued that the kind of relativism I have advocated can cohere with the claims of political liberalism. However, having a relativist foundation might be thought to change the character of the whole proposal, and this is what I now want to discuss.

Justificatory Liberalism and the Possibility of Legitimacy

Having established that relativism can provide a plausible account of the foundations that liberalism needs for the argument from reasonable disagreement to succeed, the next question concerns what this recognition does to the character of the argument. Does it change the extent to which the argument could be deemed neutral, and thus the possibility for garnering consensus? It is, it could be contended, a strength of the arguments made by Rawls and Larmore that they do not commit themselves to a particular set of philosophical foundations — this is exactly what constitutes *political* liberalism. Adding a relativist foundation would surely remove that strength.

This argument would succeed were the arguments themselves neutral and unproblematic. However, as I have argued in this chapter and chapter six, Rawls, Barry and Larmore already embody some distinctive and to my mind controversial metaethical claims. In spelling out the idea of reasonable disagreement as reasonable rejectability, how their accounts can avoid scepticism, and the authority which their accounts can command, controversial metaethical claims are inescapable, and relativism is implied in some of these claims. The open acceptance

---

[29] Having said this, I think there are situations where if an individual asserted A insincerely, or without reasons to support it — i.e. his view was procedurally underjustified — the affirmation of A would not suffice to justify the rejection of a view which clashed with it.

of relativism, or of key elements of relativism,[30] would simply be acknowledging that the proposal is a thoroughgoing one which has an account of justification as part of the parcel. A relativist could argue that it would not make the political liberal accounts less neutral or more metaethically committed precisely because the accounts are already metaethically committed, in some cases explicitly to aspects of what the relativist affirms, and thus their claim to complete neutrality is bogus. In other words, I do not see how the addition of a relativist thesis to the liberal account would harm its justification, as it already contains the seeds of one.[31] Of course, if political liberalism appears to be foundationless or neutral with regard to philosophical controversies, then even if this appearance is deceiving, it would at least prevent people from disagreeing with the foundations.[32] If a commitment to relativist, or indeed any other foundations were publicly added, this would change. Alongside those who would reject liberal principles or policies, anybody with a different metaethical view could reject the relativist component. Earlier, I attempted to provide good arguments for metaethical relativism. Nevertheless, coherence relativism recognizes that these could be reasonably rejected by some people who have differing frameworks, within which my justification appears unsuccessful. So, how could justificatory liberalism attain consensus? I think there are three possible responses.

First, it could be left to people to have their own reasons to affirm liberal conclusions. Whilst Rawls' view is that reasonable people should ideally affirm the burdens of judgement (Rawls, 1993, 54), justificatory liberalism need not endorse that conclusion. As long as reasonable people value the goals of liberalism, there is no need to seek convergence in the *reasons* they have for valuing liberalism. There are two possibilities here, and both have theoretical adherents. On one account, liberalism is affirmed as a

---

[30] Whilst I am proposing coherence relativism as a justified and plausible theory of moral justification, liberalism could conceivably provide an account of justification by combining various elements of coherence relativism and other relativist or non-relativist proposals. Consideration of the possible configurations of such elements is outside the scope of this book; however, I am contending that something like coherence relativist foundations should be added.

[31] Rather than saying that it contains the beginnings of a relativist approach, it is perhaps more correct to say that it constitutes the result; relativist conclusions are used or assumed as the starting point.

[32] This is purely a practical point about the expediency of *appearing* foundationless. As I have argued, I think there is plenty in the basic ideas of political liberalism which could justifiably be objected to.

modus vivendi; liberal ideas of tolerance and a neutral state happen to be in people's narrow self-interest, perhaps because they alone can deliver civil peace in a divided society.[33] On the other, liberal conclusions are affirmed by different people for different moral or theoretical reasons. For example, Catholics and communists might affirm the importance of equality and equality of liberty for various reasons that are valid within their divergent systems. On this account, whilst a justification for liberal principles could be offered, people would not have to accept these foundations for liberal principles, or even consider questions of whether justification was relative or not.

A second response (which can supplement the first) would be to adopt Rawls' suggestion that there will be *stages* to overlapping consensus. Rawls offers a political sociology aimed at opponents who view his position as utopian.[34] What starts as a *modus vivendi* might evolve into an overlapping consensus on not just liberal principles but their justification, through a stage of constitutional consensus. 'As a constitutional consensus, these principles are accepted simply as principles and not as grounded in certain ideas of society and person of a political conception' (Rawls, 1993, 158). This development would take place over time, partly because liberal institutions 'tend to shift citizens' comprehensive doctrines so that they at least accept the principles of a liberal constitution' (Rawls, 1993, 163) and partly because participation in such a consensus itself encourages further broadening and deepening of the consensus through requirements of generality of application and justification (Rawls, 1993, 165–6). In other words, Rawls is offering good reasons, arising from institutional and cultural change, to indicate how this shift could naturally come about. Whilst this does not talk about the foundations or justificatory components of liberalism (because Rawls maintains that his liberalism is political), a further step might be that liberal institutions would encourage a 'liberal culture' of views which saw moral justification and truth as relative, the eventual result being a society which affirmed liberalism for largely relativist reasons.[35]

---

[33] The positions of David Gauthier (1986) and John Gray (1996) perhaps approach this idea of justice as mutual advantage — of liberalism being in people's self-interest, but unstable should those interests change (Rawls, 1993, 147).

[34] Rawls provides this account in *Political Liberalism*, Lecture IV, 6–7. Here I can do no more than provide a brief sketch of his answer to this charge.

[35] The question of the mechanism which would effect such a change is a large one. It seems to me that the change could be prompted partly by the

Arguments that liberal principles, institutions and education encourage sceptical or relativist attitudes have been made by communitarian critics of liberalism such as Alasdair MacIntyre, who maintains that the enlightenment project of which liberalism is the offspring has left us in a culture of emotivism, where moral disagreements consist in mere statements of preference (MacIntyre, 1981, 6). He writes, 'the culture of liberalism transforms expressions of opinion into what its political and moral theory had already said they were' (MacIntyre, 1988, 343).[36] Whilst for MacIntyre this is a cause for despair, liberal culture need not be viewed like this. A decline in dogmatism, a willingness to countenance the validity of opposing views on their own terms and thus move to recognition of reasonable disagreement could be seen as positive consequences of liberal institutions and education.

A third response to the question of whether relativist liberalism could garner a consensus asks whether there might be an *alternative* to aiming at consensus. Gerald Gaus has argued that justificatory liberalism itself need not be the subject of a consensus in order to be legitimised. One way to instantiate the guiding intuition of liberalism, the principle of what Gaus calls Individualised Liberal Legitimacy (ILL) — 'Alpha's coercion against Beta is legitimate only if there exists a justification for it that Beta may reasonably be expected to endorse' (Gaus, 1998, 277) — is for everyone to consent to the ruling of an impartial judge. Justificatory liberalism accords with leaving difficult decisions to the judgment of this independent arbitrator. Whatever judgement resulted would be legitimised as the outcome of a process to which everyone had consented. Gaus argues

> Citizens committed to ILL in a world of pluralism require precisely this sort of umpiring of their disputes. It honors their commitment to Individualised Liberal Legitimacy because they do not act coercively against another simply on the basis of their own controversial reasoning: all have conclusive reason to submit their dispute to the umpire, who provides an impartial practical resolution of the dispute (Gaus, 1998, 279).

Representative 'adjudicative democracy' (Gaus, 1998, 279) could be the decision procedure, the independent arbitrator to which Gaus refers.

---

success of public justifications of relativism, which I go on to examine shortly.

[36] Similarly Allan Bloom contends that liberal institutions have fostered a relativism which has extinguished 'the search for a good life' (Bloom, 1987, 34) although I disagree with Bloom's diagnosis of relativism as 'the result of apathy about the state of our souls' (Bloom, 1987, 35).

As it stands, Gaus' proposal needs elaboration in order to determine whether he can answer the standard objections raised against such social contract proposals. Gaus may be able to avoid some of these since he stipulates that the agreement is only amongst reasonable people motivated by the principle of individualised liberal legitimacy.[37] I think the real problem with what Gaus proposes lies here, in that he is not answering an important prior question. Gaus stipulates that he has arrived at the same place as Rawls, 'that reasonable citizens will concur on the basic concept of a liberal regime. It was only on more specific political questions that reasonable pluralism asserts itself' (Gaus, 1998, 277). The question Gaus is answering is, 'given that people want neutrality, and given reasonable rejectability, what kind of procedure should we have to *ensure* neutrality?' However, Rawls' position has an earlier stage where my argument and analysis has been focused, and this is the question of how reasonable people holding one of a plurality of competing conceptions of the good arrive at the conclusion that the state ought to be a liberal neutral one.[38]

The strange thing about Gaus' theory is that large sections of his argument against Rawls are pitched at the level of the foundations of Rawls' theory — for example, his argument that the best liberalism 'rests on a theory of justified, reasonable, belief and argument' (Gaus, 1998, 273). But Gaus does not examine in detail whether the clear argument for a liberal 'moral epistemology', showing 'why this is to be preferred' (Gaus, 1996, 4), affects the possibility of consensus.[39] His argument for an impartial judge is a consequence of this position; it is compatible with, and justified by justificatory liberalism, but it is *not* an explanation of how justificatory liberalism might establish a consensus of people committed to ILL. It is only within this constituency that 'satisfying the principle of Liberal Legitimacy should not lead us to seek the consensus of reasonable people, but to seek arguments that are not irreconcilable with reasonable beliefs' (Gaus, 1998, 273). Gaus' proposal is one way of setting out how ILL need not require con-

---

[37] It is unclear for example whether express or tacit consent is required by Gaus; whether the agreement to set up the arbitrator is hypothetical or real; where the powers of the arbitrator to force compliance would begin and end.

[38] E.g. 'To conclude; reasonable persons see that the burdens of judgement set limits on what can be reasonably justified to others, and so they endorse some form of liberty of conscience and freedom of thought' (Rawls, 1993, 61).

[39] Although I briefly discuss below whether it affects the desirability of such a consensus.

sensus but only reasonable justification. However, it does not in itself address why or how people buy into the idea of justificatory liberalism, and in particular the idea of the 'theory of justified belief' on which it rests. Gaus' proposal is a consequence of his justificatory liberalism, but does not constitute a method for *legitimating* justificatory liberalism.

On another level, however, Gaus' proposal does bear on the possibility of a consensus on a justificatory liberalism. Gaus is concerned to maintain that reasonable justification, rather than consensus, is what is of central importance here. Another kind of legitimation can be gained not by successfully gathering a consensus, but by offering a position which is philosophically sound and in accordance with general standards of reasonableness. Such an argument can be presented in public and hope to *win*. This final idea, therefore, questions the need to attain consensus; the attempt at reasonable public justification is instead the priority.[40] A relativist will remain cautious about the success of such a move; Gaus, for one, certainly doubts that conclusive public justifications are easy to achieve. He affirms the 'deep truth' that 'justification is of fundamental importance, yet it really is hard to justify much' (Gaus, 1996, 294).[41] In fact, it is this claim about the difficulty of conclusive justification which motivates the setting up of an impartial judge. The recognition of this difficulty makes it much easier for Gaus to argue for an impartial judge from a stage where everyone already accepts reasonable rejectability and ILL.

What I think the brief discussion above suggests is the need for a twin-track 'hearts' and 'minds' strategy. On the one hand, relativist liberals should try to encourage convergence in the *hearts* of citizens around liberal principles whilst allowing for disagreement about the reasons for that convergence. Simultaneously, they must argue their case for the best reasons in support of liberalism to the justificatory *minds* of citizens, and this will involve spelling out claims about the nature of reasonable disagreement and justification.

---

[40] Simmons, 1999, offers a useful discussion of the relationship between *justifying* and *legitimising* the state.

[41] I think that Gerald Dworkin makes a similar point when he argues (with respect to the idea of neutrality) that 'we must pay more attention to the limitations of reason' (Dworkin, 1975, 140).

Conclusion

This chapter has argued first that political liberals cannot be silent on the conception of reasonable disagreement which must underwrite their argument. Political liberalism must deny the possibility of reasonable disagreement embodying clear mistakes, and instead endorse a conception of reasonable disagreement as reasonable rejectability. That is, reasonable disagreement arises because there is no view which cannot be reasonably rejected by someone. Second, I have argued that this position makes little sense, except against a background of justifiable rejectability of the kind proposed by coherence relativism. Coherence relativism offers a maximally interpersonal standard for justification of conceptions of the good which maps onto the liberal idea of epistemic reasonableness. Because it also offers a second more personal agent-relative standard of justification, coherence relativism shows how certainty can exist even in a world characterised by reasonable rejectability. As an alternative to relativism, I have considered Brian Barry's argument which founds reasonable disagreement on a lack of certainty. However, I have argued that the most plausible interpretation of Barry's position rests not on certainty but instead a relativist account of justification.

Lastly, I have considered whether a justificatory liberalism — a liberalism based on a theory of moral justification — can be the object of a consensus, and if not, how it can be legitimated. I have suggested that the legitimation of liberal principles can be separated from the legitimation of the grounds which underlie those principles, and that the former can provide a springboard for an attempt at the latter through public discussion and reasoning.[42]

These two chapters have concerned liberal arguments for neutrality. However, for many thinkers — for example, Iris Marion Young (1990) and Tariq Modood (2000), neutrality is itself a flawed ideal (Young, 1990, 114–6; Modood, 2000, 190), and should be replaced by a more truly multicultural politics. Such a politics would involve an accommodation and affirmation of difference beyond neutrality or grudging toleration. This is an issue that I cannot properly address here, but there is space to perhaps say two brief things in response. The first is to suggest that at least some of these worries could be responded to by a liberal approach that incorporated group rights, for example that of Kymlicka

---

[42] I think that a commitment to a relativist account of justification has other consequences, notably for our views towards accommodating cultural minorities and conscientious disobedience. See my 'Justification, Disagreement and the Liberal State' (Long, 2003). I mention multiculturalism briefly below.

(1989, 1995).[43] The second concerns the role of relativism in arguments for multiculturalism, and this might be thought to pose a problem for my analysis. Advocates of critical multiculturalism and broadly post-modern theories of hybridity and heterogeneity often perceive relativism or pragmatism to lie at the basis of their understanding of difference.[44] Doesn't relativism, in its support for these theories, oppose liberalism?

My answer is that it need not. First, as we have seen in chapter five, metaethical relativism says nothing *in itself* about how we should respond to other justified moral frameworks. Second, as with toleration, our commitment to multiculturalism has to be weighed against other moral judgements and principles. It may be that neutrality, or a supplemented understanding of neutrality, is a satisfactory resolution to these competing moral demands. Thus, the kind of relativism I have been discussing does not, in any straightforward way, support multiculturalist approaches. Nevertheless, the adoption of relativism might make a difference through its understanding of moral justification. A liberalism which has a central commitment to *justification* might, for example, be able to construct an argument for cultural rights from the importance of people's basic commitments and the difficulties in justifying things to people which impact on their deep commitments. If we lack compelling justification to overturn claims within cultures, this could provide a reason to retain sensitivity towards those claims.

---

[43]   I do not want to say that Kymlicka's approach is umproblematic. It has been criticised for granting both too much (Waldron, 1995; Barry 2000, e.g. 133) and too little authority to culture (Tomasi 1995, Kukathas 1992).

[44]   This is a contestable claim, but to my mind a defensible one (Goldberg, 1994, 15–9; West, 1995, 56–67; May, 1999, 22).

Chapter 8

Conclusion

This book has consisted of two parts: the first dealing with metaethical questions about the nature and defence of relativism, the second concerning questions of political philosophy and the relationship relativism has with them. In the first, I argued that relativism was a plausible account of moral justification. In the second, I argued that such a relativism could successfully underpin the arguments of political liberalism. These two parts can be viewed together as an attempt to rehabilitate relativism and put it to work. In my conclusion, I briefly recap the central claims of my argument, and offer some closing comments on relativism's reputation.

In chapter two, I distinguished between varieties of moral relativism, and examined the contemporary defences of metaethical relativism offered by Wong and Harman. I also argued that Rorty's view could be understood as relativist, and discussed some features of his position. In particular, I evaluated the ability of these views to explain aspects of our moral experience — our reaction to moral horror, moral disagreement, and demands for moral truth. I contended that these contemporary relativist approaches, whilst not vulnerable to some of the common and easy charges made against relativism, nevertheless possessed significant problems. Wong introduces a substantive moral criterion into his theory through his definition of an 'adequate moral system'. Harman invokes 'quasi-absolutism' to explain how relativists can go about their everyday moral lives just like universalists. In these ways, the approaches of Harman and Wong incorporate too great a universalist element in their attempt to provide a defensible relativist explanation of our moral life. They also fail to respond fully to two further important issues concerning our moral experience. The first of these was the ambiguity over what, if any, criticism could be offered of differing but equally justified moral systems. The second concerned indeterminacy in our choice of moral theory, specifically the absence of grounds on which to choose between the equally justified moralities predicted by relativism.

Chapter three examined competing universalist understandings of our moral life. The difference between relativism and universalism lies in the question of whether or not there is or need be a single justified morality, even if it is only a minimal or procedural one. I have discussed two types of universalist approaches; those that claim we must necessarily understand moral discourse as universal — Nagel and Habermas — and those who draw support from some kind of contingent commonality. On this schema, Hampshire's views constitute a half-way house. I have argued that the approaches of Nagel, Habermas and Hampshire face problems. If we do not grant his initial premise, then Nagel's position is unpersuasive. Also, the sceptic *can* escape Habermas' inescapable assumptions of moral discourse. Lastly, neither of the foundations Hampshire offers for his minimal moral core are compelling.

The chapter moved on to discuss more contingent varieties of universalism. Contingent universalism can take several forms, some of which can coexist with relativism. For the relativist, justification is relative to a framework, which may still be widely shared. I have suggested that this allowance by the relativist that the framework may be shared by (up to) everyone is where universalism and relativism can co-exist. The relativist can accept that contingently it may be the case that a moral framework is shared throughout the world. However she can still claim it need not be shared, and indeed that when we look at the framework in more detail, we will see ways in which it is probably not shared. Some varieties of contingent universalism can hold that this is also sufficient for a kind of universalism. These varieties exist in the space created by the overlap between relativism and universalism. I have examined how relativism can respond to the claims of contingent universalism, in particular by drawing out ambiguities in the value of commonality or convergence and its link with universality.

An examination of the methodology of reflective equilibrium in chapter four introduced a response to the problems I identified for relativist approaches in chapter two. After discussing the key features of reflective equilibrium, I argued that reflective equilibrium can be interpreted as a particular elaboration of the key relativist claim that there is no single justified morality. This analysis gives rise to what I term 'coherence relativism' — a relativist account distinct from other contemporary approaches. Coherence relativism uses a standard of consistency and coherence as a baseline to be reached by many moralities. It utilises the distinction between the internal coherence of a morality, and coherence with elements of my moral view in particular, to establish two standards of justification. The first is a maximally interpersonal one comprised by coherence and consistency, and the second a more subjective or framework-relative standard of justification composed of our deep commitments. These deep commitments provide the ground on which we can choose to change our morality or remain committed to the one we have, thus providing a response to the problem of theory choice indeterminacy.

This use of standards of justification might be thought a problem for the coherence relativist account. Coherence relativism certainly incorporates a much thinner claim about the nature of morality than either Wong or Harman's approaches. But despite the attempt to put questions of moral content aside and gauge justification by a standard of coherence, this is still only *my* standard for judging — am I not failing to justify, at this most basic level, the application of a standard of coherence? In this sense, the proposal is ethnocentric, and discriminates against those moralities which do not value reasons as support for judgements or consistency between the judgements themselves. My response to this can only be that whilst the commitment to coherence must be held reflexively, it is firstly a deep commitment — a standard by which I judge my own moral life — and secondly that there are compelling reasons for the standard to be shared. There also remains some ambiguity about the extent to which coherence or consistency admits of degrees, and how those degrees are to be judged. Whilst I accept that there will be problems in making precise or borderline judgements, the presence of grey areas or hard cases does not suffice to warrant the rejection of my proposal if the underlying idea is sound.

I also examined whether the relativist approach could allow for objectivity. I have argued that a kind of objectivity understood as maximal intersubjectivity — a wide 'community of reasons' — is available to the relativist, though a conception of objectivity as transcendence is not. The proponent of the broadest form of relativism, the statement 'everything is relative, including this statement', is often portrayed as being in a dilemma. She stands accused of either inconsistency or arbitrariness. On the 'community of reasons' approach that I have advocated, this dilemma can be resolved. Relativism can claim a form of objectivity which makes the relativist view neither inconsistent, nor purely a statement of personal preference.

Chapter five then further examined the way coherence relativism can explain our moral lives. I looked in particular at the question of how coherence relativism could allow for moral criticism when faced by equally justified moralities on the one hand, and abhorrent ones on the other. My response offered two considerations that ought to influence our answer to this question. One is the distinction I drew between the application and justification of our morality. If I am right that this split is a plausible way to think of our moral experience, there is no reason to suppose the relativist need be any less forthright than the universalist in her criticisms of moralities. The relativist will always be able to offer *evaluative criticism* based on the deep commitments of her moral system, and can back this up with *compelling criticism* when facing unjustified moralities. I have illustrated in chapter five the ways in which abhorrent moralities can fail relativist criteria of justification.

However, I have suggested that relativists who believe that justification is relevant to moral judgement will not adopt a 'shoot first, ask questions later' kind of approach. The second part of my response is to argue that, for those who affirm some kind of justification principle, relativism encourages tolerance. This argument has involved the clarification of the role that metaethics can play in moral argumentation. I have argued that this role is limited; questions of justification will only influence our moral judgements when combined with a moral commitment to the relevancy of questions of justification — what I, after Wong, have termed a 'justification principle'. Neither relativism nor universalism by themselves are meant to fill the entire space of someone's moral convictions. Instead, they contribute by providing standards to settle the question of whether competing moralities are justified or not. The relevance of this, or the weight that it is given in the final judgement, will entirely depend on the actor's moral framework (and for universalists, an external and universal standard of right and wrong will also be relevant to a judgement on the outcome). This is one way that I have argued relativism can contribute to arguments for tolerance (or more).

This discussion of tolerance led into questions about the link between relativism and political theory, which was the concern of part two. I began my examination of this area in chapter six. There I analysed contemporary liberal defences of neutrality that attempt to be *neutral* justifications of neutrality. This meant that their justifications must avoid drawing on controversial philosophical ideas. However, I have argued that the approaches of Larmore and Rawls fail to achieve the elusive status of a 'neutral' justification. Rawls' attempts to avoid issues of metaethics are undermined by his controversial accounts of both the nature of objectivity and his explanation of reasonable disagreement (the 'burdens of judgement'). These elements constitute serious barriers to Rawls' attempt to legitimise liberal principles through consensus. I also argued that the idea of a retreat to neutral ground was problematic. I suggested that if disagreement was persistent, there might well be little neutral ground to retreat to.

Where chapter six surveyed diverse approaches to justifying neutrality, chapter seven examined the underlying commonality. I argued that these 'political liberal' defences can be understood as resting on a relativist theory of moral justification. Relativism supplies an account of reasonable disagreement which preserves the liberal's non-sceptical stance and can be understood more generally as an accurate specification of the epistemic component of liberal 'reasonableness'. But even if the liberal opts instead for a sceptical basis — perhaps by retracting her claim that reasonable disagreement need not have sceptical implications — the proposal is certainly not neutral. Furthermore, I argued in my discussion of Barry that his sceptical argument for 'reasonable rejectability' needed a relativist component.

Chapter seven, having argued that political liberalism rests on controversial metaethical foundations, suggested that relativism is the set of metaethical foundations that best fits the liberal argument. This commitment is under-publicised in political liberalism, which seems to hold that silence on questions of truth suffices for 'neutrality' between philosophical controversies. It does not, not least because political liberalism *needs* a theory of moral justification to explicate the claims it makes — my focus being those concerning 'reasonable disagreement'. An analysis of the relativist component of liberal arguments indicates limits to liberal attempts to ground the proposal in consensus. The result of my argument is that liberalism can no longer claim 'neutrality' in justification. Thus, how can it command an 'overlapping' legitimising consensus? In the concluding section of this chapter I discussed briefly the ways in which a justificatory liberalism could be justified or legitimated.

Having summarised my arguments, I now want to return to where I began. This was with the claim that casual relativism is widespread in our moral dealings with others. This has not always been thought a good thing — in fact, for some thinkers it has been a cause of despair. It is only appropriate that a book concerned with relativism should end with some speculations on these wider questions concerning the effects of relativism.

The Culture of Relativism

In 1981, Alasdair MacIntyre implicated relativism in the coming of the 'new dark ages'. Society, it seemed, had lost touch with the meaning of morals. Instead, we had a situation in which there was 'no rational way of securing moral agreement' (MacIntyre, 1981, 6); 'if I lack any good reasons to invoke against you, it must seem that I lack any good reasons' (MacIntyre, 1981, 8). MacIntyre described moral debate as being vitiated by what he termed 'emotivism' — though relativism has often been described in these kinds of ways as well. This is not an isolated intellectual incident. Allan Bloom, in 1987, identified the state of students in universities as one of indifference, for 'relativism has extinguished the real motive of education, the search for the good life' (Bloom, 1987, 34). Instead, students were 'unified only in their relativism' (Bloom, 1987, 25). More recently, Charles Taylor has argued that relativism is damaging to an ethic of 'authenticity' — the ethic we ought to aim for in today's society (Taylor, 1991).

Any kind of rehabilitation of relativism must fail if it has been responsible for these problems. If relativism really is a force for evil in the world, then perhaps the fear and loathing of it is entirely justified. And it seems I must concur with at least some of the claims made by these defenders of virtue, since I suggested at the outset that relativism is deeply embedded in our culture. Having surveyed the content and consequences of relativism in the preceding chapters, I want to end by assessing this relativist culture, to see whether it is the cause for despair that such thinkers have taken it to be. I will speculate on the accuracy of this diagnosis of contemporary western society, and on the prognosis that follows from it.

As the most recent, and perhaps least opaque, of these critics, I want to begin by outlining some arguments put forward by Charles Taylor. He argues that relativism damages authenticity, the search within ourselves for a model of the good life. Taylor takes relativism to be an offshoot of a form of individualism (Taylor, 1991, 14) grounded in the idea of mutual respect. The key problem with a culture of relativism, for Taylor, is the way that it undermines any account of what it is to live a good life. It 'travesties and betrays' the condition of a free society, by maintaining that a vigorous defence of a conception of the good life is 'off-limits'. If the search for authenticity can only take place against a background of things that matter (Taylor, 1991, 18), Taylor's thought, like MacIntyre's, is that for those asserting some form of relativism, there isn't really any such background. Instead, moral life is somehow rendered arbitrary.

The first point I want to make is that to assess contemporary culture as being entirely or even mostly 'relativist' is to make a mistake. I noted in chapter two that the main context in which analytical philosophers come across relativism is on the campus. To generalise from the fact that some undergraduates — or indeed some of the chattering classes — are relativists to the view that our culture is a relativist one is a giant leap. The idea that our society is one in which people are no longer interested in settling the questions of the good life is false. We can note, for example, an increase in religious adherence to evangelical creeds in Britain, and figures indicating that religious conversions tend to be from less- demanding to more-demanding faiths. The generalisation that we live in a society which 'can't care, won't care' about the good life, which lacks commitment to values, requires more support than these theorists give it.

The second point is that, as I have argued, we needn't conceive of commitment and relativism as opposites. Relativism need not be reductive (reducing our moral commitments to psychological ones), or nihilistic (encouraging the belief that all values are worthless). There are undoubtedly reductionists and nihilists of many kinds in the world, but to group all of them under the banner 'relativism' is misleading at best. Whilst the kind of relativism I have advocated involves a personal standard of justification, this does not mean it turns morality into a question of preferences. Many systems of morality begin with our most important considered convictions and in this respect relativism is no different. Furthermore, for so many undergraduates and freshmen, relativism comes as a theory about *cultures* or the shared standards of groups. Thus, the idea that relativism comes out of *individualism* seems problematic.

What my kind of relativism does raise, however, is the possibility of failing to compellingly justify my morality to others. Thus, maybe these critics are right to say that it undermines the authority that we want to attach to talk of morals. Moral injunctions are not going to be 'unassailable' (MacIntyre, 1981, 6) and there may be situations where compelling reasons for me fail to be compelling reasons for others. However, this does not mean that morality is arbitrary for the relativist, in the sense that I have no reasons to be convinced by. The relativist simply acknowledges that it is possible for others to reject them.[1] I have suggested that this is a good thing, for it removes one reason often used to support intol-

---

[1] Johnston notes 'Whatever criteria we use for assessing whether a deed should be done, our judgement could never be unassailable, for given

erance. Taylor is partly concerned that in today's society, 'an individual lifestyle is also hard to maintain against the grain' (Taylor, 1991, 9). In a society of relativists, it might be much easier to maintain a firm conviction in your own lifestyle. Leaving room for the relativity of values, in a society of people who affirm the justification principle, is a good step towards increased tolerance and accommodation.

These minor points lead me to two more controversial, perhaps heretical, suggestions. The first is that our moral life may be *harmed* by the search for unassailable, immutable, eternal values — perhaps because it involves us in a search for something that does not exist. MacIntyre looks back to a discourse of agreement and order in the moral realm, just as Confucius did. Perhaps this order was, and is, a chimera. The second concerns the charge that relativism undermines the search for a good life. The point of these critics I take to be that relativism and the search for *the* good life are incompatible, for we are left with many ways of life that are 'mere' preferences. What if universalism and the *search* for the good life were incompatible? Universal truths *command* our assent and we obey. If the only conceivably correct moral code *commands* self-sacrifice, then in an act of self-sacrifice we are only doing what is demanded of us, not what is heroic or supererogatory. The good life requires choice and commitment; a situation of relativism, when we are always painfully aware that there are other justified ways of life, might well promote authenticity rather than diminish it. W.B. Yeats wrote that the age of objectivity ushered in by Christianity diminished the heroic virtues of the subjective age that preceded it (Yeats, 1937). Yeats' position, of course, was grounded in complicated speculation, but it nevertheless may contain an important truth. Bloom asks of relativist culture, 'Have we so simplified the soul that it is no longer difficult to explain?' (Bloom, 1987, 43). My reply is that the relativity and the openness that he condemns have *complicated* the soul, to the point where conceiving of the search for a good life as the process of discovering an unassailable, universal morality is unhelpful at best and destructive at worst.

My argument has concentrated on two areas. The first is the debate about the nature of moral justification and the plausibility of relativist justification. The second is the nature of political liberalism. Having analysed many important issues — the nature of reflective equilibrium and of relativism, the character of political liberalism, the relationship between ethics and metaethics, uni-

the nature of such judgements the logical possibility of others rejecting them can never be eliminated' (Johnston, 1989, 88).

versalism and relativism, neutrality and toleration — we are now better placed to understand and respond to the questions with which we began. Can a form of relativism be defended? How does it contribute to our response to moral diversity? I have argued that a form of relativism can be defended, and that it is relevant to the liberal argument for principles of toleration and neutrality. For many eminent thinkers, relativism is either morally or logically wrong, plain and simple. I have shown that there is nothing plain or simple in a refutation of relativism and its supposedly harmful consequences. For too many philosophers, relativism has taken the form of a spectre that must be laid to rest. My contention has been that relativism is not to be scared of, and not something we should seek to bury.

Bibliography

Ackerman B. (1980). *Social Justice in the Liberal State*. London: Yale University Press.

Ackerman B. (1989). Why Dialogue?, *Journal of Philosophy* 86, 5–22.

Allport G. W. (1979). *The Nature of Prejudice*. Reading Mass.: Addison Wesley.

Arneson R. J. (1990). Neutrality and Utility, *Canadian Journal of Philosophy* 20, 215–40.

Arrington R. L. (1989). *Rationalism, Realism, and Relativism*. Ithaca: Cornell University Press.

Ayer A. J. (1971). *The Problem of Knowledge*. Harmondsworth: Penguin.

Barry, B. (1995a). *Justice as Impartiality*. Oxford: Oxford University Press.

Barry B. (1995b). A Defence of Political Liberalism, *Ratio Juris* 8, 325–30.

Barry B. (2000). *Culture and Equality*. Cambridge: Polity Press.

Berlin I. (1991). *The Crooked Timber of Humanity*. New York: Knopf.

Bird C. (1996). Mutual Respect and Neutral Justification, *Ethics* 106, 62–96.

Blackburn S. (1993). *Essays in Quasi-Realism*. Oxford: Oxford University Press.

Blackburn S. (1999). Is Moral Justification Possible on a Quasi-realist Foundation? , *Inquiry* 42, 213–28.

Bloom A. (1987). *The Closing of the American Mind*. New York: Simon & Schuster.

Bok S. (1993). Defending Morality — a Minimalist Approach, *The Monist* 76, 349–59.

Bradley F. H. (1962). *Ethical Studies*. Oxford: Oxford University Press.

Brandt R. (1979). *A Theory of the Good and the Right*. Oxford: Oxford University Press.

Brink D. (1989). *Moral Realism and the Foundations of Ethics*. New York: Cambridge University Press.

Brink D. (1991). Rawlsian Constructivism in Moral Theory, in Corlett A. ed., *Equality and Liberty: Analysing Rawls and Nozick*. Basingstoke: Macmillan, 196–216.

Brown H. I. (1987). *Observation and Objectivity*. Oxford: Oxford University Press.

Busfield S. (2000). Irving Loses Holocaust Libel Case, *The Guardian*, April 11.

Caney S. (1995). 'Anti-perfectionism and Rawlsian Liberalism', *Political Studies* 43, 248–64.

Caney S. (1996). 'Impartiality and Liberal Neutrality', *Utilitas* 8, 273–93.

Caney S. (1999). Defending Universalism, in MacKenzie I., O'Neill S. eds. *Reconstituting Social Criticism,* Basingstoke: Macmillan, 19–34.

Coate R.A., Rosati J.A. eds. (1988). *The Power of Human Needs in World Society*. Boulder: Lynne Riener.

Confucius Trans. Lau D.C. (1979). *The Analects*. London: Penguin Books.

D'Agostino F.B. (1993). Transcendence and Conversation: Two Conceptions of Objectivity, *American Philosophical Quarterly* 30, 87–108.

Dancy J. (1993). *Moral Reasons*. Oxford: Blackwell.

Daniels N. (1996). *Justice and Justification: Reflective Equilibrium in Theory and Practice*. Cambridge: Cambridge University Press.

Darwall, S., Gibbard, A., and Railton, P. (1992). Toward Fin de Siecle Ethics: Some Trends, *The Philosophical Review* 101, 115–89.

Dawkins R. (1989). *The Selfish Gene (2nd ed.)*. Oxford: Oxford University Press.

Delgado R. and Stefancic J. (1997). *Critical White Studies: Looking Behind the Mirror*. Philadelphia: Temple University Press.

DePaul M. (1986). Reflective Equilibrium and Foundationalism, *American Philosophical Quarterly* 23, 59–69.

Devine P.E. (1987). Relativism, Abortion, and Tolerance, *Philosophy and Phenomenological Research* 48, 131–8.

Donnelly J. (1989). *Universal Human Rights in Theory and Practice*. Ithaca : Cornell University Press.

Dubow S. (1995). *Scientific Racism in Modern South Africa*. Cambridge: Cambribge University Press.

Durrant R.G. (1958). On the Description of Morality, *Journal of Philosophy*, 169–88.

Dworkin G. (1975). Non-Neutral Principles, in Daniels N. ed., *Reading Rawls*. Oxford: Blackwell, 124–40.

Dworkin R. (1985). *A Matter of Principle*. Oxford: Oxford University Press.

Dworkin R. (1996). Objectivity and Truth: You'd Better Believe It, *Philosophy and Public Affairs* 25, 87–139.

Ebertz R.(1993). Is Reflective Equilibrium a Coherentist Model?, *Canadian Journal Of Philosophy* 23, 193–214.

Elster J. (1985). *Sour Grapes: Studies in the Subversion of Rationality*. Cambridge: Cambridge University Press.

Estlund D. (1998). The Insularity of the Reasonable: Why Political Liberalism Must Admit the Truth, *Ethics* 108, 252–75.

Feinberg J. (1973). *Social Philosophy*. New Jersey: Prentice-Hall.

Fernandez J. W. (1990). Tolerance in a Repugnant World and Other Dilemmas in the Cultural Relativism of Melville J. Herskovits, *Ethos* 18, 140–64.

Feyerabend P.K. (1975). *Against Method*. London: New Left Books.

Fick M.L. (1929). Intelligence Test Reports of Poor White, Native (Zulu) Coloured and Indian School Children and the Educational and Social Implications, *South African Journal of Science* XXVI .

Finnis J.M. (1983). *Fundamentals of Ethics*. Washington: Georgetown University Press.

Fishkin J.S. (1984). *Beyond Subjective Morality: Ethical Reasoning and Political Philosophy*. New Haven, etc.: Yale University Press.

Flew A. Ed. (1984). *A Dictionary of Philosophy*. London: Pan.

Foster L. (1994). Relativism and Pluralism: The case for a Multicultural Curriculum, in Foster L. & Herzog P. eds., *Contemporary Philosophical Perspectives on Pluralism and Multiculturalism*. Boston: University of Massachusetts Press, 121–36.

Foot P. (1979). *Moral Relativism*. Lawrence: University of Kansas Press.

Frankena W.K. (1958). MacIntyre on Defining Morality, *Philosophy* 158–62.

Frankena W.K. (Goodposter K. E. ed.) (1976). *Perspectives on Morality*. Notre Dame: University of Notre Dame Press.

Galston W. (1991). *Liberal Purposes: Goods, Values and Diversity in the Liberal State*. Cambridge, Cambridge University Press.

Galston W. (1999). Value Pluralism and Liberal Political Theory, *American Political Science Review* 93, 769–78.

Gaus G. (1990). *Value and Justification: The Foundations of Liberal Theory*. Cambridge: Cambridge University Press.

Gaus G. (1995). The Rational, the Reasonable, and Justification, *The Journal of Political Philosophy*, 3 234–58.

Gaus G. (1996). *Justificatory Liberalism*. New York: Oxford University Press.

Gaus G. (1999). Reasonable Pluralism and the Domain of the Political, *Inquiry* 42, 259–84.

Gauthier D. (1986). *Morals by Agreement*. Oxford: Oxford University Press.

Geertz C. (1989). Anti-Anti-Relativism, in Krausz M ed. 1989, *Relativism: Interpretation and Confrontation*. Notre Dame: Notre Dame University Press, 12–34.

Gewirth A. (1978). *Reason and Morality*, London: University of Chicago Press.

Giddens A. (1994). Reason Without Revolution? Habermas's Theorie des Kommunicativen Handelns in Bernstein R. J. ed. 1994, *Habermas and Modernity*. Cambridge: MIT Press, 95–121.

Gilligan C. (1982). *In a Different Voice: Psychological Theory and Women's Development*. Cambridge: Harvard University Press.

Glazer N. (1975). *Affirmative Discrimination: Ethnic Inequality and Public Policy*. New York: Basic Books.

Goldberg D. T. (1993). Introduction: Multicultural Conditions, in Goldberg D.T. ed. *Racist Culture: Philosophy and the Politics of Meaning*. Oxford: Blackwell, 1–41.

Goldberg D.T. (1994). *Multiculturalism: A Critical Reader*. Oxford: Blackwell.

Gould S.J. (1994). Curveball. *New Yorker*, Nov. 28, 139.

Gray J. (1996). *Post-liberalism: Studies in Political Thought*. London: Routledge.

Griffin, J. (1996). *Value Judgement: Improving Our Ethical Beliefs*. Oxford: Clarendon Press.

Griffin R. ed. (1995). *Fascism*. Oxford: Oxford University Press.

Gutmann A., Thompson D. (1990). Moral Conflict and Political Consensus, *Ethics* 101, 64–88.

Habermas J. (Trans. McCarthy T.) (1984–7). *The Theory of Communicative Action Vol 1: Reason and the Rationalization of Society. Vol 2: Lifeworld and System: a Critique of Functionalist Reason*. Boston: Beacon Press.

Habermas J. (1990). *Moral Consciousness and Communicative Action*. Cambridge: Polity.

Habermas J. (1996). *Between Facts and Norms: Contributions to a Discourse Theory of Law and Democracy*. Cambridge: Polity.

Hampshire S. (1983). *Morality and Conflict*. Oxford: Blackwell.

Hampshire S. (1989). *Innocence and Experience*. Cambridge: Harvard University Press.

Hampshire S. (1999). *Justice is Conflict*. London: Gerald Duckworth & Co.

Hare R.M. (1972). *The Language of Morals*. Oxford: Oxford University Press.

Harman G. (1975). Moral Relativism Defended, *Philosophical Review* 84, 3–22.

Harman G. (1977). *The Nature of Morality: An Introduction to Ethics*. New York: Oxford University Press.

Harman G. (1982). Human Flourishing, Ethics and Liberty, *Philosophy and Public Affairs* 12, 307–22.

Harman G. (1996). Part I: Moral Relativism, in Harman G., Thomson J. J. 1996, *Moral Relativism and Moral Objectivity*. Cambridge: Blackwell, 1–64.

Harman G. (1998). Response to Critics, *Philosophy and Phenomenological Research* LVIII, 207–14.

Harré R., Krausz M. (1996). *Varieties of Relativism*. Oxford: Blackwell.

Harrison G. (1976). Relativism and Tolerance, *Ethics* 86, 122–35.

Hernstein R.J. and Murray C. (1994). *The Bell Curve*. New York, Free Press.

Herskovits M. (1972). *Cultural Relativism: Perspectives in Cultural Pluralism*. New York: Random House.

Holmgren M. (1989). The Wide and Narrow of Reflective Equilibrium, *Canadian Journal of Philosophy* 19, 43–60.

Horton J. and Nicholson P. (1992). Philosophy and the Practice of Toleration, in Horton J. and Nicholson P. eds. *Toleration: Philosophy and Practice*. Aldershot: Avebury, 1–14.

Hursthouse R., Lawrence G., Quinn W. eds. (1995). *Virtues and Reasons; Philippa Foot and Moral Theory*. Oxford: Oxford University Press.

Jameson F. (1991). *Postmodernism or, The Cultural Logic of Late Capitalism*. Durham: Duke University Press.

Jamieson D. (1993). Method and Moral Theory, in Singer, P. ed. (1993), *A Companion to Ethics*. Oxford: Blackwell, 476–87.

Johnston P. (1989). *Wittgenstein and Moral Philosophy*. London: Routledge.

Jones P. (1989). Liberalism, Belief and Doubt, in Bellamy R. ed. 1989, *Liberalism and Recent Legal and Social Philosophy*. Stuttgart: F. Steiner, 51–69.

Kagan S. (1997). *Normative Ethics*. Boulder: Westview Press.

Korsgaard, C. (1996). *The Sources of Normativity*. Cambridge: Cambridge University Press.

Krausz M. Meiland J. W. eds. (1982). *Relativism: Cognitive and Moral*. Notre Dame: University of Notre Dame Press.

Kuhn T. (1970). *The Structure of Scientific Revolution*. Chicago: University of Chicago Press.

Kukathas C. (1992). Are there any Cultural Rights?, *Political Theory* 20, 105–39.

Kymlicka W. (1989a). *Liberalism, Community, and Culture*. Oxford: Clarendon Press.

Kymlicka W. (1989b). Liberal Individualism and Liberal Neutrality, *Ethics* 99, 883–905.

Kymlicka W. (1995). *Multicultural Citizenship: A Liberal Theory of Minority Rights*. Oxford: Oxford University Press.

Larmore C.E. (1987). *Patterns of Moral Complexity*. Cambridge: Cambridge University Press.

Larmore C.E. (1996). *The Morals of Modernity*. Cambridge: Cambridge University Press.

Levy J. (1997). Classifying Cultural Rights, in Shapiro I. and Kymlicka W. ed., *Ethnicity and Group Rights*. New York: New York University Press, 22–66.

Lilla M. (2000). Review of 'Justice is Conflict' in *London Review of Books*.

Locke J. (Horton J. Mendus S. eds.) (1991). *A Letter Concerning Toleration*. London: Routledge.

Long G. (2003). Justification, Disagreement and the Liberal State, *CRISPP* 6, 32–49.

Lyons D. (1976). Ethical Relativism and the Problem of Incoherence, *Ethics* 86, 107–21.

MacIntyre A. (1970). What Morality is Not, in Wallace G., Walker A.D.M. eds., *The Definition of Morality*. London: Methuen, 26–39.

MacIntyre A. (1981). *After Virtue*. London: Duckworth.

MacIntyre A. (1988). *Whose Justice, Which Rationality*. London: Duckworth.

Mackie J.L. (1977). *Ethics: Inventing Right and Wrong*. London: Penguin.

Macklin R. (1999). *Against Relativism: Cultural Diversity and the Search for Ethical Universals in Medicine*. New York: Oxford University Press.

Margolis J. (1991). *The Truth about Relativism*. Oxford: Blackwell.

May S. (1999). Critical Multiculturalism and Cultural Difference: Avoiding Essentialism, in May S. ed., *Critical Multiculturalism: Rethinking Multicultural and Anti-Racist Education*. London: Falmer Press, 11–41.

McCarthy T. (1978). *The Critical Theory of Jürgen Habermas*. London, Hutchison & Co.

McGuinness B. ed. (1982). *Wittgenstein and his Times*. Oxford: Blackwell.

Mendus S. (1988). Introduction, in Mendus S. ed., *Justifying Toleration*. Cambridge: Cambridge University Press, 1–21.

Mill J. S. (1891). *Principles of Political Economy*.

Mill J. S. (1991). *On Liberty and Other Essays*. Oxford: Oxford University Press.

Modood T. (2000). Anti-Essentialism, Multiculturalism, and the 'Recognition' of Religious Groups, in Kymlicka W., Norman W. eds., *Citizenship in Diverse Societies*. New York: Oxford University Press, 175–95.

Moser P.K. (1993). *Philosophy after Objectivity: Making Sense in Perspective*. Oxford: Oxford University Press.

Nagel T. (1978). *The Possibility of Altruism*. Princeton: Princeton University Press.

Nagel T. (1986). *The View From Nowhere*. Oxford: Oxford University Press.

Nagel T. (1991). *Equality and Partiality*. Oxford: Oxford University Press.

Nagel T. (1997). *The Last Word*. Oxford: Oxford University Press.

Neisser U. (1976). *Cognition and Reality*. San Francisco: Freeman.

Nielsen K. (1993). Relativism and Wide Reflective Equilibrium, *The Monist* 76, 316–31.

Norris C. (1996) *Reclaiming Truth: Contribution to a Critique of Cultural Relativism*. London: Lawrence & Wishart.

Nozick R. (1974). *Anarchy, State, and Utopia* Oxford: Basil Blackwell.

Nozick R. (1981). *Philosophical Explanations*. Oxford, Clarendon Press.

Nussbaum M. (1996). Non-Relative Virtues – An Aristotelian Approach, in Nussbaum M. and Sen A. eds. *The Quality of Life*. Oxford: Clarendon Press, 242–69.

Pierce W. (1978). *The Turner Diaries*.

Plato (Burnyeat M. ed., Trans M.J. Levett) (1990). *The Theaetetus of Plato*. Indianapolis: Hackett.

Preston J.M. (1992). On Some Objections to Relativism, *Ratio* 5, 57–73.

Putnam H. (1981). *Reason, Truth and History*. Cambridge: Cambridge University Press.

Putnam H. (1988). *Representation and Reality*. Cambridge, Mass.: MIT Press.

Putnam H. (1990). *Realism with a Human Face*. Cambridge, Mass.: Harvard University Press.

Rawls J. (1951). Outline of a Decision Procedure for Ethics, *The Philosophical Review* 60, 177–97.

Rawls J. (1972). *A Theory of Justice*. Oxford: Oxford University Press.

Rawls J. (1980). Kantian Constructivism in Moral Theory, *Journal of Philosophy* 77, 515–72.

Rawls J. (1993). *Political Liberalism*. New York: Columbia University Press.

Rawls J. (1999a).The Independence of Moral Theory, in Rawls J. *Collected Papers*. Harvard: Harvard University Press, 286–302.

Rawls J. (1999b) The Law of Peoples, with 'The Idea of Public Reason Revisited'. Cambridge, Mass.: Harvard University Press.

Raz J. (1975). *Practical Reasons and Norms*. London: Hutchinson.

Raz J. (1986). *The Morality of Freedom*. Oxford: Clarendon Press.

Raz J. (1990). Facing Diversity: The Case of Epistemic Abstinence, *Philosophy and Public Affairs* 19, 3–46.

Raz J. (1991). The Claims of Reflective Equilibrium, in Corlett A. ed. *Equality and Liberty: Analysing Rawls and Nozick*. Basingstoke: Macmillan, 110–35.

Raz J. (1994). *Ethics in the Public Domain*. Oxford, Oxford University Press.

Renteln A. (1990). *International Human Rights: Universalism versus Relativism*. London: Sage.

Rhees R. (1982). Wittgenstein on Language and Ritual, in McGuinness B. ed., *Wittgenstein and his Times*. Oxford: Blackwell.

Rorty R. (1979). *Philosophy and the Mirror of Nature*. Princeton: Princeton University Press.

Rorty R. (1991). *Objectivity, Relativism and Truth*. Cambridge: Cambridge University Press.

Rorty R. (1998). *Truth and Progress*. Cambridge: Cambridge University Press.

Rousseau J-J. (1993). *The Social Contract and Discourses*. London: Everyman.

Sandel M. (1982). *Liberalism and the Limits of Justice*. Cambridge: Cambridge University Press.

Scanlon T.M. (1995). Fear of Relativism, in. Hursthouse R., Lawrence G., Quinn W. eds., *Virtues and Reasons; Philippa Foot and Moral Theory*. Oxford: Oxford University Press.

Scheffler S. (1992). *Human Morality*. New York: Oxford University Press.

Scheffler S. (1994). The Appeal of Political Liberalism, *Ethics* 1994, Vol.105, No.1 SI, 4–22.

Schoek H. and Wiggins J. W. eds. (1961). *Relativism and the Study of Man*. Princeton: Van Nostrand.

Simmons A.J. (1999). Justification and Legitimacy, *Ethics*109, 739–71.

Smith J.F. (1994). A Critique of Adversarial Discourse: Gender as an Aspect of Cultural Difference, in Foster L. & Herzog P. eds., *Contemporary Philosophical Perspectives on Pluralism and Multiculturalism*. Boston: University of Massachusetts Press, 59–82.

Solovyov V., Klepikava E. (1995). *Zhirinovsky – The Paradoxes of Russian Fascism,* London: Viking.

Sparkes A. W. (1991). *Talking Philosophy: A Wordbook*. London: Routledge.

Sprigge T.L.S. (1990). *The Rational Foundations of Ethics*. London: Routledge.

Stout J. (1990). *Ethics after Babel: The Languages of Morals and Their Discontents*. Cambridge: James Clarke & Co.

Strauss L. (1961). Relativism, in Schoek H. and Wiggins J. W. eds., *Relativism and the Study of Man*. Princeton: Van Nostrand.

Stroud S. (1998). Relativism and Quasi-Absolutism, *Philosophy and Phenomenological Research* LVIII, 189–94.

Sturgeon N.L. (1994). Moral Disagreement and Moral Relativism, *Social Philosophy and Policy* 11, 80–115.

Taylor C. (1991). *The Ethics of Authenticity*. Cambridge, Mass: Harvard University Press.

Taylor C. (1992). *Multiculturalism and the Politics of Recognition: An Essay*. Princeton: Princeton University Press.

Taylor C. (1996). Explanation and Practical Reason, in Nussbaum M. and Sen A. eds., *The Quality of Life*. Oxford: Clarendon Press, 208–31.

Thompson J. J. (1996). Part II: Moral Objectivity, in Harman G., Thomson J. J. 1996. *Moral Relativism and Moral Objectivity*. Cambridge: Blackwell, 65–125.

Tilley J.J. (1998). The problem for Normative Cultural Relativism, *Ratio Juris* 11, 272–90.

Tomasi J. (1995). Kymlicka, Liberalism and Respect for Cultural Minorities, *Ethics* 105, 580–603.

Unger R.M. (1976). *Knowledge and Politics*. New York: Free Press.

Waldron J. (1989). Legislation and Moral Neutrality, in Goodin R. and Reeve A. eds. *Liberal Neutrality*. New York: Routledge, 61–83.

Walzer M. (1983). *Spheres of Justice: A Defence of Pluralism and Equality*. Oxford: Martin Robertson and Co. Ltd.

Walzer M. (1985). *Interpretation and Social Criticism*. Cambridge, Mass.: Harvard University Press.

Walzer M. (1994). *Thick and Thin: Moral Argument at Home and Abroad*. Notre Dame: Notre Dame University Press.

Warnke G. (1987). *Gadamer: Hermeneutics, Tradition and Reason*. Cambridge: Polity Press.

Wenar L. (1995). Political Liberalism: An Internal Critique, *Ethics* 106, 32–62.

West D. (1995). Continental Philosophy, in Goodin R. and Pettit P. eds., *A Companion to Political Philosophy*. Oxford: Blackwell, 39–72.

White S.K. (1988). *The Recent Work of Jürgen Habermas*. Cambridge: Cambridge University Press.

White S.K. (1991). *Political Theory and Postmodernism*. Cambridge: Cambridge University Press.

Wiggins D. (1996). Objective and Subjective in Ethics, with two Postscripts on Truth, in Hooker B. ed., *Truth in Ethics*. Oxford: Blackwell, 35–50.

Williams B. (1973). *Morality: An Introduction to Ethics*. Harmondsworth: Penguin.

Williams B. (1981). *Moral Luck*. Cambridge: Cambridge University Press.

Williams B. (1985). *Ethics and the Limits of Philosophy*. London: Fontana Press.

Winch P. (1958). *The Idea of a Social Science and its Relation to Philosophy*. London: Routledge & Kegan Paul.

Wong D.B. (1986). *Moral Relativity*. Berkeley: California University Press.

Wong D.B. (1993). Relativism, in Singer P. ed., *A Companion to Ethics*. Oxford: Blackwell, 442–50.

Wong D.B. (1994). Coping with Moral Conflict and Ambiguity, in Foster L. & Herzog P. eds. *Contemporary Philosophical Perspectives on Pluralism and Multiculturalism*. Boston: University of Massachusetts Press, 13–38.

Yamamoto T. (1979). *Hagakure*. Tokyo: Kodansha.

Index

A

abhorrent moralities: see moral horror

absolutism: 26

accommodation: as response to diversity, 253, 262

Ackerman B.: 197

affirmation: as response to diversity, 253

Allport G. W.: 174, 177

application of a morality: contrasted with justification of, 7, 9, 107, 114, 163-167, 178; see also criticism, compelling and evaluative

Arneson R. J.: 196, 197

Arrington R. L.: 26, 36, 38n

Ayer A. J.: 210n

B

Barry B.: 4, 14n, 182n, 211n, 220, 221, 227, 241, 254n, 259; on political liberalism and scepticism 233 – 241, 244-247

Berlin I.: 18

Blackburn S.: 14-15, 44

Bloom A.: 250n, 260, 262

Bok S.: 98n

Bradley F. H.: 156

Brandt R.: 119n, 133n

Brink D.: 103n, 115n, 118n

Brown H.: 148

C

Caney S.: 26, 40, 54, 123, 124, 129, 132, 206n; on contingent universalism 98-99, 104, 109n, 111

cognitivism: 19

coherence: 3, 7, 50, 64, 114, 171, 257; and reflective equilibrium 115-120, 125, 130, 132, 133, 136; and relativism: see coherence relativism

coherence relativism: 138-145, 205, 229n, 231; and abhorrent moralities 180-181; as a foundation for liberalism 241-253; and indeterminate theory choice 161-171; and moral criticism 176-178; and objectivity 151-159; and tolerance 183, 184, 187, 189-191

coherentism: 118

conceptions of the good: 196-197, 223; disagreement between 223, 238-240; reasonable rejection of 242-3, 245

considered moral judgements: 99, 100; role in coherence relativism 139, 147n, 157, 158, 176, 178; role in reflective equilibrium 116-121, 131-137; weak and strong constraints on 122-130